Teaching, Pedagogy, and Learning

Teaching, Pedagogy, and Learning

Fertile Ground for Campus and Community Innovations

Edited by
Jeffery Galle and Rebecca L. Harrison

ROWMAN & LITTLEFIELD
Lanham • Boulder • New York • London

Published by Rowman & Littlefield
A wholly owned subsidiary of The Rowman & Littlefield Publishing Group, Inc.
4501 Forbes Boulevard, Suite 200, Lanham, Maryland 20706
www.rowman.com

Unit A, Whitacre Mews, 26-34 Stannary Street, London SE11 4AB

Copyright © 2017 by Jeffery Galle and Rebecca L. Harrison

All rights reserved. No part of this book may be reproduced in any form or by any electronic or mechanical means, including information storage and retrieval systems, without written permission from the publisher, except by a reviewer who may quote passages in a review.

British Library Cataloguing in Publication Information Available

Library of Congress Cataloging-in-Publication Data

ISBN: 978-1-4758-3288-4 (cloth : alk. paper)
ISBN: 978-1-4758-3289-1 (pbk. : alk. paper)
ISBN: 978-1-4758-3290-7 (electronic)

∞™ The paper used in this publication meets the minimum requirements of American National Standard for Information Sciences—Permanence of Paper for Printed Library Materials, ANSI/NISO Z39.48-1992.

Printed in the United States of America

For my beloved children Samuel and Ruby Erben who teach me daily the real power of inquiry-based learning.

Remain Montessori children always, my sweet ones.

—Mama

Contents

Foreword   ix
Stephen Bowen

Acknowledgments   xi

Introduction: Partnering for Success: Institute for Pedagogy in the Liberal Arts as a Galvanizing Journey for Faculty Development   xiii
Jeffery Galle and Rebecca L. Harrison

PART I: INQUIRY AND CAMPUS CULTURE   1
Foreword by Virginia S. Lee

1   Institut[ing] Innovation: Courses, Curriculum, and Faculty Expertise   3
Jeffery Galle

2   IGL Certification: A Model for Institutionalizing Inquiry-Guided Learning   23
Devon Fisher, Daniel W. Kiser, Jennifer Heller, and David Ratke

3   Implementing Inquiry-Guided Labs in an Introductory Nonmajors Science Course   45
Caralyn B. Zehnder, Kalina Manoylov, Christine Mutiti, Sam Mutiti, and Allison VandeVoort

4   Resolving Early Career Paradoxes at the IPLA   71
Lia Schraeder

PART II: PEDAGOGIES OF COMMUNITY 89
Foreword by Catherine Chiappetta Swanson

5 Inquiry-Based Learning: Partnering to Increase
   Student Engagement 91
   *Rebecca L. Harrison, Angela Suzanne Insenga,
   and Heather Giebeig*

6 Constructing a Social Justice Pedagogy through
   Contemplative Service-Learning 117
   Patricia Owen-Smith

7 Common, yet Uncertain, Ground: Listening as Service-Learning 143
   Emily R. Yowonske and C. Aiden Downey

Index 161

About the Contributors 167

Foreword

There seems never to be enough time in the yearly schedule for faculty to discuss teaching. Lunchtime conversations and the occasional mentoring session rarely allow for much depth. Most faculty will tell you they have an unmet need to learn more about innovations in college-level teaching and to hear from their colleagues about their experiences with specific pedagogies. An essential first step is to set aside time.

To make good use of that time, the faculty needs to hear about a given pedagogy from experts who have a comprehensive perspective and can present the rationale, goals, and concepts, and summarize others' experiences efficiently. There must be time for discussion with the experts and with colleagues from a number of institutions about their contexts and how the pedagogy may be useful to them and their students. Ideally, there will be time to develop a plan to test these innovations in the faculty's classes.

Oxford College's Institute for Pedagogy in the Liberal Arts (IPLA) was created to meet this need. It is a four-day program, Tuesday through Friday, held during the week following Emory's commencement exercises—on the Monday of that week, usually the third week in May. The inaugural institute in 2007 was a test of the concept involving just twenty participants, all from Oxford College. In the decade that followed, participation expanded to as many as 125, including faculty from across the United States and from several foreign countries. Active learning pedagogies have always been the focus. Early topics were problem-based learning and team-based learning (TBL), but beginning with the 2010 institute, inquiry-guided learning emerged as the overarching pedagogy that produced the most faculty enthusiasm and offered the greatest promise for enhancing student learning.

It has been gratifying to see how much faculty value their participation in IPLA. Some return to participate year after year. Some use what they have learned to start a new program of scholarship on teaching and learning, and others have used their IPLA experience and contacts to lead institutional change. The institute has resulted in a number of publications and presentations at other meetings as participants share their experiences in implementing what they learned at IPLA.

The present volume, *Teaching, Pedagogy, and Learning: Fertile Ground for Campus and Community Innovations* edited by Jeffery Galle and Rebecca L. Harrison, brings together seven case study narratives reporting on pedagogical innovations at the institutional and community levels launched by IPLA. For those who could not attend IPLA, these will help them catch up. Those who have will recognize the IPLA approach and find fascinating results in the post-IPLA implementations. Both groups of readers will find this to be an invaluable and inspiring resource as they think about how to improve their students' learning.

—Stephen Bowen
Dean of Oxford College (2005–2016)

Acknowledgments

This volume has been two years (and several professional lives) in the making. The initial idea can be traced back to IPLA 2012 and the questions of Rebecca Harrison and Angela Insenga as we shared lunch together. They commented on the unique structure of the institute and asked whether anyone had organized a scholarly writing project on the course and curricular products emerging from IPLA. We left that lunch with potential answers to their question hanging in the air. By IPLA 2014, the idea had become a project, and the request for proposals issued in January 2015 solicited a highly diverse, creative set of ideas which has turned into two books.

We wish first to thank our contributors who have described the journeys they have made within individual courses and/or on institutional initiatives arising from the institute. They met our deadlines with grace and humor, and their work makes this book possible. Second, we would like to thank Tom Koerner and Carlie Wall of Rowman and Littlefield who saw in the original proposal not one but two books and who have supported us during the revision and editing process.

This project has benefitted from our spirit of friendship and collaboration first shared by us as co-editors and, more broadly, as a group of IPLA colleagues across many institutions. More personally, I would like to thank colleagues of mine at Oxford College of Emory University whose passion for teaching and the learning of their students has inspired this book. Colleagues there are people who have become friends and mentors, colleagues like David Gowler and Ken Anderson, to mention only two of nearly a hundred who have had a hand in building the institute. A special thanks goes to Dean Stephen Bowen, who wrote the foreword for this book, and whose vision for the IPLA and the Center for Academic Excellence (CAE) is deeply appreciated. When the CAE and IPLA were just getting off the ground, my first academic dean Kent Linville and his administrative assistant Lynn Harwell gave me unconditional support every day, which was vital to the growth of the CAE and the Institute for Pedagogy in the Liberal Arts. Finally, I would like to thank my spouse Jo Kuhn Galle for her unfailing patience in this project and her creative insights into my work at the unique and special college I call home.

—Jeff

I owe many debts of gratitude for my part in this book. My wonderful colleague David Newton, former chair of the Department of English and Philosophy, always found a way to support both my training at IPLA and my resulting curricula projects. The University of West Georgia's President Kyle Marrero and Randy Hendricks, during his tenure as college dean, also provided much-needed funding that made the field study with our local secondary partners possible. And, Cher Hendricks, the forward thinking, energetic director of the UWG Center for Teaching and Learning, sponsored our 2014 team sojourn to IPLA that jumpstarted both my field study and this book. I am especially grateful to these UWG colleagues, my graduate students Eli Miles and Abbie Driver, and the many others who go unnamed here, for their professional support.

More personally, I owe a heartfelt debt of gratitude to two individuals who have been my mainstays throughout this book project, certainly, but also in my personal journey in becoming a true inquiry-based learning (IBL) practitioner. Angela Insenga, my dear friend and colleague, thank you for supporting me with both honesty and laughter all these years in our many IPLA journeys and for always being my pedagogical yoda. Lastly, my deepest gratitude goes to my spouse, Patrick M. Erben, without whom none of this would be possible. He continues to tirelessly support my work and inspires me daily with his energy, optimism, and vision for a better world. Thank you for the last twenty years; I can't wait to see what the next twenty bring. *Der Himmel ist die Grenze meiner Liebe.*

—Rebecca

Introduction

Partnering for Success

Institute for Pedagogy in the Liberal Arts as a Galvanizing Journey for Faculty Development

Jeffery Galle and Rebecca L. Harrison

This collection began in 2010 when, quite appropriately, we first met in the role of student and teacher. As a newly hired faculty member seeking pedagogical innovations for her pre-service English education majors, I walked into my first Institute for Pedagogy in the Liberal Arts (IPLA) workshop at Emory Oxford co-taught by Jeffery Galle. That seminar—one devoted to hands-on work with full-format inquiry practices—politely challenged me to reassess deeply rooted, traditional philosophies about teaching and learning, and, perhaps most importantly, to come to see that asking students to answer questions and engage in discussions about texts through traditional categories of my discipline were not by their *nature* profitable inquiry practices.

Galle's seminar contextualized for participants how tangible paths for establishing authentic, student-centered, critical learning environments capitalize on the potency of cognitive dissonance by establishing settings where students learn "by confronting intriguing, beautiful, or important problems, [and] authentic tasks that will challenge them to grapple with ideas, rethink their assumptions, and examine their mental models of reality" (Bain, 2004, p. 18). In coming to terms with my own expectation failures about teaching, those conversations led to a new way of seeing students as stakeholders in the learning process and inquiry as a living pedagogical practice key for building sustainable curricula for twenty-first-century learners.

The 2010 workshop also began to foster regular discussions between us, dialogues that would continue to grow over the next four years and many sojourns to Oxford's campus, about IBL's potential[1] in reforming secondary and collegiate curricula alike, and the ways in which the pedagogical innovations cultivated at IPLA could benefit a plethora of teaching audiences and environments. The possibilities for bringing these individual faculty innovations to light and, thus, the work and mission of the institute came to be the common thread of our discussions in 2014, an IPLA focused squarely on IBL practices with an arm dedicated to broader institutional and communal change. There, over a lively talk about the cross-discipline curricular implementation of Oxford's recently acquired sustainable farm and the import of the final phase of SoTL paradigm (the scholarly production of teaching innovation), our editorial collaboration was born. This book is the result of that partnership.

Teaching, Pedagogy, and Learning: Fertile Ground for Campus and Community Innovations brings together narratives of pedagogical innovation aimed at increasing student engagement and performance and bolstering faculty teaching effectiveness and satisfaction. These transdisciplinary, transpedagogical chapters all emerged from faculty experiences at the annual IPLA, offered by Oxford College of Emory University. The book spotlights two significant points: first, faculty need pioneering, supportive contexts within which they can conceive, develop, revise, and publish innovative teaching experiments using the same principles of experiential and active learning that have become the foundation of learning for student success; and, second, strong institutional partnership with faculty development affords one way to achieve this outcome.

The seven chapters in this book are written by seventeen diverse scholar-teachers across eleven academic disciplines and nine institutions—from K-12 schools to small liberal arts colleges to tier-one research institutions—for whom the IPLA experience at Oxford spring-boarded significant pedagogical growth. While the authors all share the foundational IPLA experience, they spotlight the work from conception to implementation to revision that goes into impactful course and institutional innovation by faculty who practically seek out and implement new approaches.

Why are IPLA's story and these individual faculty journeys important to other instructors, institutions, faculty development officers, and teaching centers? IPLA's unique, concurrent session conference model, which avoids antiquated large group lecture-style delivery of pedagogical information, serves to model the unlimited possibilities for transforming classroom spaces when faculty are provided with fertile ground for training in active learning techniques.

The chapters in this book encapsulate in a few pages what amounts to years of faculty and institutional work. Their stories of change and discovery through the common exploration of signature pedagogies and teaching strategies can have widespread influences on others seeking similar growth in our radically shifting global educational contexts.

As highlighted by our authors, perhaps the most important way to gauge the impact of this institute is to identify and delineate the influences on various kinds of faculty work in a range of contexts: (1) the development of pedagogies and course materials that are the specialty area or special focus of the individual faculty; (2) the development of pedagogies and course materials specific to an area, a particular discipline, such as problem-based learning (PBL) in the sciences; and (3) at the broader institutional level, the development of pedagogies and course materials that will enable the success of a campus-wide curricular initiative at the undergraduate or graduate level (e.g., a general education requirement or a particular upper-level curricular pedagogy that groups of faculty need to study).

This collection takes up these contexts where pedagogical experimentation, as our authors show, gives birth to meaningful local and communal change. Though finished essays, their pedagogical projects are by their very nature still works in progress, as experimentation with scholarly teaching and learning that fosters long-lasting, impactful change takes time, reflection, and revision.

Much like IPLA's wide-ranging pedagogical outreach mission, this book is designed to benefit individual teachers working in K-12 environs through all facets of university-level instruction and faculty developers. It seeks to help, for example, K-12 teachers who may be struggling to pair more inquiry-based practices with the common core, as well as new, first-year college instructors who are suddenly charged with full-time teaching loads with little pedagogical support. Conversely, it also hopes to inspire senior faculty, many of whom may feel a stagnancy in their teaching, to reassess their signature courses and pursue new avenues for increased student and personal growth, or faculty administrators who, in taking stock of strategic initiatives and lagging outcomes, are looking to reinvest and spearhead larger institutional change. That is to say that these seven chapters are of value in themselves as products of the efforts of individual scholar-teachers but also for those interested in cultivating change.

The array of purposes that faculty and faculty teams bring to the annual IPLA institute may be partly attributed to the variety of programs that each IPLA is able to offer. As our authors attest, pedagogies deemed of vital interest to faculty range across a broad spectrum of inquiry-based approaches, a range that encompasses the liberal arts disciplines, the sciences, secondary school contexts, and a number of professional schools as well.

A scholar like Ken Bain and his groundbreaking work on establishing natural, critical learning environments and cooperative classrooms through the use of expectation failures, for example, offer insights to faculty from every locale. Similarly, the approach of Eric Mazur to active peer teaching, especially in large classroom contexts, crosses all disciplines and educational contexts. Scholar-teachers also gravitate to sessions hosted by scholars who have founded a particular pedagogical approach, like Larry Michaelson's team-based learning, which highlights the intersection of effective group work with relevant problems, a method that resonates meaningfully with faculty outside of the colleges of business where TBL had its start.[2]

As IPLA's programming has become more varied over the first decade of its existence, the range of applications to IPLA has also changed. Each year has seen new applications from institutions across Georgia and the southeast, as well as the nation and beyond.[3]

There remains tremendous potential for improving instruction in higher education and in fomenting stronger connections to our public school partners and local communities. These growth areas certainly trace forward to deeper exploration of teaching and learning, but they also trail backward to the roots of education in the K-12 system. *Teaching, Pedagogy, and Learning* explores further the ways that dedicated practitioners from every level and every type of training can engage in pedagogical connections and strategies across traditional borders.

In facilitating the pedagogical innovations of courses from the liberal arts alongside those of professors from medical schools, colleges of business and education, schools of nursing, public health, law, or theology, this volume furthers the potential for the cross-pollination of ideas, problem awareness, and joint ownership of proposed solutions to classroom challenges. For too long and with too many negative effects, education has occurred in separate and disconnected places.

How, then, does this volume connect to and intervene in existing scholarship? While the *Going Public* movement which began fifteen years ago encouraged and provided venues for faculty to present on and publish their individual experiments with teaching and learning, those opportunities have been, generally, isolated to conferences, like the International Society for the Scholarship of Teaching and Learning, or to pedagogy-centered journals, such as *College Teaching* (CT), or the *International Journal for the Scholarship of Teaching and Learning* (IJSOTL).[4]

These advances notwithstanding, the *Going Public* movement has yet to lead to a substantial body of collected essays that is simultaneously pluralistic, transdisciplinary, transpedagogical, and transinstitutional. And, while the literature involving innovation in teaching is fairly extensive, recent publications in this area fall into two main categories: single author and collected editions.

A number of recent single author texts contribute much to the market. Texts such as Ken Bain's *What the Best College Teachers Do* (2004), Art Zajonc's *Meditation as Contemplative Inquiry: When Knowing Becomes Love* (2010), Jim Lang's *On Course: A Week-by-Week Guide to Your First Semester of College Teaching*, (2010), and John Bean's *Engaging Ideas: The Professor's Guide to Integrating Writing, Critical Thinking, and Active Learning in the Classroom* (2011), all establish a type of discourse on teaching inspired by each author's primary pedagogical expertise. Though insightful texts, the strategies they offer emerge from and are limited to data and research produced by one predominant scholar with significant experience in the field. They are also written for a largely passive (but receptive) reading audience. Though invaluable, the findings, the suggestions, and, indeed, the voice from each work are the products of a single person's imagination and analysis.

Such monolithic approaches to pedagogical innovation are augmented by other more collaborative forms and models, which are gaining in popularity. Virginia S. Lee's seminal collection *Teaching and Learning through Inquiry* (2004) presents twenty chapters that open the discourse on teaching to the expertise of many other scholar-teachers across a variety of disciplines; each chapter either narrates an experience within a particular college course or writes from within another area of expertise. In a similar vein, Tim Riordan and James Roth's edited collection *Disciplines as Frameworks for Student Learning* (2004) presents essays by the faculty of Alverno College who identify key pedagogical concepts of specific disciplines that provide conceptual frameworks for students to work within and learn. *Exploring Signature Pedagogies* (2008), edited by Regan Garung and Nancy Chick, likewise spotlights essays authored by faculty across the Wisconsin system who individually present narratives describing ways to foster disciplinary habits of mind in undergraduate students.

These four books are highly valuable and represent just a small sampling of the existing discourse on the scholarly production of teaching and the need for more attention to collaboration, diversity, and multiple voices. Yet, they are also by their nature simultaneously restricted to specific program, university, and/or system initiatives.

Teaching, Pedagogy, and Learning, in its outgrowth from the diverse, sweeping scope of the IPLA experience, begins to fill this niche, and, given its origins with the common IPLA experience, intercedes in the existing discourse on teaching in unique ways. Profiting from IPLA's mission to provide a varied group of faculty with the opportunity to work in small groups with internationally renowned experts of a particular pedagogy, our authors have studied with the very experts who have written the groundbreaking literature mentioned above.

Bain, Lang, Mazur, and Lee, among many noted others, have taken off the proverbial gloves during their residency at IPLA and narrowed the distance from keynote scholars to hands-on mentors working with individual faculty on grassroots projects with the purpose of developing individual narratives of pedagogical innovation and scholarship. The participating faculty, across disciplines and institution types, have then implemented these experiments in their classes and have written individual narratives of their efforts and course revisions that now, with the publication of this book, talk back to and in concert with those scholars with whom they studied. In so doing, their innovative pedagogical ideas are emerging from multiple points: not just top down from expert to novice, but from burgeoning scholar-teachers who are becoming—in the truest sense of the word—practitioners of the conceptions of the scholarship of teaching and learning. This book, therefore, is a first in many ways.

These case study narratives model teaching strategies across disciplines in the humanities and fine arts, social sciences, sciences, and education, but they also present models for larger institutional shifts that impact communities at the local, department, and university level. In toto, the collection evidences how innovative ideas must be fostered and applied at the ground level with individual faculty before "innovative" becomes innovation.

This collection, as the first of two books spotlighting faculty teaching experiments from the common IPLA experience, is divided into two parts, each prefaced by an internationally renowned master scholar-teacher who served as an IPLA mentor. The chapters in part I, *Inquiry and Campus Culture*, present and highlight the IPLA model as an engine of large-scale department and university change, as well as its impact on individual faculty development.

Jeffery Galle's opening chapter, "Institut[ing] Innovation: Courses, Curriculum, and Faculty Expertise," recounts the Institute's inception and development. He outlines both its structural design and its impact on individual course development and teaching strategies among its interdisciplinary and transinstitutional cohorts.

Further, the chapter stresses the vital contributions of IPLA (and its central relationship with the CAE) to Oxford's mission as the teaching college inhabiting Emory University's original campus—to serve as a leader in pedagogical innovation for the larger research university and beyond. For Galle, Emory Oxford's new sustainable farm—the centerpiece of pedagogical explorations in sustainability at the 2014 Institute—serves as a fitting metaphor for IPLA's significance: a fertile, yet wide open space that spurs creativity, a foundation for growth in teaching and learning, and a place for envisioning and engaging tall order projects.

"IGL Certification: A Model for Institutionalizing Inquiry-Guided Learning," by *Devon Fisher, Daniel W. Kiser, Jennifer Heller, and David Ratke*, details the processes that lead to the university-wide adoption of inquiry-guided learning (IGL) at Lenoir-Rhyne University. The authors describe the creation of a semester-long IGL certification program for faculty, its theoretical underpinnings, and the practical steps needed for its implementation. It notes the challenges and successes of the program, including the establishment across the campus of a common vocabulary for talking about IGL and a growing commitment of faculty to using the method. Finally, they present preliminary assessment results that point to the ongoing success of the certification program.

Caralyn B. Zehnder, Kalina Manoylov, Christine Mutiti, Sam Mutiti, and Allison VandeVoort in "Implementing Inquiry-Guided Labs in an Introductory Nonmajors Science Course" trace a pedagogy innovation project at Georgia College and State University proceeding from the problem that too many students equate learning science with fact memorization. The authors decided to use IGL to communicate their excitement about science to their students, majors and nonmajors alike.

In 2014, a team from Georgia College attended a three-day IGL workshop embedded within the IPLA conference, where they learned how to apply key IGL concepts to their own program. One specific outcome was the revision of the "Introduction to Environmental Science" laboratory course to include inquiry-guided labs. This process included the creation of new assessment methods to measure the effect of these changes on student learning. The chapter focuses on the process followed to implement these changes, the structures in place that supported this work, the assessment tools used, and the team's future work.

Lia Schraeder's chapter, "Resolving Early Career Paradoxes at the IPLA," candidly reflects on the problem that many early career collegiate faculty face: moving into full-time, four/four load teaching positions with little formal training in pedagogical approaches conducive to the discipline and student engagement. Her chapter problematizes both graduate assistant training and academic cultures, which too often leave early career faculty feeling isolated, with few opportunities to talk productively about struggles with pedagogy.

Faced with this situation and a diverse student body struggling to balance work, family, and school life, the author recounts how IPLA served as fertile ground for robust pedagogical training and provided her with a nurturing community of scholars devoted to building positive and engaged classroom practice. Finally, Schraeder discusses putting this new teaching tool kit into practice with her history survey course, World History II, which moved her students to understand history as far more than a rote "memorization class" and led to the highest evaluations and class retention rates of her career.

The narratives in part II, *Pedagogies of Community,* look outward, tracing the outreach potential of pedagogical innovation when, as the authors highlight, strategies learned at IPLA are brought to and applied in K-12 education and local communities. The section opens with "Inquiry-Based Learning: Partnering to Increase Student Engagement" by *Rebecca L. Harrison, Angela Suzanne Insenga, and Heather Giebeig.*

The authors recount using IPLA's 2014 focus on IBL to launch a community-based research project centered on building meaningful connections between collegiate and public school faculty. They explain the efficacy of implementing IBL practices in public schools and argue for the vital role that college faculty can play in bridging distances—perceived and real—between these intrinsically linked spaces. The chapter details their project's procedures, which provided a two-day institute for K–12 teachers and deployed an instrument for their on-site assessment of IBL's impact in secondary classrooms. The resulting quantitative and qualitative data analysis of IBL's effects in the participants' classes, finally, the authors conclude, reveal the virtually unlimited potential of inquiry practices in secondary schools.

Patricia Owen-Smith's "Constructing a Social Justice Pedagogy through Contemplative Service-Learning" proceeds from the premise that the triad of cognitive-affective learning, service-learning, and contemplative pedagogy have all been fundamental to the original conception and subsequent development of IPLA. All three models pursue a participatory and transformative epistemology that is counternormative in its fundamental inversion of traditional institutional and pedagogical approaches.

The author briefly reviews the history of service-learning, definitions that have emerged from this history, and how this history informs the ways in which service-learning programs and courses contribute to citizenship and engagement. The meaning of "social justice," specifically as it relates to a contemplative service-learning pedagogy, is explored. Central to this chapter is a consideration of how the use of specific contemplative practices addresses problems that currently exist between the service-learning and social justice relationship and how they might deepen and bring integrity to this relationship. The chapter concludes with a central question driving contemplative service-learning: "what does it mean to be human and what is our responsibility to answering this question?"

Lastly, *C. Aiden Downey and Emily Yowonske* in "Common, yet Uncertain, Ground: Listening as Service-Learning" explores how pairing inquiry guided learning with community-based learning challenges preconceived assumptions about local communities in ways that foster relationships and meaningful learning. The chapter spotlights listening as service, an outgrowth of narrative inquiry, and the students' work in the neighboring Clarkston community: a refugee-resettlement site and one of the most diverse cities in the country.

Their class project, The Clarkston Roving Listener Project, spotlights Downey's undergraduate course's struggle to rethink service-learning. Yowonske, a student from the course, recounts their efforts to gather the oral histories of Clarkston school students, an effort that branched out to the larger Clarkston community in the culminating "Banquet of Stories" celebration. In so doing, this class's work—an outgrowth of IPLA—created a "sustainable community fixture" that honored communal diversity and helped Clarkston youth, many of whom are refugees from countries like Sudan, find voice and agency.

Taking one step back from the narratives of this volume to the institute itself, the authors can say that the IPLA has provided a venue for innovation and collegiality. For Oxford College, the institute has contributed to crystallizing its own identity. From within a leading research institution like Emory, the evolution of Oxford College as a valued, contributing member of the university is an important story in itself. This introduction, then, should not end without expressing the deepest possible thanks to Steve Bowen, whose support as the Dean of Oxford College and whose vision for IPLA and the Center for Academic Excellence have made this book possible.

Over the past twenty years, this small college located at the geographical birthplace of Emory in Oxford, Georgia, has distilled its mission, a commitment to liberal arts–intensive undergraduate education. With teaching and learning as the primary focus, it is natural for Oxford faculty to create innovative designs like the Ways of Inquiry program and develop a number of vital programs in service-learning, leadership development, and other experiential learning pedagogies.

Yet, the story is one in progress; it is not complete. In a college website news report that summarized his work and achievements as college dean, Dean Bowen looked ahead to the college's future:

> I often hear it said that "Oxford is in a good place," and of course I agree. But Oxford has not yet fulfilled its potential or realized its mission. Progress over the last decade has strengthened the college and removed many constraints. The challenge for the future will be to build on that strength and seize the opportunities inherent in a small college that enrolls only freshmen and sophomores, embedded in a leading R1 university…My advice is to be ambitious, take some risks, and build a purposefully structured educational program that pursues the goals of liberal education head on and with minimal compromise. In the world of higher education, that is Oxford's singular promise.

This college possesses a singular drive and hunger for excellence in teaching, as Bowen's statement attests. Even with past successes, the future possibilities call for renewal and commitment. The following chapters indicate the direction of the college and its aspiration to inspire great teaching and excellent learning both within the college and beyond.

NOTES

1. The chapters in this book make use of several related terms, "inquiry," "inquiry-guided learning" (IGL), and "inquiry-based learning" (IBL). They all share the fundamental requisite feature of question-making on the part of students. IGL allows more faculty guidance and scaffolding, hence the word *guided* indicating a level of faculty support. IBL tends to focus more on student independence. Despite their different emphases relative to the degree of student responsibility for their own inquiry and efforts, both IGL and IBL engage students where they are, ask a great deal of students, and foster appreciation of disciplinary thinking. Thus, throughout the book, readers will see references to IBL, IGL, and inquiry.

2. The IPLA has hosted a number of scholars who are recognized as founders of a particular pedagogy, and this has elicited a great deal of support for IPLA from those who had not heard of the institute. Even more compelling is that, over time, faculty who have studied at IPLA with someone like Michaelson have gone on to produce work in the pedagogy and then led sessions at IPLA in later years. This process of students of a pedagogy becoming experts in the pedagogy is one of the achievements of the institute that will be mentioned later.

3. The first IPLA cohort in 2007 was composed of faculty from Oxford College and the sessions were led exclusively by Oxford College faculty. In succeeding years, the faculty of the college continued to lead sessions of IPLA, as also other faculty from Emory's other divisions began to lead as well. Complementing these Emory faculty, other scholars from outside Emory who possessed significant knowledge in specific pedagogies were invited to lead sessions. The participants of IPLA likewise demonstrate great diversity in terms of institutional type, geographical location, and disciplinary focus.

4. Also, this movement began to pave the way for institutions, including R1, to count professional development in pedagogy toward tenure and promotion.

REFERENCES

Bain, K. (2004). *What the best college teachers do.* Cambridge, MA: Harvard UP.
Bean, J. (2011). *Engaging ideas: The professor's guide to integrating writing, critical thinking, and active learning in the classroom.* San Francisco: Jossey Bass.
Bowen retires, leaving tremendous Oxford legacy. Retrieved May 17, 2016 from http://oxford.emory.edu/news/bowen-retires-leaving-tremendous-oxford-legacy/

Garung, R. and N. Chick. (2008). *Exploring signature pedagogies: Approaches to teaching disciplinary habits of mind.* Sterling, VA: Stylus.

Lang, J. (2010). *On course: A week-by-week guide to your first semester of college teaching.* Cambridge, MA: Harvard UP.

Lee, V. (2004). *Teaching and learning through inquiry: A guidebook for institutions and instructors.* Sterling, VA: Stylus.

Riordan, T. and J. Roth. (2004). *Disciplines as frameworks for student learning: Teaching the practice of the disciplines.* Sterling, VA: Stylus.

Zajonc, A. (2014). *Meditation as contemplative inquiry: When knowing becomes love.* Herndon, VA: Lindisfarne Books.

Part I

INQUIRY AND CAMPUS CULTURE

Foreword

Virginia S. Lee

As an independent consultant, over the past twelve years, I have found most rewarding assignments that allowed me to collaborate with a single campus, working together over several years toward a larger, transformative vision for the institution. The Institute for Pedagogy in the Liberal Arts (IPLA) 2014 and some of its fruits in the form of the chapter contributions in *Inquiry and Campus Culture* culminated four years of engagement with my colleagues at Oxford College of Emory University. The association has been very important to me.

Not only has it been gratifying to see the growth of a culture of inquiry at Oxford College through its own "Ways of Inquiry" program. Equally gratifying has been seeing the extension of the college's influence to other campuses through its annual IPLA, whether through individual faculty members, through academic departments, or through campus-wide initiatives.

The chapters that follow document undergraduate education change efforts at the individual course, program, and institution-wide level, all stimulated by IPLA, as Galle describes. The IGL (i.e., inquiry-guided learning) Certificate described by Devon Fisher and his colleagues at Lenoir-Rhyne University (Hickory, NC) and the development of inquiry-guided labs for nonmajors documented by Caralyn Zehnder and her colleagues in the Department of Biology and Environmental Sciences at Georgia College and State University (Milledgeville, GA) in chapters two and three emerged from the three-day institute on "Inquiry as a Way of Learning in Colleges and Universities," a one-time innovation of IPLA 2014, led by Phil Levy (United Kingdom), Rachel Spronken-Smith (New Zealand), Catherine Chiappetta Swanson (Canada), and me. Change at the program and university-wide level is more difficult to orchestrate, but potentially more powerful, because it is institutionalized and affects a wider swath of faculty members, students, and staff.

But change at the course level through the work of an individual faculty member can also be an important stimulus for change under the right circumstances. In her chapter Lia Schraeder, Department of History, Georgia Gwinnett College (Lawrenceville, GA) describes the impact of IPLA's intensive two-day workshops on a faculty member in the early and important formative stage of her career and her highly successful revision of an introductory World History survey course. Two-day workshops have been the mainstay of IPLA offerings since its inception, because they can influence participants' teaching practices so powerfully.

This volume describes how Oxford College has found another means of leveraging and extending the impact of its IPLA by providing a venue for the scholarship of teaching and learning of its participants. I hope instructors and students on other campuses benefit from the important work described in the pages that follow.

Chapter One

Institut[ing] Innovation

Courses, Curriculum, and Faculty Expertise

Jeffery Galle

> I thought I was a good teacher until I discovered my students were just memorizing information rather than learning to understand the material. Who was to blame?
>
> —Eric Mazur, Harvard University

What it means to be a good teacher is at the heart of Mazur's observation. In the second week of May each year, the Institute for Pedagogy in the Liberal Arts (IPLA) establishes a venue within which university colleagues explore a number of ways to respond to this question. This chapter traces the development of the institute at Oxford College as one part of the college's response to the question of what it means to be a teaching and learning college that happens to be happily housed within a preeminent research university.

Identity, mission, values—these are the words that are mentioned frequently in conversations about the evolution of Oxford College and its key initiatives such as the IPLA. Aspiring to be a national model for undergraduate education, the college seeks to identify pedagogies and practices that enhance learning. The institute's structure and programming have enabled faculty to develop expertise in specific pedagogies, all founded on the fundamental precept of inquiry. The chapter also offers brief examples of innovation in practice and ends with some consideration of significance, next steps, and impacts of the institute within and beyond Emory.

THE ORIGINS OF THE INSTITUTE FOR PEDAGOGY IN THE LIBERAL ARTS

First envisioned during the 2005 strategic planning process of Oxford College of Emory University, the IPLA celebrated its tenth anniversary in May 2016. Through IPLA, the college has addressed two central questions that the strategic planning process set out to answer: in what ways can the college provide significant pedagogical training, discussion, and support for the faculty of Oxford College as a division within Emory with special expertise in the pedagogies of teaching and learning, and what contributions to the larger academic world, including all divisions of Emory University, can Oxford College make?[1] Thus, the college has sought to further its own distinctiveness as a division within the research university through programs and events that focus on teaching, learning, and related scholarship. Success in defining a clear and useful role within Emory University has also framed current and potential contributions to the higher education community.

During IPLA 2013, a small group of participants walked to the five-acre grassy knoll that was soon to become the Oxford College organic farm. The session on Pedagogy as Sustainability, led by Tom Kelly, took advantage of the fledgling organic farm as the context in which to imagine the possibilities of sustainability projects across the curriculum. Participants sat in chairs on the grass of the empty lot and began to envision the organic farm and their own courses or new courses. Participating faculty left that afternoon with a sense of the possible for what could be created when faculty are given the opportunity and the support to innovate learning experiences.[2]

That moment, described in detail across many conversations, represents the ethos of the college: creativity, commitment to teaching and learning, and a fearless engagement with tall order projects. Today, the IPLA conference as well as the thriving organic farm are vibrant examples of a culture of creative possibility, optimism, and hard work. This inviting field of grass is an appropriate metaphor for the vision of the 2005 Strategic Plan which foresaw the potential for Oxford College as a nationally recognized learning and teaching institution.[3]

Two steps in the process of establishing the vision were the creation of the Center for Academic Excellence (CAE) and the IPLA. In 2007, the inaugural IPLA was offered to approximately twenty faculty members of the college. Before the second institute of 2008, the director of the teaching center, the CAE, was hired, and the responsibility for organizing and extending the institute fell under the domain of the CAE.

The backstory to these developments—strategic planning, the IPLA, and the CAE—really begins with Emory's move from its original site in Oxford,

Georgia, to the Druid Hills campus in Atlanta in 1918. From its founding in 1836 until 1918, Emory resided on the Oxford, Georgia, site. The move to Atlanta raised the question of what was to be done with the college on the birthplace site. Would all of Emory be in Atlanta, or would the Oxford campus remain a part of Emory yet be separate? The ways that the university and the Oxford campus responded to these questions actually represent the history of the college after Emory's move to Atlanta.

After the move, from 1918 until the strategic planning period of 2004–2005, Oxford College of Emory University underwent several iterations. The compelling story has been told by Joseph C. Moon in *An Uncommon Place: Oxford College of Emory University, 1914–2000* (2003). In the decades following Emory's move to the Druid Hills campus, Oxford College underwent several different blueprint designs. For a decade, the Academy at Oxford was a high caliber university preparatory institution.

A four-year program composed of the last two years of advanced high school study and the first two years of college study was then developed; this program lasted another dozen or so years. By the late twentieth century, Oxford was more aligned with the central mission of the university itself, but the overlap between Emory College and Oxford College remained a question for some.

In 2003–2004, President James Wagner challenged the college to identify and articulate its distinctiveness within the larger university, which already possessed a topnotch four-year program in Emory College. What was needed was for Oxford College to articulate its mission and vision for a two-year program within a range of Emory baccalaureate possibilities. Out of this challenge, the strategic planning process of 2004–2005 emerged.

Over many decades, the college had developed signature features—high quality teaching, strong relationships shared by faculty, students, and staff, and a pronounced co-curricular experience for students. Successes in the late 1990s had resulted in the school receiving Carnegie status, and the institution scored in the top percentage in all five categories of the National Survey of Student Engagement, something rare for any institution. As the college evolved, the key elements of success became clear: student and faculty interaction, academic rigor, a focus on the liberal arts, and the benefits of scale where everyone in the small residential college essentially knew everyone else.

The college began to articulate its own identity as a learning community. With the university's increasing support under President Wagner, and through the efforts of Oxford College faculty and its dean, Dr. Stephen Bowen, the college was poised for a period of even greater creativity. Much like the situation described above at the organic farm, the faculty worked to produce a vision that blended the best qualities integral to the Oxford experience with a sense of open-ended possibilities. That historical moment led to the codifying of the core values of the college and its curriculum as Liberal Arts Intensive (LAI), the creation of the CAE, and the founding of the IPLA.

The inaugural IPLA of 2007 represented, in one sense then, the culmination of a number of historical efforts. This volume, produced more than a decade after the inception of IPLA, contains a few of the catalyzing experiences of participants over the years of the institute. The chapters also suggest multiple ways that such efforts and initiatives can extend institutional identity, enrich relationships beyond institutional boundaries, and provide pivotal means for the faculty of the college to export their teaching expertise to a larger audience.

MAXIMIZING CREATIVITY THROUGH STRUCTURE

The graduate school course seminar model in which students engaged with the professor as the disciplinary expert offered the most engaging, learning rich standard for every session. As IPLA grew, organizers were mindful of retaining the seminar, small group model, keeping the size of each session at twelve to fifteen participants.

Since the IPLA of 2007, the four-day institute has changed in the number of session tracks and the diversity of pedagogies offered, but it has retained its fundamental structure of a pair of two-day workshops, each composed of individual pedagogical programs led by a scholar recognized for work in a particular pedagogy. IPLA organizers have experimented with the overall number of admitted participants by increasing the number of sessions rather than adding many more participants to each one. Hence, the number of accepted participants has remained in the sixty-to-seventy range for most years.[4]

Common meals, keynote addresses, and working lunches have augmented the sessions and provided more integration of the thinking, discussion, and pedagogies. Individual participants working on personal course design have been the fundamental purpose, but in IPLA 2014, a second concurrent three-day institute for institutional teams dedicated to the exploration of inquiry-guided learning (IGL) was offered. Scholars from institutions around the world that possessed an IGL curricular feature led groups of faculty and staff from participating institutions that had planned to develop inquiry in some institutional unit.

Thus, as individual faculty or institutional teams, passionate teachers from around the country self-select to participate in the IPLA workshop experience, and confirmation of the ways that the institute fuels their passion is supported by the number of repeat applications by faculty who express in their application a clear (and emphatic) plan for ways to use each annual iteration of the IPLA.

Two successful aspects of the IPLA structure immediately come to mind from frequent evaluations and mention of the IPLA in external sources, such as Jim Lang's column in the *Chronicle*.[5] These two components are the successive two-day sessions (making this a four-day institute) and the consequence of the four three-hour blocks of instruction over the two days.

In the IPLA of 2007, the organizers offered three session tracks on Tuesday/Wednesday and then repeated the same three programs on Thursday/Friday, thus enabling participants to switch to a new track on Thursday/Friday. This structure worked well the first two years as most of the twenty or so participants came from Oxford College. As interest in IPLA grew, adding an additional track for each two-day session allowed for a higher number of accepted faculty while retaining the seminar discussion model. Thus, by the third year, IPLA offered eight entirely different programs—four on Tuesday/Wednesday and four on Thursday/Friday.

The way in which each two-day session is structured is left to the creativity of each facilitating scholar, but some general patterns have emerged. Essentially, scholars and participants have three-hour blocks of time on two successive mornings and afternoons, thus creating four blocks of three hours.

Generally, facilitators contextualize the session on the morning of the first day with faculty attendees receiving essential guiding questions, materials, and an intellectual frame up front. Then, sessions shift toward more individual work and projects on the second day. By the final afternoon, faculty have time to present a course idea, make a presentation, or even offer a complete unit in summary fashion to the full group for feedback.

This model is repeated on Thursday/Friday but with a different signature pedagogy, a different scholar facilitator, and a different set of participants. By the end of the week, all participants make significant progress on two different pedagogies or course ideas and carry away pedagogical innovations to increase student success.

While participants do not receive training in all eight programs sessions, the overwhelming majority prefer going deep into two signature pedagogies while spending significant time with other faculty who have selected other pedagogies. In an email following IPLA 2015, a research librarian at the Goizueta Business School Library wrote: "Great conference—I'd never been through such an intensive multi-hour session format before, but it's incredibly valuable to really take a deep dive into content and work through it with actionable outcomes vs touching the surface as so many conferences do with 1-hr sessions on similar topics" (M. Anderson-Strait, personal correspondence, May 29, 2015).

PROGRAMMING: PEDAGOGIES FOR COURSES AND CURRICULUM

Given the structure of IPLA's eight session tracks across the first ten years, approximately 600 faculty across the ranks and from a variety of institutions have undertaken the "deep dive." When one considers that a traditional annual conference in a discipline often draws two or three thousand attendees, one might think that IPLA is much ado about little.

Yet upon closer examination, the 600 individuals who have attended in the first few years have also experienced two sets of two-day session tracks, which effectively doubles the individual faculty projects undertaken. With this number of projects emerging from in-depth programs, the participants frequently follow up by email posts or, for Emory faculty, at successive teaching programs across the year that, thanks to IPLA, they have "changed the way they teach." Faculty who have attended the IPLA have in many cases become experts in particular pedagogies. A number of faculty who studied inquiry, team-based learning (TBL), or problem-based learning (PBL), for example, are now publishing chapters and articles on these pedagogies. Also, faculty teams who have attended the IPLA report that new features now exist at their home institutions.

These outcomes of the institute can be traced back to the attention being given to programming that addresses disciplinary, college, and institutional curricular needs. The director and the other organizers ensure that the sciences, social sciences, and humanities faculty have a number of options to consider when they apply. It is vital that second choices for each two-day session be useful and good for the variety of faculty applying. Thus, disciplinary needs are fundamental.

Another factor in programming has been to consider the types of home institutions of applying faculty. The faculty that form each cohort come from residential liberal arts colleges, large research institutions across the nation, state colleges and universities, Historically Black Colleges and Universities (HBCU) in the southeast, and K-12 teachers from a variety of locales. Such a diverse IPLA cohort means these participants form a significantly different group of teachers than would be found at disciplinary conferences where attendees are presenting, networking, and listening to colleagues within a narrow strand of the higher education scene.

At IPLA, faculty from all disciplines and educational environments gather together to study teaching strategies and engage in meaningful, collaborative dialogue for student success. Some of the IPLA-inspired discipline-specific projects include the following:

- A biologist from a research university refines a PBL approach to her lab.
- An anthropologist from a residential liberal arts college develops a TBL component for her large introductory anthropology class.
- A historian from a prestigious HBCU shifts the pedagogy in an upper-level history class to a "Reacting to the Past" approach.
- A secondary school social studies teacher develops an inquiry unit for her sophomore students.
- A professor of classics who participated in a previous TBL session returns to lead an upcoming IPLA session on TBL. In so doing, he refines his TBL approach.
- A secondary school English teacher adds an oral debate component to her literature classes after participating in an IPLA session on debate as a pedagogical exercise.
- A professor of political science at a major research university attends two successive IPLAs in teaching and learning with technology sessions and creates five new pedagogical exercises for his large political science introductory classes.
- A professor of French participates in a session track on developing a travel course and develops a proposal for his administration to consider.

This handful of examples, which could be extended by hundreds more, demonstrates how the IPLA collective cohort touches every discipline and most educational contexts. Retaining the small group seminar sessions, providing common times at meals for conversation, and asking that each participant develop a concrete project in each of the two-day sessions have fostered broader engagement across the cohorts and deeper integration of the materials of each IPLA session into the professional lives of participants.

The CAE director and a small group of organizers read detailed evaluations after each session in preparing the slate of session tracks for each succeeding IPLA. In this way, the stories of individual faculty figure prominently during the planning and creation of individual IPLA session tracks: faculty may request a particular topic, scholar, or a session track/pedagogy that addresses a particular course challenge; faculty from particular disciplines or academic areas may express the desire for more study of a pedagogy that addresses a disciplinary need; and sometimes faculty request a session track that addresses a general institutional interest or need. As these (and other) requests recur with greater frequency, a clearer idea of the potential response to widespread need can be discerned and addressed by IPLA.[6]

Another type of faculty work drives the creation of other session programs. For example, many times a signature pedagogy for a particular discipline such as PBL in the sciences is requested by a senior faculty member, department head, or division chair for the development of junior faculty.[7] Science faculty of Emory College and Oxford College have led invaluable sessions on PBL over the years of IPLA, much to the benefit of STEM faculty who have doctorates in a very specialized field but feel a level of frustration when faced with structuring coursework that will place students in the best position to learn through doing. Colleagues at the Emory School of Medicine have participated in PBL and TBL session tracks very often with great enthusiasm.

In a similar way, such pedagogies as "Reacting to the Past" (IPLA 2012) have stimulated innovations by faculty from the humanities and social sciences. Yet this pedagogy is not one like PBL that is so essential to the teaching within specific disciplines. As faculty from language studies, history, political science, and sociology, for example, have expressed the need for pedagogies that address the specialized contexts and content of their areas, some scholars have developed generalized teaching strategies such as those found in sessions such as "Tactics for Teaching the Liberal Arts" (IPLA 2013). The diverse projects that have acquired the general name Digital Humanities (IPLA 2012) now invite partnerships between humanities faculty and other academic areas in the creation of teaching resources and sites that are limited only by the imagination of those involved. Yet another example is TBL (IPLA 2010), which was initially developed within business courses to foster collaboration and competitiveness and has now moved well beyond this disciplinary purpose.

A particular pedagogical approach founded in one particular discipline often moves beyond its historical roots, undergoes some modification, and emerges again in other disciplines and contexts. Such is the story of oral debate, PBL, and TBL. Others are readily conducive to multiple academic contexts almost immediately as has been the case with Mazur's Peer Instruction methods and the use of clickers and other such instruments that discern student learning during individual classes.

All of these sessions and pedagogies not only invite faculty to work on content and delivery particular to their own individual courses, but they also connect faculty to the multiplicity of ways of teaching *and* learning within their respective disciplines. The mixture of faculty, again, is the idea to underscore as IPLA creates diverse audiences (from every educational context) and a set of pedagogies that are often readily used or adapted for these very diverse faculty and course contexts.

INQUIRY: THE GOLDEN THREAD OF THE INSTITUTE

The Boyer Report (1987) offers ten suggestions for improving undergraduate education, and the first two suggestions align well with the programming of the Oxford College institute. Boyer's Report, supported by the Carnegie Foundation, and entitled *Reinventing Undergraduate Education: A Blueprint for America's Research Universities*, encourages beginning research work by students in the first year and constructing an inquiry-based freshman year as well.

Inquiry involves students being challenged by problems, issues, and scenarios that are complex, multifaceted, and conducive to more than one answer or solution. Then, students apply disciplinary concepts and methodology to begin to formulate answers to the problem at hand. Learning how to form researchable questions; how to seek, identify, and evaluate answers to these questions; and in so doing acquire disciplinary knowledge—these are the fundamentals of good inquiry for academic disciplines.

Within each session's pedagogy, there is focus on active learning, student work, research in the discipline, and researchable questions. Whether the session has in its title PBL, case-based studies, TBL, or IGL, the elements of inquiry remain significant parts of the session. In fact, if one were to choose the single most important pedagogical approach, then inquiry would be that golden thread.

The 2010 IPLA was the first to offer specifically entitled inquiry sessions, and in this first rendition, there were two sessions which were each led by a pair of Oxford College faculty who had worked to develop inquiry courses and individual course units since the college's adoption of its own Ways of Inquiry curriculum in 2008. In each session, the college faculty shared the institution's journey into inquiry as a central pedagogy, described the particulars of the Ways of Inquiry, and discussed with participants what the application of this pedagogy to their own courses would entail.

IPLA 2011 saw its first IGL external scholar, Jill Lane, who had authored IGL materials at Penn State's Schreyer Institute before becoming AVP of Assessment at Clayton State in Georgia. Lane guided faculty through a discussion of distinct questions or issues: "What Is Inquiry-Based Learning (IBL)?" "Why Use IBL?" "Stating Goals and Objectives," "Analyzing Your Potential Students," "Designing an Instructional Plan with Activities and Assignments," and "Developing Assessment." This session challenged faculty to consider IBL in terms of a design challenge, a pedagogical process from definition through assessment.

In the following year (IPLA 2012), IGL expert Virginia S. Lee led a very popular session entitled "Easing into Inquiry-Guided Learning." The very title indicated that transformative pedagogies require time and sustained effort to develop. As the session description articulated: "For instructors accustomed to traditional models of teaching, inquiry-guided learning requires a significant and exciting shift in perspective about the teaching and learning process. The learning outcomes advanced by IGL are more complex. And, promoting learning through inquiry also entails a broader repertoire of teaching and learning strategies and assessment methods." While the college faculty had already developed an IGL requirement, this IPLA moment with Virginia Lee certainly helped faculty from Oxford College recognize the ambitious nature of their curricular program.

Then, two years later in IPLA 2014 an international group of inquiry scholars led an array of sessions ranging from course designs for individual courses to institutional initiatives involving IGL. With the focus of an entire institute dedicated to IGL, a full range of issues was explored—the student experience of inquiry, the need for academic scaffolding within individual courses, the assessment of an array of outcomes—which went on to become aspects of this culminating institute.

INNOVATION IN PRACTICE: INSTITUTE FOR PEDAGOGY IN THE LIBERAL ARTS AND INDIVIDUAL COURSES

The attention to programming, pedagogy, structure of sessions, and other important elements, (e.g., common meals, evening discussions, and entertainment) have provided the frame and the setting for the actual work of the participants in each institute. Innovation comes about through the interplay of several good forces: scholars and participant seminar discussions, the pedagogical content of a session, the course or particular challenge the individual faculty has brought, and the interplay of ideas from multiple sessions and indeed multiple years of the institute. Faculty who attend every IPLA arrive with a set of course challenges and questions already in mind. They have selected sessions that piqued their interest and offered a possible solution to challenges at hand.

The way these forces interact is best illustrated in the various chapters in this volume; yet, two brief examples also highlight the many processes at work in the institute. Participants, for instance, may wish to explore an entirely new pedagogy to apply to existing courses and challenges. Faculty may also elect to work specifically on one or more elements of a course: the course description and its goals, the work and assignments, or assessment of the student learning. The intertwining of pedagogy within the sessions of successive institutes and these course elements, then, can be a fascinating story of innovation in itself.

The American Literary Survey II is a university reading course in which students, frequently in large sections, read and discuss anthologized works published from 1855 to the present. Literary Criticism, however, is frequently an upper-level or graduate course that requires a great deal of theoretical knowledge before the work of the course can be undertaken. Redesigning these two courses for students in the first two years of undergraduate study within an inquiry-driven curriculum thus presents exciting and significant challenges.[8]

A fundamental reality presented by the survey course is the volume of readings inherent given its chronological scope. These readings cover a century and a half of anthologized texts and span all genres. To compromise the nature of a survey by selecting only a few key texts to explore literary issues in a more traditional inquiry mode is a desirable option.

Colleagues at successive IPLA, along with the guidance of inquiry scholars Jill Lane, Virginia S. Lee, and others, supported development of an inquiry unit comprising the research project for each student. Colleagues asked, "What is the work of your discipline that you can draw on for this survey course?" As a result of these conversations at successive IPLA, the academic discourse surrounding the literary canon became the topic from which student research projects developed. The readings themselves remained the same, as supplemental readings on the literary canon and a number of associated issues would set up an inquiry research project for each student.

Scholars who led a "Backward Design" session encouraged participants to begin with the outcomes of the course in mind and to work backward to devise appropriate assignments and student support. With each student's research project exploring an aspect of canon formation as the primary inquiry outcome for this course, the question that arose was what early assignments and disciplinary *scaffolding*[9] for the research question would prepare students to be successful in this research project?[10] Over two years and much to the credit of successive IPLA scholars and participants, the course evolved and a number of original student projects emerged.

As a second example, the challenge presented by the course in Literary Criticism also involved course content and the difficulty of identifying an appropriate disciplinary feature that would become an inquiry unit. Literary Criticism often becomes a survey of successive schools of criticism covered by scholars in their work, for example by Robert Conn Davis in his *Contemporary Literary Criticism*, by the editors of the *Norton Anthology of Literary Theory*, or on a more introductory level in such texts as Barry's *Beginning Theory*, Tyson's *Critical Theory Today* and her *Learning for a Diverse World*, Bressler's *Literary Criticism: An Introduction to Theory and Practice*, and a host of other handbooks. Such a Literary Criticism course, as exciting and challenging as it can be, is one which is driven by the concepts, templates, and interpretive strategies of successive schools rather than one that seeks to develop student inquiry and the skills necessary to their own development as interpretive critics.

In 2010, the first time Literary Criticism was taught in the inquiry style, the course proved to be more of a traditional course in Literary Criticism. The heavy content of the Literary Criticism drew most of the attention and time. On the syllabus and certainly in my daily class assignments, this course looked very inquiry driven; yet in practice, students spent less time doing the work of the discipline than asking introductory questions about the literary schools. The assignments invited major redesign.

IPLA sessions on assessment strategies led to the exploration of such ideas as low-stakes writing assignments that enabled students to learn course content in smaller increments. The minute paper allowed the instructor to quickly ascertain student familiarity and knowledge of specific theoretical frameworks. Instruction could then target precisely where student understanding was lacking.

With the minute paper, students free-write on a topic, one that they have read about but not discussed in class. The instructor can thereby discern student comprehension of terms and concepts before the class discussion. This course took on significantly different inquiry assignments using these brief in-class writing assignments. Many of the changes were directly attributable to the sessions of IPLA institutes.

The course continued to rely on close reading, but the improved feedback to the instructor allowed more time to be dedicated to increasing the sophistication of student questions. This is a key difference that emerged from IPLA conversations, ones that emphasized having the students *do* the work and thereby become more adept at interpretive strategies through reflection on their own process.

The presence of the annual institute and the relationships fostered with many scholar-teachers at each individual institute and throughout each academic year contributed greatly to solving the challenges that specific courses presented, obstacles that in being overcome provided essential support for the college's Ways of Inquiry curriculum (see appendices 1.1 and 1.2).

WHERE FROM HERE: EXPORTING FACULTY EXPERTISE AND IMPACTS BEYOND EMORY

Since its inception, IPLA has retained its two-day structure with the four blocks of time, its intentionally sized groups for each session track, and the seminar discussion format modeled after graduate courses dedicated to collaborating on significant teaching and learning matters led by a scholar recognized for expertise in the pedagogy at hand. These elements and the growing slate of pedagogical offerings each year have led to several outcomes.

Oxford College has acquired momentum toward the goal of being a leader in undergraduate education. Faculty who have attended the IPLA have acquired pedagogical expertise in strategies essential to the effective teaching of their disciplines, and many of them have presented and published in the pedagogy and are becoming recognized expert consultants.

The impact of the institute upon other institutions is also clear to judge from the products that have been explored at the IPLA and then brought to fruition at home institutions. Such innovations as curricular changes, a new Quality Enhancement Plan, modifications of undergraduate curricula, and the introduction of inquiry into a wide range of undergraduate courses are examples of these institutional initiatives.

Within Oxford College many developments are clear—new courses are now being offered (particularly those involving IGL). Scholarship of Teaching and Learning (SoTL), presentations and publications by the faculty have markedly increased, perceived teaching challenges have often been remedied, collegiality has been strengthened within the college and extended beyond the college as well, and Oxford faculty have been recognized as leaders in pedagogical innovation both within and beyond Emory University.

Enabling positions of leadership in pedagogy, extending innovation and knowledge of teaching, providing a context within which faculty from many institutions can reflect, share, and develop—all of these support the initiatives of the last strategic planning process. In a research institution, the focus on teaching can be surpassed by the goal of knowledge production. So at Oxford College, the distinctiveness within Emory's research focus is to intentionally study and produce knowledge about teaching and learning. This is Oxford's core value, and the IPLA is one way for the identity of the college to find form both within and beyond Emory.

After a decade of institutes and significant development, the college anticipates a number of tracks/sessions on national issues: pedagogical opportunities for postdocs and for secondary school faculty, sessions on research archives, programs focusing on student flourishing, and in-depth exploration of new technologies like digital humanities and social media. Experiential learning and diversity issues will continue to be compelling topics for further exploration as well.

Finally, such institutes as the IPLA may set an example of programming for other teaching centers. As the teaching center responsible for the annual IPLA, the CAE has received acknowledgment in a number of ways. With the growth of numbers of participating Emory faculty and of faculty from an increasing number of institutions within the United States and elsewhere, the reputation of the IPLA and the CAE as Emory resources has grown.

The wisdom of many leaders of Emory University who saw fit to retain its home and to delineate and articulate a clear role for Oxford College within the larger university and beyond can now, thus, pay dividends as Oxford College continues to develop its potential for its special focus on learning, teaching, and related scholarship.

Appendix 1.1

WAYS OF INQUIRY: A GENERAL EDUCATION REQUIREMENTS PROPOSAL FOR HIGHLIGHTING AND STRENGTHENING THE DISTINCTIVENESS OF OUR CURRICULUM*

Michael K. Rogers and David B. Gowler

INTRODUCTION

This proposal seeks to highlight Oxford College's mission of providing an excellent foundation for four-year undergraduate liberal education and to direct attention to what is our focus, the critical beginnings that students make at Oxford College. The most important beginnings in the curriculum are the courses that introduce the student to a disciplinary way of thinking, of seeing, of valuing, and of feeling. Thus the proposal is to have certain introductory courses designated as "Ways of Inquiry" (INQ) courses and to require a certain number of them throughout the General Education Requirements (GER). The idea of Ways of Inquiry needs to be elaborated and a common understanding developed through broad faculty discussion, but its distinctive Oxford identity is reflected in the Oxford College Vision Statement from the 2005 Strategic Plan:

> Oxford, attracting people to *a place* in the heart of Emory; *a community*, diverse, caring for humanity, nature, and one another, driven by inquiry and dedicated to excellence in undergraduate liberal arts education; *a college*, providing a peerless and transformative learning environment, renowned for the leadership, service, achievement, and support of its graduates (italics in the original).

WAYS OF INQUIRY

The key emphasis, particularly appropriate to a curriculum focused on freshmen and sophomores, is on introductory courses. Introductory courses, where suitable, should introduce the student to the way of inquiry of the discipline, subject, or field. The introduction need not be complete, but it should lay the foundation for future learning. Any tension between giving enough "content" to form a basis and covering everything would need to be worked out by each instructor. Sometimes questions may be raised that cannot be answered until a later course. Indeed, many important questions still do not have satisfactory answers. But the courses should be *elementary*, that is, centered on the elements of the discipline.

A goal in the GER should be to equip the students with introductions to the "most important" ways of inquiring into the world. Introductions into disciplines in each of the broad categories of our divisions seem important to give the student a good foundation for learning. At first glance, Ways of Inquiry classes might seem focused entirely on the first component of Oxford College's LAI Philosophy and Goals: *Knowledge and Understanding*: "Knowledge of human cultures and the natural world through a breadth of study in the humanities, mathematics, sciences, and social sciences." Yet breadth of study, we believe, is in a dialogical relationship with the other components of the LAI Philosophy and Goals, such as *Reasoning and Imagination*, which include "inquiry and analysis, critical and creative thinking, written and oral communication," and so forth. An introductory course in a particular subject seeks to assist students to become better readers, writers, and thinkers within the context of that field but with an eye on another, more comprehensive goal: becoming better readers, writers, and thinkers.

This proposal thus seeks to address a common ailment in discussions of general education: Ernest Boyer and Arthur Levine argue that faculty usually try to determine how general education can contribute to the study of a particular discipline. Faculty rarely question, however, how separate disciplines can "contribute to a truly *general* education."[11] A "Ways of Inquiry" approach attempts to address both of those questions but primarily the latter.

In a Ways of Inquiry approach, attempting to reach the goals of general education is begun within a particular and introductory context: First, by "way" is meant a way of doing things. It implies there is a culture of how things are done in each discipline/subject/field. An introductory course should introduce a student to the way of the discipline.[12]

By "inquiry" is meant the seeking of knowledge in the discipline. The way of inquiry is roughly how knowledge is sought in the discipline. It includes things like the following:

- How to ask questions
- What sorts of evidence to seek
- How to relate ideas
- How to solve problems
- How to read
- How to measure

Such elements of inquiry need to be grounded in the discipline by introducing fundamental questions, principles, assumptions, concepts, terminology, and so on. These lists are meant only to suggest a picture of what is meant by a way of inquiry. The ways of each discipline ought to be elaborated by the individuals in the discipline and then further illuminated by discussions with others both inside and outside that discipline. A discussion often excites our powers of imagination and invention and also lets us understand what others think, such as we discovered at the INQ workshop on January 31, 2009. Indeed, we seemed to make progress toward a general understanding of how introductory inquiry would work in a variety of courses.

The ways of inquiry have been discussed above mainly in the context of introductory courses. It is clear that students would advance along such ways in upper-level courses, ones we often describe as "for the major." At Oxford College, with our exclusive focus on the critical first two years of undergraduate education, this emphasis on introductory courses is particularly germane.

To address other essential concerns of general education, Ways of Inquiry courses also incorporate, whenever possible, the following three, often overlapping, elements:

1. *Values discernment, ethical issues, and social responsibility.*
   Boyer and Levine describe the agenda for general education as "those experiences, relationships, and ethical concerns that are common to all of us simply by virtue of our membership in the human family at a particular moment in history."[13] The focus on ethical engagement runs throughout Oxford College's Strategic Plan and continues through our LAI Philosophy and Goals, which states that "knowledge must be anchored in ethical engagement" and includes "values in action" goals such as "civic knowledge and ethical engagement." Civic knowledge, self-understanding, and ethical engagement thus are critical elements of Oxford College's "transformational" LAI program.
2. *Interdisciplinary opportunities where students connect ideas.*
   Ernest Boyer argues that general education is not "complete" until interdisciplinary bridges are opened between disciplines, students appreciate the interconnectedness of knowledge, and that knowledge is also applied to life beyond the campus.[14] He goes on to write: "The central question is ... whether students are helped to see integration across the disciplines and discover the shared relationship common to all people. In such a program, the academic disciplines should be viewed as a means to a larger end" (p. 100).

3. *An "experiential" context, where knowledge is applied to issues outside the classroom.*
Ways of Inquiry courses not only familiarize students with the kinds of questions raised by scholars in a particular discipline, but they also focus on the methods by which scholars wrestle with answering those questions. Yet general education courses should also, where possible, exceed the boundaries of singular disciplines, explore the interconnectedness of disciplines (#2 above), and apply those concerns to life outside the classroom, such as in response to issues that we all face in our individual and communal lives. This experiential context may range from classroom discussions about issues past and/or present to experiences outside the classroom (e.g., TPSL or off-campus courses).

Appendix 1.2

WAYS OF INQUIRY COURSE PROPOSAL FORM: INFORMATION REQUIRED FOR COURSES CLASSIFIED AS WAYS OF INQUIRY

Courses driven by inquiry are designed to be transformative in that students not only learn elemental concepts, principles, assumptions, and terminology of a particular discipline, but they understand and question the way knowledge is sought by actively learning and practicing the discipline's approaches to inquiry. These explorations often engage ethical issues and social responsibility, make connections across disciplines, and create contexts for experiential learning. Ways of Inquiry courses, although primarily focused on ways of seeking knowledge rooted within a discipline, also strive to develop students' abilities in areas that in some ways transcend disciplines: reading critically, writing cogently, communicating effectively, and independently pursuing knowledge through inquiry.

Faculty desiring a course be labeled "INQ" for the purposes of the General Education Program (GEP) should first become familiar with what a "Ways of Inquiry" course is meant to entail. The "Ways of Inquiry" vision statement, sample syllabi submitted by the INQ task force, and Virginia Lee's book are all sources that can be used to this end. Then, answers to the following questions should be submitted (along with a class syllabus) as evidence that a course should be classified as INQ. Answers should be as detailed as possible, citing specific intentionally designed activities, assignments, or pedagogies to be used in the class, as appropriate.

Asking the "Right" Questions

1. What fundamental questions will students learn to ask and use consistently when dealing with this discipline? Please describe intentionally designed activities, assignments, or pedagogies that are meant to accomplish this.

Using the "Right" Tools

2. What methods of analysis and argument will students learn to help them investigate questions and "discover knowledge" in this discipline? Please describe intentionally designed activities, assignments, or pedagogies that will allow students to practice these techniques.

Increasingly Independent Investigation

3. Students should demonstrate their increased abilities (over time) in using the tools of the discipline. How will students' investigations become more independent over the course of the semester (be specific)?

Connections to Something Bigger

4. What specific "real-world" questions, interdisciplinary connections, and/or ethical issues will students explore in an attempt to deepen their understanding and appreciation of the class content?

NOTES

* Excerpt.

1. The very title of the 2005 Strategic Plan reveals the college's purpose: "Distinctive and Distinguishing: A Strategic Plan for Oxford College and Its Role within Emory."

2. The vision for the college in the 2005 Strategic Plan unabashedly stated thus: "Becoming a national model for engaged student-centered learning."

3. In the late 1990s, Oxford College organized a campus initiative focusing on teaching excellence. The Advisory Council on Teaching (ACT) was initiated and led by Dean Kent Linville, and grew in importance and outreach to faculty in the college. The college participated in the Carnegie Campus Program, a program with more than seven hundred institutional participants, eighty of which were to be designated as Carnegie Teaching Academies. Finally, Oxford undertook participation in the National Survey of Student Engagement (NSSE) during the same period, and by 2007–2008 had received scores in the top 10 percent in all five categories that the NSSE measures.

4. Over the years, more sessions have been added, and from time to time, the caps have been raised when pedagogy permitted it.

5. See Jim Lang article in *The Chronicle of Higher Education*.

6. IPLA has sought to meet specific course challenges through a number of pedagogical tracks over the years. A high number of individual requests, for example, involve the array of tools within the teaching with technology menu. At every IPLA, at least one (and often two) session programs offer faculty opportunities to develop and present in the technology showcase, a pedagogical project involving one or more technological programs or tools. Tracks led by the director of academic computing with frequent appearances by faculty experts in specific technologies have become annual standard features of the IPLA. These seminars offer the general exploration of multiple technologies that lead to the culminating showcase at which individual participants demonstrate the technological project and explain how it will accompany or be integrated into one of the courses taught by the faculty. This teaching and learning with technology session traditionally features such technological programs as blogs, Camtasia, videos, social media, and digital humanities, to mention only a few of the most recent sessions.

7. While some pedagogies fit nicely into one or two particular disciplinary approaches, others have been adopted and adapted by numerous disciplines. These in the second group, I tend to think of as signature or *uber*-pedagogies.

8. To be awarded an Inquiry designation at Oxford College, the professor must create course units that call for work within the discipline, questions and issues facing literary experts, and then structure these units in such a way as to be appropriate but challenging for students in the first two years.

9. In the field of education, the term *scaffolding* refers to a process in which teachers model or demonstrate the problem-solving process, then step back and offer support as needed. Psychologist and instructional designer Jerome Bruner first used the term "scaffolding" back in the 1960s. (Study.com website, Accessed July 6, 2015).

10. In a 2014 version of the course, Tom Csicsila's book became one of many resources and a number of articles involving the canon were added. The most essential support, however, involved the refashioning of the structure of the class. Early in the class, we read and discussed short articles on the canon, asking questions such as: what is the canon? Should we have one or multiple canons, and from a social justice perspective who should be included or excluded? How is one formed? How does a text come to be included and why? And, finally, do texts drop out of the canon and why? Students progressed through the readings from the mid- to late-nineteenth century, through Realism and Naturalism, and during the first readings of the twentieth century, they began to debate these and other questions relative to texts that we had read.

11. See Boyer and Levine (1981, p. 25).

12. The use of the term *discipline* creates some difficulties of definition, but here it is shorthand for such categories as *discipline, field, or subject*.

13. See Boyer and Levine (1985, p. 19).

14. See Boyer (1987, p. 91).

REFERENCES

Bain, K. (2004). *What the best college teachers do*. Cambridge, MA: Harvard.

Barry, P. (2009). *Beginning theory: An introduction to literary and cultural theory.* Manchester, England: Manchester University Press.

Boyer, E. (1987). *College: The undergraduate experience in America.* New York: Harper & Row, 1987, p. 91.

Boyer, E. and Levine, A. (1981). *A quest for common learning: The aims of general education.* Washington, DC: The Carnegie Foundation for the Advancement of Teaching, p. 25.

Bressler, C. (2002). *Literary criticism: An introduction to theory and practice,* 3rd ed. Upper Saddle River, NJ: Prentice Hall.

Csicsila, J. (2004). *Canons by consensus.* Tuscaloosa, AL: University of Alabama Press.

Davis, R. and Schleifer, R. (1998). *Contemporary literary criticism: Literary and cultural studies.* New York: Pearson.

Lee, V. (Ed.). (2004). *Teaching & learning through inquiry.* Sterling, VA: Stylus.

Mazur, E. (2016). Retrieved June 26, 2016, from http://mazur.harvard.edu/abstracts/#2.

Moon, J. (2003). *An uncommon place: Oxford College of Emory University, 1914–2000.* Marietta, GA: Bookhouse Group.

Oxford College of Emory University Strategic Plan. (2005). Retrieved May 30, 2016, from file:///C:/Users/Jeff/Desktop/Oxford%20College%20important%20materials/2005%20Oxford%20Strategic%20Plan(1)%20(1).pdf.

Tyson, L. (2001). *Learning for a diverse world: Using critical theory to read and write about literature.* New York: Routledge.

Tyson, L. (2006). *Critical theory today: A user-friendly guide.* New York: Routledge.

Chapter Two

IGL Certification

A Model for Institutionalizing Inquiry-Guided Learning

Devon Fisher, Daniel W. Kiser, Jennifer Heller, and David Ratke

In the fall of 2013 and in the spring of 2014, Lenoir-Rhyne University offered an interdisciplinary humanities course titled "Sacred Spaces of Hickory."[1] The students who enrolled in this general education course were juniors or seniors majoring in nonhumanities fields. For their final projects, they worked in groups to develop web content explaining to a general public why they thought that a space of their choice could be considered sacred. This content included photographs, recorded oral histories of people associated with the space, a written narrative, and, ultimately, an edited four- to six-minute video telling the space's story.

The students far surpassed course expectations. Rather than choosing obvious sites like the churches of downtown Hickory, North Carolina, students focused on spaces like the Hickory Motor Speedway, Club Cabaret (a gay bar in Hickory), and Plaza Latina (a strip mall of businesses owned by Latino/a business owners). Those who did choose churches took unexpected approaches, investigating, for instance, the social activism of Exodus Missionary Outreach Church, a congregation that focuses on welcoming all who enter their doors, including those recently out of prison and recovering from addiction. The professor who taught the course considered it a remarkable success.[2] Just as important, so did the students.

One nursing major sums up what other students expressed both formally in student evaluations and informally in conversation and emails, reflecting that the biggest lesson she learned was to "never be afraid of not having the right answer. As it turns out, it's not 'getting the right answer' but the experience that teaches you the most" (Anonymous, personal communication, December 5, 2013). What accounts for the deep learning that occurred in that course? In a word—"inquiry."

LR chose to focus on inquiry-guided learning (IGL) pedagogies as its quality enhancement plan (QEP) in its most recent reaffirmation cycle. The QEP is a requirement of the Southern Association of Colleges and Schools Commission on Colleges (SACSCOC), the university's accrediting agency. SACSCOC (2015) describes the QEP as follows: "Engaging the wider academic community and addressing one or more issues that contribute to institutional improvement, the plan should be focused, succinct, and limited in length. The QEP describes a carefully designed and focused course of action that addresses a well-defined topic or issue(s) related to enhancing student learning."

The "Sacred Spaces" course was an early part of the effort of making that change at an institutional level. Assessment at the course level suggests that student interest, engagement, and learning increased substantially because, within the framework of the course, they were able to ask their own questions about which places in Hickory were sacred. This freedom to engage in sustained inquiry on a topic of their choosing motivated students to become active participants in the learning process and to engage in higher-level thinking skills.

This type of classroom experience reflects the goals of LR's QEP. The team that developed the idea of IGL as a campus-wide initiative hoped to transform student learning by challenging faculty to rethink the very concept of teaching. This effort coincided with an influx of new faculty; the university saw significant growth in faculty hiring between 2005 and 2012, the year in which full implementation of the QEP began. The QEP became a way to facilitate—and even to require—conversations about what constitutes "good teaching." And, it became a way for new faculty to define and commit to the future of LR's vision of education.

After the initial push to implement the QEP, and despite some successes like the one described above, faculty often reported that they were unsure of whether they were "doing" IGL. They lacked both a clear vision of what IGL meant in the context of LR as well as a shared vocabulary with which to talk about it. In response, the institution sent a small team of key faculty and administrators to the 2014 "Inquiry as a Way of Learning in Colleges and Universities" seminar, where they developed an IGL certification program designed to further institutionalize IGL pedagogies at LR.[3]

This chapter details the steps the institution took to implement its IGL certification program, describes the preliminary assessment results, and offers final conclusions. The lessons learned at LR can benefit similar institutions and, more broadly, any college or university seeking to move toward active and engaged pedagogies like IGL. Before turning to the certification program itself, however, it may be helpful to offer some background on LR and the process that led to administrative efforts to institutionalize IGL.

BACKGROUND AND QUALITY ENHANCEMENT PLAN

LR is a small university (approximately 1,500 undergraduate students and 800 graduate students) located in Hickory, NC, about sixty miles north of Charlotte. Historically, the university has primarily served undergraduate students. Since its inception in 1891, the university has emphasized the liberal arts, though professional programs like nursing and education have long been an important part of the curriculum. More recently, like so many other institutions, LR has focused on graduate education and professional programs, though the university continues to value its commitment to the liberal arts. Reflecting this changing dynamic, LR restructured in 2008, and it changed its name from "Lenoir-Rhyne College" to "Lenoir-Rhyne University." At that time, the university reorganized into four colleges: the College of Arts & Sciences, the College of Education & Human Services, the College of Health Sciences, and the College of Professional & Mathematical Studies.

In 2012, the university expanded its graduate programming significantly with the opening of a graduate center in Asheville, NC, and a merger with Lutheran Southern Theological Seminary in Columbia, SC. LR's efforts to increase IGL had to accommodate these institutional changes, taking into account the diversity represented by the programs, both undergraduate and graduate, in four colleges ranging from traditional liberal arts to cutting-edge professional programs.

As noted above, LR's foray into IGL began in 2009 as so many institutional changes do: with the impending visit of our accrediting agency. A team of nine faculty and staff worked over the 2009–2010 academic year to explore possible QEP topics, ultimately choosing to focus on campus-wide implementation of IGL pedagogies. A team of eight faculty from across campus piloted implementation of IGL pedagogies in their spring 2011 courses, and after their notable successes, the committee recommended to the faculty a proposal for a QEP focused on IGL pedagogies titled *Rise Up! Dig Deep!: Nurturing a Culture of Inquiry at LRU*, which the university's faculty assembly endorsed in November, 2011.[4]

THE CHALLENGES OF IMPLEMENTING INQUIRY-GUIDED LEARNING AT A SMALL UNIVERSITY

LR's IGL-centered QEP was ambitious primarily because it targeted the two things that are most important to a university and perhaps most difficult to change: faculty pedagogy and student-learning habits. Moreover, IGL by definition lacks the clarity that faculty find in other more traditional pedagogies. LR's faculty understand what a lecture is, and if asked, could say with confidence how they use this technique in their classrooms. Similarly, some more recent constructivist pedagogies offer fairly clear definitions and processes for implementation. For instance, many practitioners of problem-based learning cite Boud and Feletti's (1997) seminal *The Challenge of Problem-Based Learning* as providing a series of four steps that, taken together, outline this pedagogy.[5]

In recent years, LR's faculty have become more familiar with some of these constructivist pedagogies, especially within a redesigned core curriculum that places a premium on active learning, requiring students to take courses that include clearly defined service and experiential learning components. Yet, as the faculty began to learn more about IGL, a sense emerged that we collectively were struggling to understand what, exactly, constituted "inquiry" on our campus.

The struggle that faculty faced has much to do with the fact that IGL remains a somewhat nebulous term even in the scholarly literature on the subject. Virginia Lee (2012), whose work was instrumental in the development of Lenoir-Rhyne's QEP, makes the case as follows: "Unlike popular teaching strategies such as TBL or cooperative learning, IGL comprises a suite of teaching strategies and defies definition as a single heuristic, a prescribed set of practices, or a formula for classroom practice" (p. 7). Even the name of the pedagogy invites questions rather than answers. Inquiry: questions—but whose? The professor's, the individual student's, or that of the class? Guided: facilitated in some way—but who or what does the guiding?

The lack of a clear definition of IGL raised several barriers during the first two years of the implementation of LR's QEP. First, faculty in disciplines like nursing, which must satisfy external accrediting agencies, expressed concern that what they perceived as fairly vague models of inquiry would not enable their students to learn significant amounts of required content.

A second barrier emerged among faculty who were committed to making LR's QEP successful. After reviewing the QEP and attending an initial faculty development event (a two-day workshop in January 2012 led by Virginia S. Lee), many faculty expressed a sense of bewilderment—a sense of being unsure whether assignments or courses they had designed "counted" as IGL. In many ways, this was unsurprising; Lee (2012), in fact, identifies this as a typical response of faculty seeking to implement IGL pedagogies (p. 7).

A third barrier proved perhaps more challenging. The nebulous definitions of IGL enabled some faculty simply to say, "I [or my program] am already doing that and have been for years; it's only recently that someone labelled it as 'inquiry-guided learning.'" Students in these classes may ask and answer questions, but faculty may not have adopted the *full* suite of techniques essential to successful use of IGL. In particular, they may not have fully grasped the emphasis that IGL pedagogies place on scaffolding, on the professor's role as supportive guide, and on the value of student reflection on the learning process.

The assumption that one is "already doing it" created a second challenge for this particular subset of faculty. That assumption short-circuits entirely the faculty development process that LR's QEP called for. Faculty do not participate in activities designed to help them implement IGL pedagogies effectively when they assume that they already do so.

In addition to these three barriers, LR's efforts to institutionalize IGL suffered because incentives to participate in the various faculty development activities relied on the intrinsic motivation of faculty. To be blunt, the effort to change campus culture ran headlong into the realities of our existing campus culture. Faculty teaching undergraduates at LR teach twenty-four credit hours per year[6]; those who teach fewer hours have substantial administrative expectations that replace some of those courses.

In addition to high expectations for teaching, many faculty maintain active research agendas, and most have significant service commitments to the university. In these ways, LR is similar to many small colleges and universities. Given this campus culture, it was perhaps predictable that it would be difficult to get 72 percent of faculty to commit to participate in a long-term peer-learning community (perhaps one of the more unrealistic benchmarks of the QEP), particularly when faculty already experienced the additional challenges created by a somewhat unclear understanding of what, exactly, IGL was.

Despite these barriers, LR experienced some successful faculty development efforts, though perhaps fewer than we had hoped. A small but dedicated group of eight to ten faculty participated regularly in a peer-learning community focused on IGL in the university's general education program. These faculty, representing six of the university's programs (English, religious studies, psychology, philosophy, theater, and history) met twice a month over the course of an academic year. At those meetings, the group reviewed the literature about IGL.

After a year's worth of meetings, the consensus among this group was that these sessions provided a valuable space in which to learn more about using inquiry to guide student learning. Even that group, however, continued to struggle with a sense that LR faculty lacked a common vocabulary for understanding and talking about IGL pedagogies. In short, after two years, it seemed clear that LR was in the position that Lee (2012) describes of many universities who "adopt IGL ... even as they are struggling to understand what it is" (p. 7).

PLAN DEVELOPMENT: THE 2014 INSTITUTE FOR INQUIRY AS A WAY OF LEARNING

In early 2014, Devon Fisher, LR's Director of Teaching and Learning (a position that includes oversight and assessment of the university's QEP) formed a team to attend the "Inquiry as a Way of Learning in Colleges and Universities" seminar. This seminar, led by Virginia S. Lee, Philippa Levy, Rachael Spronken-Smith, and Catherine Chiappetta Swanson, was conducted in May 2014 as part of that year's Institute for Pedagogy in the Liberal Arts (IPLA). Colleges and universities sent teams of four to the seminar to work with leading scholars in the field of IGL to identify obstacles to the implementation of IGL at an institutional level and to develop strategies for overcoming those obstacles.

LR's team consisted of four individuals (the co-authors of this piece) who were uniquely suited to bring about institutional change: Dr. Devon Fisher, who assumed responsibilities as Lenoir-Rhyne's Director of Teaching and Learning in January 2014; Dr. Daniel Kiser, dean of the College of Arts & Sciences; Dr. Jennifer Heller, chair of the School of Arts & Letters; and Dr. David Ratke, chair of the School of Humanities and Social Sciences.[7] The makeup of this team focused heavily on the liberal arts because assessment efforts of LR's QEP focused on the university's general education curriculum, which is taught primarily by faculty in liberal arts disciplines.

Working with the institute's organizers—and especially with Catherine Chiappetta Swanson, who was assigned to work with LR's team—team members realized that any efforts to institutionalize IGL at LR would require two things. First, LR would need a framework and a vocabulary for talking about IGL that would meet the needs of its varied constituents. This framework would need to account equally for an introductory anatomy course in which the primary goal is for students to learn a great deal of information about the human body and for an upper-level history seminar in which students focus on creating original arguments based on their analyses of primary texts.

Even with such a framework, our efforts to institutionalize IGL would require incentives for faculty to participate in the process of learning about IGL and implementing it in their classes. To address these challenges, LR's team developed a proposal for a semester-long IGL certification program that would create the needed framework for talking about IGL as well as the incentives needed to gain faculty buy-in.

During the three-day institute, LR's team looked at several frameworks for inquiry as models for the needs of our own campus. First, as noted above, the framework had to accommodate the diverse needs of different types of programs and courses. Second, the framework had to clarify who asks the questions that stimulate the inquiry. Faculty at LR seemed to have accepted the idea that IGL necessitates that *students* are the ones pursuing answers to questions, but they have been less clear about who poses the questions in the first place. Some faculty felt that IGL necessitated a fairly open form of inquiry in which student interest drives the questioning. Others believed that, by virtue of their expertise, faculty may be better positioned to pose meaningful questions to which students can then pursue answers. LR needed a model that acknowledges that both of these positions hold merit.

Finally, LR needed a framework that emphasized the importance of inquiry as a process that requires the participation of both professor and student. LR has a fairly open admissions policy that allows a variety of students with a wide range of experiences to study at the university. Frequently, those students arrive having had little real experience with inquiry—at least in a formal educational environment.[8] Because of this diversity, one legitimate way of doing IGL—having students independently pursue answers to questions—often proved ineffective, especially in general education courses.

In order to account for students who may struggle with independent inquiry, LR's model thus needed both to teach students the inquiry process and to allow professors to provide the appropriate level of support at the right times. In short, the university needed a framework that made clear, as Hmelo-Silver, Duncan, and Chinn (2006) put it, that IGL pedagogies "are not minimally guided instructional approaches but rather provide extensive scaffolding and guidance to facilitate student learning" (p. 99).

In the end, LR adapted two different ways of thinking about inquiry. The first, based on the work of Levy (2012, p. 20), provides a framework for thinking about the purpose and the origin of inquiry (see figure 2.1).[9] The second is also adapted from Levy (2012, p. 18), though our adaptation is also indebted to Justice et al. (2007, p. 203).[10] The connections between Levy's work and Justice's are so strong that LR faculty refer to this second image as the "Justice circle" as a way both of distinguishing the two images and of acknowledging Justice's work (see figure 2.2). Our use of the Justice circle by way of Levy provides an essential way of thinking about the process of inquiry.

In the framework the LR team adapted from Levy, the x-axis identifies who poses the question—the professor or the student. The y-axis maps out the purpose of the inquiry: inquiry done for the purpose of mastering an already existing body of knowledge or done for the purpose of creating new knowledge. As the grid suggests, this framework leads to four different ways of doing inquiry:

1. Identifying. The professor poses questions to which students pursue answers for the purpose of mastering knowledge that already exists.
2. Pursuing. Students pose their own question, and they then pursue answers for the purpose of mastering knowledge that already exists.

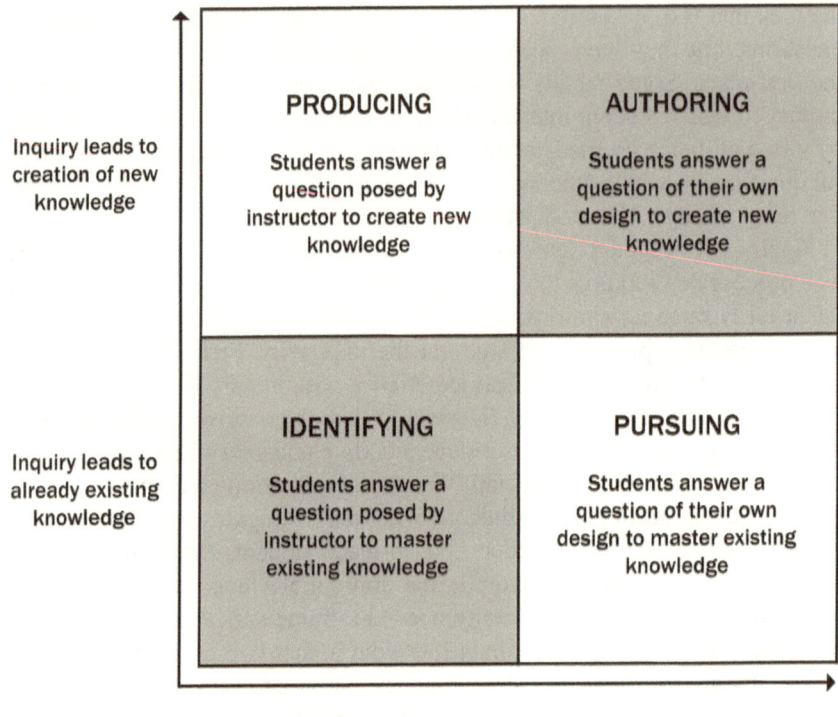

Figure 2.1. LR's Inquiry Framework

3. Producing. The professor poses questions to which students pursue answers for the purpose of creating new knowledge.
4. Authoring. Students pose their own questions, and they then pursue answers for the purpose of creating new knowledge.

Levy's model thus provides different types of inquiry with varying levels of professor and student input.

This framework has a number of benefits in the context of a university like LR. It acknowledges that inquiry may take place for different purposes, accommodating programs that require students to master existing knowledge and those that emphasize the creation of new ideas. Furthermore, it acknowledges that questions may originate with either the professor or the student. Above all, this framework validates each type of activity as being a legitimate form of IGL while providing a common vocabulary that can be used across the university.

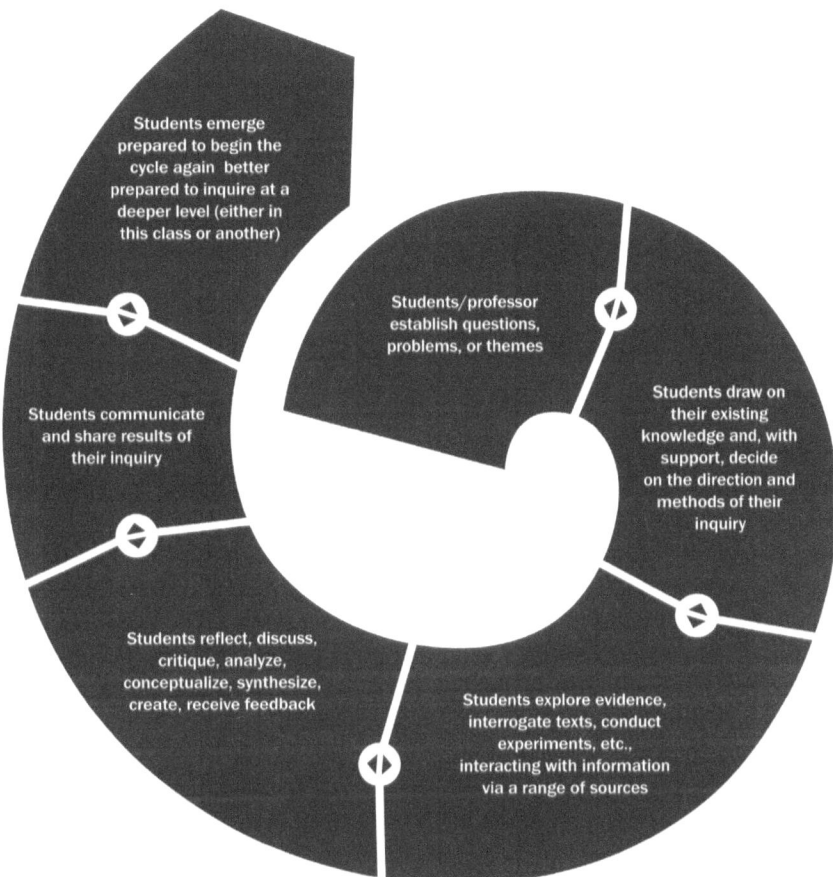

Figure 2.2. LR's Inquiry Circle

Levy's model does not, however, provide a way of thinking about the process of inquiry. For that reason, we added a version of the inquiry circle developed by Justice et al. (2007, p. 203), which illustrates the process by which a student moves through the inquiry process.

This model makes two main revisions to Justice's original. First, making it a spiral rather than a circle indicates visually the expectation that as students engage in the inquiry process, they will become progressively more adept at posing questions and answering them in insightful ways. Second, while the overall motion of the inquiry process is forward (as indicated by the large arrows), students can also backtrack in the process (as indicated by the smaller arrows pointing in both directions).

LR's use of this model emphasizes the professor's role as a guide, helping as students begin to identify questions, providing support as they formulate those questions, providing feedback, and serving as an audience for the student's work. Justice's inquiry circle forces the professor to decide the appropriate level of support for students at every step of the way. The blend of these two models gave us the background and the vocabulary needed to implement the semester-long certification program that now forms the core of LR's efforts to institutionalize IGL.

THE INQUIRY-GUIDED LEARNING CERTIFICATION PROGRAM

After the "Inquiry as a Way of Learning" seminar, the LR team proposed a semester-long IGL certification program open to faculty across the university designed to accomplish two main goals. First, it would provide an opportunity to present the common framework for inquiry that the LR team developed. Second, it would address the issue of faculty feeling overburdened and thus reluctant to commit to a peer-learning community by clearly defining the time commitment involved and by providing some external incentives.[11]

The provost's enthusiasm for the idea confirmed what we had already concluded during the three-day IPLA institute: that a supportive chief academic officer can be one of the most important drivers of change across an institution. Not only did the provost agree to a trial implementation of the IGL Certification program in the 2014–2015 academic year, he worked with the university's budget committee to increase the Teaching and Learning Committee's budget sufficiently to provide each participant with a modest stipend upon completion of the terms of the contract associated with the program (see appendix 2.1).

The IGL Certification Program invites six faculty each term to participate in a semester-long program of faculty development designed to provide support as they implement IGL pedagogies in a specific class. Applications are solicited early in the fall and spring semesters, and the university's Teaching and Learning Committee reviews those applications to identify an appropriate cohort. This process is not intended to be competitive. Instead, participants are chosen from the applicant pool with an eye toward developing a diverse yet functional group. Over time, any professor who wishes to will have the opportunity to participate in the program.

Creating effective cohorts requires navigating several logistical challenges. First, the simple matter of geography comes into play, as the fall 2015 cohort demonstrates. There were twelve applicants for the six-person cohort, and three of those applicants were from the university's seminary, which is located in Columbia, SC, a two-hour drive from the Hickory campus. Given the significant investment in time and cost to drive between campuses, the selection committee agreed that it made the most sense to invite all three of those faculty to participate in one cohort. This decision facilitated carpooling when a full meeting of all participants was necessary,[12] and it created a critical mass for the purpose of classroom observation.

The experience of faculty from Columbia illustrates that even when carefully considered, logistical challenges can occasionally be insurmountable. Midway through the fall semester, Columbia was hit with severe flooding, and, in the aftermath, faculty determined that the effort to clean up homes, campuses, and communities was such that they needed (quite understandably) to step away from the IGL certification program. Other institutions will, of course, have their own logistical difficulties that must be taken into consideration when creating cohorts.

Second, the diversity of faculty can both facilitate and hinder the certification process. The certification program integrated Arts & Sciences faculty with faculty from our professional schools. Faculty teaching in the Arts & Sciences tended to value the "authoring" category of Levy's model, while faculty in our professional schools, who often must follow rigid curriculum due to external accrediting agencies, valued the "identifying" and "pursuing" categories. Conversations about these differences had the benefit of leading faculty to ask how the categories to which they did not immediately gravitate might nevertheless be helpful in their classrooms.

At the same time, the diversity in faculty presented challenges. In particular, getting the right mix of graduate and undergraduate faculty in a cohort is important because of the different concerns those professors have in the classroom. For instance, faculty who teach undergraduates in the general education program face a challenge often not encountered in graduate courses; they have to convince students that the questions we ask about our various content areas are worth asking in the first place.

The final—and by far the most important—consideration in developing cohorts is the personalities of the individuals participating. In a small group setting that includes study, discussion, and classroom observation, all participants must feel at ease with each other. Using the university's Teaching and Learning Committee as a selection committee proved helpful here. As that committee is a standing faculty committee of representatives elected from each college, it was able to consider carefully any potential personality conflicts.

Once the cohort is selected, the members meet before the start of the particular semester during which faculty will implement IGL pedagogies through a four-hour session introduction and planning workshop. Participants prepare by reading Lee's (2012) "What Is Inquiry-Guided Learning" and Levy's

(2012) "Developing Inquiry-Guided Learning in a Research University in the United Kingdom." Faculty are then introduced to LR's Framework for Inquiry, exploring it through a thirty-minute analysis of sample course materials. Participants work in groups of three to analyze syllabi and assignments, identifying places where they see significant inquiry and noting which of the four types of inquiry they are observing.

The remainder of the initial session focuses on principles of backwards design based heavily on the work of Wiggins and McTighe (2005).[13] Participants identify outcomes for their courses and work backwards from that point to identify appropriate inquiry tasks that will allow students to demonstrate that they have met those outcomes. They develop appropriate scaffolding (tasks that provide the necessary foundations so that students will be capable of conducting the inquiry that will demonstrate mastery of course outcomes) and work together to create effective inquiry-based assignments. At the close of the session, participants share how they plan to use the LR framework for inquiry to shape their courses.

Over the course of the following semester, the cohort meets thrice for one-hour sessions designed to foster a fuller understanding of IGL pedagogies. The first of those meetings focuses on scaffolding in more detail. The second and third, in keeping with the spirit of IGL, are largely determined by the needs of each cohort. One cohort, for instance, explored the issue of managing groups in the IGL classroom. Another studied ways to generate student interest in the questions that form the basis for inquiry. Allowing each cohort autonomy to pursue its own interests under the IGL umbrella both generates greater interest and models the inquiry process.

As the semester progresses, participants engage in classroom observations. Each participant agrees to observe two other members of the cohort and to allow his/her own class to be observed by two participants. This observation is formative rather than summative. Prior to the observation, the person being observed provides the observer with a syllabus and a narrative establishing the context of the specific class session. Following the observation, they meet for a follow-up session in which they discuss the class and the use of IGL techniques in it, and they set goals for the observee.

The final three-hour session of the certification program takes place shortly after the semester ends. The first hour is left open for discussion of any lingering issues participants wish to address. The final two hours serve two important purposes. Some of the time is set aside for assessment purposes. Participants join in a focus group in which the cohort assesses their perception of the value of the certification program and begins to assess the extent to which they have incorporated IGL pedagogies into their classes.

The remainder of the final session encourages participants to engage in a process of reflection designed to mirror the final stage of Justice's inquiry circle. Participants spend twenty minutes reflecting in whatever way they feel appropriate on what they have learned and how they plan to implement it moving forward. Each participant then has five minutes to share that knowledge with the rest of the cohort.

The overall trajectory of the certification mirrors both parts of the framework for inquiry that LR has adopted. Early in the semester, many of the questions that the cohort tries to answer are posed by the Director of Teaching and Learning in order to help participants become more familiar with the Levy and Justice models. As the semester progresses, the responsibility for posing questions increasingly passes to the participants as they identify areas where they would like additional reading and discussion.[14]

If one goal of the program is to model for participants different ways of inquiring, another is to model Justice's inquiry circle. As faculty set about doing the work of implementing IGL in their classes, they pass through the various stages of that circle—almost always with the stops and starts that the LR adaptation of that circle includes. And, as our initial assessment results show, faculty across the board did, in fact, emerge from that process ready to begin again with greater skill and confidence.

ASSESSMENT AND RESULTS

Measuring the success of this effort requires us to consider the impact of the program at several different levels. From a global perspective, we must ask whether the program has facilitated large-scale implementation of IGL at LR. Narrowing our focus, we must ask whether the certification program has been successful in providing faculty with a meaningful framework for thinking about inquiry and with appropriate incentives for participation in the program. And at the narrowest level—and perhaps the most challenging to measure—we must ask whether the program has led to meaningful change in student learning.

Our initial analysis suggests that the certification program has made progress toward institutionalizing IGL at LR. During the first two years, a total of twenty-one faculty participated in the program, and it is currently beginning its fifth semester with six additional faculty. Thus, the IGL Certification program has reached over 20 percent of the university's full-time teaching faculty.[15] The ease with which this many faculty have been immersed in a semester-long learning community is itself an argument for why the certification process makes sense at a small institution. The relatively small number of faculty makes it easier to bring about cultural change.

A particularly interesting—and unanticipated—result of the certification program at the global level is a significant change in culture in individual programs. Two-thirds of the university's full-time history faculty have completed the program as have half of LR's full-time English faculty. And, in religious studies, one professor helped to design the certification initiative, and the other two completed IGL certification in the first year. Thus, while it may be too early to say that the certification program is leading to full-scale institutionalization of IGL, we can say with some degree of certainty that it is succeeding at the individual program level.

One particular challenge to institution-wide change is that the certification program has been available only to full-time faculty at LR. This decision was made in large part because the stipends associated with the program constitute a significant part of the Teaching and Learning Committee's annual budget, and as such, we hoped to get the greatest benefit possible from those limited funds. We therefore decided to invest first in development opportunities for the faculty who teach the highest number of classes and who have a long-term investment in LR.

While we initially focused on full-time faculty, we recognize nevertheless that at LR, as at so many other colleges and universities, adjunct faculty teach many of our courses, particularly in the general education program. Making them part of the initiative would significantly benefit LR's student body. As a first step in this process, the university's Teaching and Learning Committee is in the process of developing a set of criteria by which adjunct faculty who teach significant course loads over multiple semesters will be eligible for the program.

The second criteria for success—providing faculty with a meaningful framework for talking about inquiry and with incentives for learning about and implementing them—has been assessed through semi-structured interviews conducted with the participants in the first two cohorts.[16] Conversations with participants in the certification program revealed three important trends:

1. *The IGL certification program succeeded in creating a community of practitioners who inquired together about improving their teaching.*

    Participants valued the opportunity to approach development of teaching skills as a form of inquiry. When asked what they found most valuable about the certification program, nine of the ten participants specifically mentioned that learning within a community contributed significantly to their developing knowledge of IGL, and they spoke specifically of the importance of having a cohort in which a range of disciplines was represented. One participant, for instance, noted that it was particularly helpful to "hear different interpretations of the frameworks for IGL through the different lenses of practitioners in different disciplines."[17]

    In addition to the cohort experience, participants reported that they valued the classroom observation process; five of the ten specifically mentioned this part of the program as being valuable. One participant noted that even though she knew classroom observation was important, she would not have made time for it except that it was a required part of the program. She went on to say, though, that not only did she benefit from the experience, she and her observation partners continued to have discussions about their class sessions throughout the semester.

The cohort did have one setback with classroom observation; we did not, in the first semester, have adequate protocols for observation of fully online, asynchronous courses. The one participant whose class was in this format reported that the lack of meaningful feedback in an observation setting was one of the disappointing aspects of the experience. Despite that setback, the data suggest that one benefit of a certification program based on a small cohort is that participants come to view the study of pedagogy as its own form of worthwhile inquiry.

2. *The certification succeeded in creating a common vocabulary and framework for inquiry specific to Lenoir-Rhyne University.*

The decision to include two frameworks for inquiry and to tailor them to LR's specific needs provided participants an essential tool for planning meaningful learning experiences for students. None of the participants chose to share with their students either the Levy framework or the Justice inquiry circle. However, participants pointed to those frameworks as essential tools for their own thinking. Interestingly, most participants gravitated toward one framework or the other, but they did so in fairly even numbers, with just over half (six of the ten) speaking of a preference for the Levy model.

Comments by participants suggest that this split may have to do with a different understanding of the professor's role in the inquiry process. Four of the six who expressed a preference for the Levy framework used that framework to help themselves conceptualize ways to move students toward becoming independent inquirers. In other words, the Levy framework's emphasis on who asks the question provided faculty a way of thinking about how best to push students to move from being inquirers who answered other people's questions to being inquirers who generated their own questions.

Those who expressed a preference for the Justice inquiry circle, in contrast, tended to reject the polarity of "professor or student" asking the question. One participant expressed this fairly succinctly; she prefers the Justice framework specifically because it blurs that line, and she perceives herself and her students as all "muddling through this together."

Regardless of whether they gravitated toward the Levy framework or the Justice circle, each of the participants spoke about the importance of these models in planning their courses over the semester, and five of the

ten noted that the two models jointly provided a framework that was helpful in communicating with colleagues across disciplines.
3. *Incentives were an essential part of the program's success in the first year.* None of the participants suggested that external incentives were a primary factor motivating them to participate in the certification program. Nevertheless, based on participant feedback, it appears that external incentives were critical to its success. The combination of a small stipend connected to a contract helped participants prioritize the certification program over other commitments. One participant specifically noted that this formalization forced the entire cohort to "step up the level of commitment."

   A perhaps surprising trend in the qualitative data suggests why this "stepped up" level of commitment is so important. One participant noted that the readings assigned in the program initially seemed unhelpful but that upon reflection, those readings became increasingly meaningful as conversations developed over the course of the semester. Three other participants expressed similar thoughts. These responses offer a compelling reason for incentivizing the IGL peer-learning community; participants, because they felt a contractual obligation to continue with the certification program, persisted with the material until they reached a level of knowledge and experience where it became useful.

Across the board, then, the participants agreed that the program provided them with a useful framework for designing courses and for talking about inquiry with their colleagues, and they confirmed the need for some form of external incentive.

Beyond the goals of institutionalizing IGL and providing faculty with a framework for inquiry, we hoped that the IGL certification program would lead to meaningful change in both instructor practice and student learning. Preliminary results suggest that we have succeeded in this regard. Participants in the certification provide samples of student work produced in their classes which an assessment team then assesses using rubrics designed to measure higher-order thinking skills. At present, there is insufficient data to begin this assessment, primarily because many of the courses in which instructors have focused their IGL efforts are taught only once a year.

In addition to these measures, LR uses its student ratings of instructions to measure student perceptions of the extent to which they are asked to do five tasks: to analyze materials, to synthesize ideas, to evaluate information and arguments, to apply theories and concepts, and to memorize facts. Although we would like to report that the IGL certification led to noticeably higher student evaluations in these categories (with the exception of memorizing facts where we would ideally hope to see lower scores), that has not been the case—though there also has not been any discernible decline.

There may be several reasons for the numbers observed in student ratings in classes using IGL pedagogies. First, the faculty who have been part of the first two cohorts have, over the past five years, consistently scored fairly high in these questions on the evaluation instrument, and hence there simply wasn't much room for improvement.

Second, the certification program invited faculty to focus their IGL efforts on a single course. Given the variability of student evaluations from course to course, we have chosen not to look at that microlevel, and the evaluation results thus may include courses that did not use IGL pedagogies. One of the goals of the initiative is for faculty who have been through the certification program to expand their use of IGL pedagogies beyond a single course, and it may simply take more time for them to implement those strategies in multiple courses.

A final yet very important piece of data drawn from the student evaluation instrument is that faculty who have been involved in IGL at some level (whether in the certification program, our earlier peer-learning communities, or the pilot group for LR's QEP) score significantly higher on this set of questions than faculty who have had no formal involvement with IGL. This correlation confirms that our efforts in developing the IGL certification program have been well founded.

In addition, faculty perceive that the IGL certification program has led to meaningful student learning. Faculty consistently reported that IGL pushed students into new roles that forced them to take greater responsibility for and ownership of their ideas. One participant noted that the approaches he developed in the certification program "forced [students] to take [approaches] that Biblical scholars use and try to use them," rather than simply holding fast to beliefs that they had learned from home and church. Another commented that the IGL approach challenged students to be aware that their learning takes place in the context of a larger scholarly conversation and that this, in turn, made them take greater ownership of their own ideas.

In terms of their own practice, perhaps the most meaningful data that we can provide is that when asked whether they intended to use IGL in future revisions of the class upon which they had focused during the certification program, all ten participants responded with an unambiguous "yes." They also said that, going forward, they expected to integrate IGL pedagogies into other courses. One participant spoke about how IGL had created a "paradigm shift" in his teaching. Another talked about the ways in which IGL "gives an organizing framework" to his ideas about teaching.

TAKEAWAYS: LESSONS TO BE LEARNED FROM THE LENOIR-RHYNE'S EXPERIENCE

After two years, LR's IGL certification program has been successful in beginning the process of institutionalizing IGL across the university. The university's experience may prove useful not only to colleagues at colleges and universities with a similar profile but also to those at other types of institutions who hope to begin the process of making large-scale changes toward more active learning strategies. The experiences of LR faculty suggest five key takeaways.

First, what counts as "inquiry"—and thus what counts as "inquiry-guided learning"—has a great deal to do with context. Scholars in English programs simply do inquiry differently than those in occupational therapy, and they in turn understand inquiry differently than those in the performing arts. Accordingly, any attempt to institutionalize IGL must be sensitive to these disciplinary differences; moreover, those leading these kinds of institutional changes must be vigilant as they develop frameworks and vocabularies, ensuring that no legitimate form of inquiry is marginalized.

Second, a single framework for IGL may be insufficient. One of the clearest messages from participants in LR's certification program was that having two different ways of thinking about inquiry facilitated communication and learning among their colleagues. While some participants were mystified that their colleagues found the Levy model (or the Justice circle) useful, they agreed that the dual models provided two important things: ideas they could use in their own planning and a vocabulary so that they could talk to colleagues in other disciplines about inquiry.

Third, having faculty participate in a clearly defined, multidisciplinary cohort facilitated learning about IGL. In some ways, this was unsurprising given the research that suggests the importance of peer-learning communities in higher education. Nevertheless, the consistency with which participants identified this cohort experience as being the most valuable part of the certification program was surprising. Participants valued the cohort experience because they were challenged by the different perspectives they encountered on the inquiry process. They perceived the certification program as a collaborative exercise in inquiry that led each individual to reflect upon his/her own teaching practices.

Fourth, appropriate intrinsic and extrinsic incentives are essential. In an ideal world, every professor would willingly participate in efforts to improve pedagogy from a desire to be a more effective practitioner. As participants in the two different cohorts reported, however, despite a strong intrinsic motivation, the extrinsic incentive of a stipend and a contract provided an official stamp of approval that their efforts were appreciated and needed. While it may not always be possible to provide financial incentives, those extrinsic motivators could take other forms—public recognition, consideration in promotion and tenure decisions, and the like.

Fifth, small universities like LR may be uniquely suited to bring about institutional change. LR's relatively small size made swift implementation of a new initiative possible in ways that may not be the case at larger universities. LR's team planned the certification program at the "Inquiry as a Way of Learning" seminar at IPLA in mid-May of 2014, sent a proposal to the Provost by June 1, and had a pilot program running by mid-August. The university's size also facilitated quick, meaningful results in terms of numbers as a significant percentage of the full-time faculty participated in the program within a fairly short timeframe.

Much of this chapter has been about the process of developing institutional structures that will facilitate large-scale changes in pedagogy across a university. In the end, though, those changes end up being less about institutional structures and more about a series of small changes. One participant, describing how her thinking about teaching has changed, noted: "this way of thinking is working its way through every course that I teach when I design it." Statements like this point to the success of the program, showing how meaningful change can occur when individuals are given the support that they need to develop new ways of thinking about teaching and learning.

Appendix 2.1

INQUIRY-GUIDED LEARNING CERTIFICATION PROGRAM CONTRACT

Purpose: IGL Certification at Lenoir-Rhyne is intended to serve three purposes. First, it provides an opportunity for faculty to explore IGL and to develop strategies for implementing them. While the training focuses on one course of the instructor's choosing, the goal ultimately is for faculty to apply those IGL pedagogies broadly in their teaching. Second, IGL certification provides an incentive for faculty to try new pedagogies. Third, the certification process provides documentation of efforts taken by faculty to enhance student learning.

Faculty who participate in IGL certification agree to participate in training sessions, to implement IGL pedagogies in at least one class during the semester in which training occurs, to implement IGL pedagogies as appropriate in future semesters, and to participate in assessment of IGL at Lenoir-Rhyne University. Specifically, faculty agree to the following:

1. To choose one class in which the faculty member will implement IGL pedagogies.

2. To participate in a total of ten hours of training/reflection: a four-hour training session in the semester or summer prior to that class, four one-hour discussion groups during the semester of that class, and a two-hour session at the conclusion of that class.
3. To observe a classroom session of at least two of the other participants in the IGL certification cohort and to make their own classroom available for at least two visits by other participants.
4. To participate in assessment activities in the following ways:
    a. Joining in focus groups with other IGL faculty in the semester following the implementation of the course.
    b. Providing to the Office of Institutional Research the course syllabus, major assignments, and student submissions for those assignments no later than one month following the completion of the course. In cases where major assignments involve presentations or other forms of non-written communication, faculty will inform the director of teaching and learning so that he/she can arrange to have those presentations observed. (Note: these materials will be used exclusively for assessment purposes.)
5. To implement IGL pedagogies where possible and where appropriate in future courses, particularly those in Lenoir-Rhyne's core curriculum and to provide to the Office of Institutional Research the documents required for assessment noted in point #3 above.
6. To serve as mentor to a faculty member in the next cohort going through the IGL certification process.

In return, Lenoir-Rhyne University will provide a stipend of ____ to be paid upon completion of items 1, 2, 3, and 4 above and will provide support for the faculty member through the Center for Teaching and Learning.

NOTES

1. From here forward, the authors use LR and first-person plural to represent the institutional changes undertaken collectively by the faculty at Lenoir-Rhyne University in this effort.
2. Students' work can be seen at www.sacredspacesofhickory.org.
3. This seminar ran concurrently with and as part of the 2014 IPLA.
4. The title of LR's QEP reflects the university's marketing campaign at the time—"Rise Up."
5. See for instance Duch, Groh, and Allen (2001, p. 7) as well as Amador, Miles, and Peters (2006, pp. 10–11) for discussions of Boud and Feletti's model.
6. As of AY 2016–2017, that load will decrease to twenty-one hours.

7. Within the university's College of Arts & Sciences, there are three subdivisions: the School of Arts & Letters, the School of Humanities and Social Sciences, and the School of Natural Sciences.

8. This inexperience with the inquiry process does not correlate with the academic potential of students. Indeed, even our most prepared students find IGL approaches frustrating because it is so different from what they have experienced in prior educational settings. At times, they are the *most* frustrated because, unlike some of their classmates, they have learned how to succeed in contexts that do not require significant independent inquiry.

9. Although LR based its work on Levy (2012), the image that the team adapted was published earlier; see Levy and Petrulis (2012) for the original publication of the image and for additional discussion of it. Modifications to Levy's model include defining the key terms ("identifying," "pursuing," "producing," and "authoring") on the graphic itself and removing a portion of the graphic intended to indicate different levels of support that the instructor might provide. These changes were made primarily to simplify the graphic, making it easier for faculty to use.

10. LR's team drew from both models, and Levy herself acknowledges that her version of the inquiry circle is closely related to Justice's (2012, p. 17).

11. In our discussions of external motivators, the LR team agreed that this must be handled carefully. Our hope was that the intrinsic motivation of wanting to become a better teacher would remain the driving force; extrinsic motivations should be an added bonus—something that perhaps encourages faculty to prioritize participation in something that they already recognize as valuable. In short, we did not wish for the extrinsic motivators to be so significant that we might attract faculty who actually were not interested in the content of the certification program.

12. As a purely practical matter, all participants agreed that faculty from Columbia would travel to Hickory for our initial meeting, that they would participate in the one-hour sessions via videoconferencing software, and that Hickory faculty would travel to Columbia for the final long session at the end of the semester.

13. See Wiggins and McTighe (2005) for a fuller discussion of backward design principles.

14. Interestingly, in each of the first two cohorts, a guiding question for the semester developed organically from conversation. For the first group, the overarching question was "what does it mean for a professor to guide students in the learning process?"; for the second, it was "how do we respond to students who seem to lack the motivation to engage fully in the inquiry process?"

15. As of the end of the 2014–2015 academic year, 124 individuals have full-time faculty status at Lenoir-Rhyne; seven of those are in nonteaching roles.

16. Semi-structured interviews hover between informal conversation and a strictly scripted interview; while the interviewer has developed a set of fairly open-ended questions, those questions guide a conversation rather than being a strict template to which the interviewer rigidly adheres. As Galletta (2013) notes, this style of interview places the interviewer in the role of using probing questions, some scripted and some in response to the participant's answers, to "support the unfolding of the participant's

narrative" (p. 47). Ten of the twelve participants in LR's IGL certification program were able to participate in these interviews.

17. All quotes are by LR IGL participant faculty and are from anonymous, personal communication in 2015.

REFERENCES

Amador, J. A., Miles, L., and Peters, C. B. (2006). *The practice of problem-based learning: a guide to implementing PBL in the college classroom.* San Francisco, CA: Anker.

Boud, D. and Feletti, G. (1997). *The challenge of problem based learning,* 2nd ed. London: *Kogan Page.*

Duch, B. J., Groh, S. E., and Allen, D. E. (2001). Why problem-based learning? A case study of institutional change in undergraduate education. In B. J. Duch, S. E. Groh, and D. E. Allen (Eds.), *The power of problem-based learning* (pp. 3–11). Sterling, VA: Stylus.

Galletta, A. (2013). *Mastering the semi-structured interview and beyond: From research design to analysis and publication.* New York: New York University Press.

Hmelo-Silver, C. E., Duncan, R. G., and Chinn, C. A. Scaffolding and achievement in problem-based and inquiry learning: A response to Kirschner, Sweller, and Clark (2006). *Educational Psychologist, 42*, 99–107.

Justice, C., Rice, J., Warry, W., Inglis, S., Miller S., Sammon, S. (2007). Inquiry in higher education: Reflections and directions on course design and teaching methods. *Innovative Higher Education, 31*, 201–214.

Lee, V. S. (2012). What is inquiry guided learning? *New Directions for Teaching & Learning, 129*, 5–14.

Levy, P. (2012). Developing inquiry-guided learning in a research university in the United Kingdom. *New Directions for Teaching and Learning. 129*, 15–26.

Levy P. and Petrulis, R. (2012). How do first-year university students experience inquiry and research, and what are the implications for the practice of inquiry-based learning? *Studies in Higher Education, 37*, 85–101.

Southern Association of Colleges and Schools Commission on Colleges. (2015). *General information on the reaffirmation process.* Retrieved from http://www.sacscoc.org/genaccproc.asp.

Wiggins, G. and McTighe, J. (2005). *Understanding by design,* expanded 2nd ed. Alexandria, VA: Association for Supervision and Curriculum Development.

Chapter Three

Implementing Inquiry-Guided Labs in an Introductory Nonmajors Science Course

Caralyn B. Zehnder, Kalina Manoylov, Christine Mutiti, Sam Mutiti, and Allison VandeVoort

This chapter traces a pedagogy innovation project at Georgia College (GC) proceeding from the problem that too many students equate learning science with fact memorization. The authors decided to use inquiry-guided learning (IGL) to communicate their excitement about science to their students, both majors and nonmajors. In 2014, a team from GC attended a three-day IGL workshop embedded within the Institute for Pedagogy in the Liberal Arts (IPLA) conference, where they benefitted from IGL experts and learned how to apply key concepts to their own program.[1] One specific outcome was the revision of the "Introduction to Environmental Science" laboratory course to include inquiry-guided labs. This process included the creation of new assessment methods to measure the effect of these changes on student learning. The chapter focuses on the process followed to implement these changes, the structures in place that supported this work, the assessment tools used, and the team's future work.

Every year, over 400 undergraduate students, largely nonscience majors, enroll in GC's "Introduction to Environmental Science" (ENSC 1000/ 1000L—lecture/lab) course. Most students enroll to fulfill their general education science requirements, and for the majority of the nonscience majors, this is one of the only college-level science classes that they will take. The purpose of the lab is to give students the opportunity to use hands-on activities that explore environmental concepts and problems.

However, an analysis of the lab activities showed that many of the labs were "cookbook style" labs where students follow the instructions in the lab manual and come up with the same results, year after year (Luckie et al.,

2013). In the past, students have described the labs as *"high school-like labs," "pointless and boring,"* and *"full of busy work."* This is distressing because if these labs give students a poor impression of science, then they will likely carry this impression with them after graduation.

In addition, many GC students enroll in ENSC 1000 because they are interested in environmental issues. Therefore, if the lab activities are not engaging, then Environmental Science (ENSC) faculty are missing an opportunity to take environmental issues and problems that students care about and use them as "hooks" to get students interested in science.

In response to this problem, a team of ENSC faculty at GC revised the ENSC 1000 lab course. A major component of this revision was getting students to complete inquiry-guided research projects. IGL is an active learning pedagogy that presents students with questions that they must then answer following discipline-based research methods (Lee, 2012). IGL can communicate the excitement of science to students.

IGL is especially suited to the discipline of environmental science because many of the environmental issues facing our planet today are complex. Students need skills that are explicitly developed by the use of IGL in order to grapple with and solve these problems. IGL goes beyond content knowledge and helps students learn to think like scientists. It enables students to experience the processes of knowledge creation.

Rather than have students memorize the steps of the scientific method, students apply the scientific method by answering questions independently. The instructor is a facilitator, instead of the source of all knowledge. In IGL, students learn about the content that they are researching, and, more importantly, they participate in the research process itself thereby gaining first-hand experience with the scientific method, in the case of science courses.

In the spring of 2014, a team of ENSC faculty attended an IGL workshop as part of the IPLA conference at Oxford College. Throughout the workshop they learned about developing, implementing, and assessing IGL from a team of internationally renowned facilitators. In addition, they had the opportunity to collaborate with other teams from the United States and Canada who were working on similar projects. Their IPLA experience provided them with a firm foundation of knowledge about IGL and the motivation and excitement to continue on with the course revision once they returned to campus.

THE ENVIRONMENTAL SCIENCE
PROGRAM AT GEORGIA COLLEGE

GC is the state's designated public liberal arts university. Approximately 6,000 undergraduate and 800 graduate students enroll in liberal arts and sciences, business, education, and health sciences programs. The ENSC program at GC is a relatively small, young program. Initiated in 2002, the program has had approximately 100 majors enrolled for each of the past five years. A majority of the ENSC majors are traditional college students, eighteen to twenty-four years old. The ENSC program is one of two undergraduate majors within the Department of Environmental & Biological Sciences; the other being the much larger biology major (approximately 400–500 majors).

INQUIRY-GUIDED LEARNING

IGL is an active learning pedagogy that presents students with questions that they must then answer following discipline-based research methods (Lee, 2011). IGL should be driven by questions or problems, based on seeking new knowledge, and be student-centered, with teachers acting as facilitators (Spronken-Smith and Walker, 2010).

IGL shares many attributes with other active learning pedagogies such as case studies and PBL (Prince and Felder, 2006). It includes a range of teaching strategies that promote student learning through active and increasingly independent investigations of questions, issues, or problems, many of which do not have a single answer, as is also the nature of many environmental issues.

This approach is beneficial for both ENSC majors as well as students who are nonscience majors. The question-centered approach provides a more realistic view of science—not as a dogmatic list of rules and terms, but rather as a changing, troubleshooting focused discipline (Beck and Blumer, 2012). This is beneficial to students who desire to be scientists, as it gives them a more accurate view of their future career. Equally important, however, is its benefits to nonmajors, who will develop into citizens who understand the uses and applications of science and how science applies to everyday scenarios.

At the IPLA workshop, participants discussed and reflected on the motivation for including IGL in specific courses and programs. These motivations included using IGL to give students the opportunity to develop skills and attributes beyond course content knowledge. An inquiry-based approach fosters development of critical and creative thinking, problem-solving, quantitative skills, computing skills, and team work, which are among the skill sets that employers are seeking.

In 1995, researchers stated that students were entering a labor force in which employment patterns were changing rapidly and that graduates needed to demonstrate and develop skills and knowledge that would help them survive in an uncertain world of employment (Jenkins and Healey, 1995). Two decades later, the world of employment continues to evolve and is indeed more uncertain than ever. Faculty need to provide their students with the skill sets and dispositions that allow students to succeed in the information-driven economy.

As presented and discussed at the IPLA workshop, IGL focuses on quality above quantity and depth above breadth. Multiple calls for reform in higher education have focused on this very idea (Brewer and Smith, 2011; Olson and Riordan, 2012). In this digital age, information is readily available, and educators are quickly realizing the need to shift from "quantity" to "quality." You can think of *quantity* as focusing on teaching and producing graduates with a solid grasp of many scientific facts, but who are unable to come up with solutions when faced with challenges in the real world. *Quality*, however, focuses on equipping students with skills such as being able to locate and evaluate information, review literature, construct an argument, research questions, and clearly communicate results.

Students who participate in IGL often report a sense of ownership over the ideas generated and are often more enthusiastic about coursework (Hyatt, 2012). This is particularly true when questions or questioning is driving the process of learning. According to Lee, students are motivated to learn when they have a question to which they want an answer (Lee, 2004).

However, many students entering college are accustomed to the numbing passivity of traditional schooling and the challenge, therefore, is reigniting the spirit of curiosity and interest, as often seen in very young children who naturally love to learn. A sense of ownership can also result when faculty provide guidance in the formulation of questions, so that inquiry is more of a developmental process. This is important because first-year students may not be able to ask good, robust questions that can yield good inquiry. It is expected that, over time, guidance by faculty as a driver of learning decreases while inquiry by the students increases.

In addition to learning content, IGL supports learning outcomes that are often integral to college and university mission statements such as cultivating the attributes of curiosity, initiative, and risk taking; promoting critical thinking; and developing into lifelong learners (Lee, 2004). By participating in IGL, students develop intellectually and grow into more mature thinkers who are able to deal with ambiguity and uncertainty (Lee, 2004).

IGL is not only important in single courses; it is most influential and beneficial to students when it is infused throughout the curriculum (Spronken-Smith et al., 2011b). This has been shown to be successful in a variety of academic programs, both science-based and humanities-based, especially in programs with a highly interdisciplinary component (Lee and Ash, 2010). The curriculum-based approach allows for students to encounter IGL multiple times and in a variety of scenarios, based on the course content and the expertise of the faculty.

The implementation plan used by the ENSC program at GC includes scaffolding IGL through a variety of courses encountered by ENSC students as they progress through their undergraduate career. This was part of a broader, college-wide focus on program assessment and curriculum mapping. While other programs at GC use IGL and other active learning pedagogies, there was no institution-wide push for increased use of IGL.

While it is not realistic that every class be IGL-centered, faculty can employ a curriculum mapping approach to assess when and how often students encounter courses that implement IGL within a specific program (Zehnder et al., 2016). The GC implementation plan for introductory-level courses focuses on guided inquiry, where instructors provide the questions to the students in order to facilitate inquiry. As ENSC students progress through the curriculum, they will be provided with opportunities to be less reliant on faculty providing questions and will be better equipped to ask their own questions through open- or discovery-oriented inquiry (Hmelo-Silver, Duncan, and Chinn, 2007).

Having students participate in IGL in introductory, intermediate, and upper-level courses will allow them to progress through the IGL hierarchy of decreasing dependence on faculty support and help build intellectual independence and a love of learning. ENSC faculty have spent the majority of their efforts thus far on implementing IGL into the introductory ENSC course, as well as identifying the upper-level courses where they were already using IGL. Future work will include implementing IGL across the ENSC curriculum and ensuring that all students participate in a research experience within the environmental science major.

INQUIRY-GUIDED LEARNING IN INTRODUCTION TO ENVIRONMENTAL SCIENCE LABS

Introduction to Environmental Science (ENSC 1000) is a general education science course regularly taught by faculty in the ENSC program. Each year, over 400 students, the majority of them nonscience majors, enroll in the course along with the co-requisite lab (ENSC 1000L) and, typically, at least half of the class is composed of freshmen. The lecture portion of the class is taught by ENSC faculty, and the majority of the sections have sixty students per section. The exception is the majors-only section which is capped at twenty-four students per section.

ENSC faculty all use the same student-learning outcomes (SLO) in ENSC 1000 and follow the same schedule, but they do not have a common exam or shared activities. In each semester, about ten lab sections are taught by biology graduate teaching assistants, who are supervised by the program coordinator. All lab sections share a syllabus, follow the same schedule, assign similar tasks, and give a common exam.

THE COURSE REDESIGN PROCESS

Faculty in the ENSC program regularly use the process of backward design (Wiggins and McTighe, 2005; Zehnder et al., 2016) for both course design and curriculum development. Basically, this process means "planning with the end in mind" by first focusing on SLO, then moving on to plan course activities and assessment instruments based on these SLO.

Therefore, this process began by first examining the ENSC 1000L SLO and revising these outcomes. Table 3.1 shows the old and revised SLO. Because this course is in the "core" at GC, there are certain requirements associated with these SLO. In addition, these SLO align with the general education learning outcomes at GC and also the program goals of the environmental science curriculum.

For a number of years outcome 1 was not adequately assessed: *Students will understand how environmental processes and problems are interconnected with aspects of human society and cultural institutions.* Further

Table 3.1. A Comparison of Old and Revised Student-Learning Outcomes for Introduction to Environmental Science Lab (ENSC 1000L)

Old student-learning outcomes As a result of this course, students will be able to:	Revised student-learning outcomes As a result of this course, students will be able to:
Understand how environmental processes and problems are interconnected with aspects of human society and cultural institutions.	Make critical observations, develop hypotheses, and test them using the scientific method.
Make critical observations, develop hypotheses, and test them using the scientific method.	Present scientific ideas and results in both written and oral formats.
Be able to accurately, clearly and precisely present field and lab collected data using appropriate figures, tables, and graphs.	Use appropriate technology to collect, analyze, interpret, and present environmental data.
Be able to present scientific ideas and results in both written and oral formats.	Use descriptive statistics to explain and present data.
Use appropriate technology to collect, analyze, interpret, and present environmental data.	
Use descriptive statistics to explain and present data.	

reflection on the outcome showed that the inability to properly assess this outcome stemmed from the fact that it was poorly written, vague, and not measurable. Faculty could not determine what a student would have to do to demonstrate that they had met this outcome and could not come up with a common activity that instructors could use that aligned with this outcome. Therefore, this outcome was discarded in order to focus on the outcomes that better aligned with what students needed to learn from this course.

Outcomes 3 and 4 were considered redundant because both outcomes were met using the same activities and assessed using the same instruments: group lab reports and group oral presentations. Outcome 3 was perceived as narrower and included within outcome 4; so, they decided to discard outcome 3.

As faculty discussed these SLO and examined how a lab revision focused on IGL would map to these outcomes, they realized a group inquiry project with a formal lab report and group presentation would meet all four SLO. Since this would be a large, high-stakes project, both in terms of time and grades, they decided to have the IGL projects in the latter half of the semester. This provided students with opportunities to practice activities and have low-stakes assessments in the first half of the course before embarking on a large group project at the course conclusion. In addition, faculty wanted to build the appropriate scaffolding into the course so that students would receive feedback multiple times throughout the semester.

Once faculty decided to place the IGL module in the latter half of the course, they then needed to move on to the hard part: focusing on an IGL module, designing new lab activities, creating assessment instruments, and creating a plan to implement the new ideas. Fortunately, they came across an excellent education essay in *Science* magazine (Hyatt, 2012). In this chapter, Dr. Hyatt describes how she facilitated IGL in her biology course. In her course, students read prompts that start with a question, include two to three paragraphs of background information, and provide a list of possible supplies. Students then collaboratively design experiments, write research proposals, implement their experiments, and collect and analyze their data (Hyatt, 2012).

The ENSC faculty decided that this model would be a great fit for ENSC 1000L because it is populated predominantly by nonscience majors, many of whom say that they "don't like science" or that they "are worried about taking a college-level science class." The Hyatt model follows a guided-inquiry approach (Bonnstetter, 1998; Staver and Bay, 1987) whereby students are provided with questions from their instructor, but the students design their own approach to answer these questions.

Faculty thought that this guided-inquiry approach would support science majors too. Most of the science majors who enroll in ENSC 1000 tend to have little to no experience with designing experiments and answering open-ended questions. In fact, some of the science majors struggle with these types of activities more than the nonscience majors. Faculty think that this is because these students have taken multiple science classes already and excelled at memorizing terms and hence are frustrated by this new approach and the open-ended nature of the inquiry questions.

Prior to these revisions, the ENSC 1000L course had five weeks of water-themed labs at the end of the semester. A few years ago, faculty had deliberately decided to focus on water because there are multiple aquatic environments around GC for students to sample from (streams, lakes, and the Oconee River). Students are also interested in water and water quality, and there are numerous ways for untrained students to measure it (pH, dissolved oxygen, nitrate concentrations, phosphate concentrations, fecal coliform bacteria levels, temperature, etc.) and collect interesting, useable data. They decided to replace these water-themed labs, which were mostly cookbook in nature, with an IGL student research project focused on water.

DESIGNING THE INQUIRY-GUIDED LEARNING QUESTIONS

Faculty used an inquiry-based approach to design the new IGL questions. Five upper-level environmental science majors were recruited to help redesign the ENSC 1000L labs. The faculty wanted student input in question generation because they felt that students would be best able to come up with questions that would interest other students. In addition, they felt that this would be a great learning opportunity for these students.

In September of 2014, they announced this opportunity to all ENSC majors and asked interested students to submit an application to participate in an "Inquiry-Guided Lab Designing Workshop." Workshop participants were expected to attend five two-hour long meetings spaced throughout the fall 2014 semester, work collaboratively with other group members, and commit to creating three to four IGL questions for ENSC 1000L. Twelve students applied to take part in this project, and five were selected based on their application essays.

Before these students could write their own inquiry questions, they had to learn about inquiry itself. During the first meeting, the workshop facilitator presented students with a handout on inquiry and everyone discussed the "Model of the Inquiry Process" (Justice et al., 2002) and the "Qualities of a Good Inquiry Question" (Justice et al., 2007). In addition, students read the Hyatt essay (Hyatt, 2012) and discussed how this model could be applied to ENSC 1000L. The five students were then divided into two groups, and each group was instructed to write four IGL questions before the next meeting.

Designing appropriate IGL questions takes time. The first draft of questions was not useable because some of the questions were either too limited, for instance, "How much water on the planet is freshwater?"—a question that is answered via a table or pie chart in most environmental science textbooks. Other questions were too broad, for example, "What are the effects of building on a floodplain?" Multiple meetings were spent discussing and evaluating IGL questions.

While many of the students had participated in undergraduate research projects and understood how to apply the scientific method, they struggled with writing questions that could lead others down the inquiry path. In addition, none of the students had experienced IGL in any previous courses, though many of them had experienced case studies and problem-based learning, and so it was understandably hard for them to design good questions. However, after a lot of hard work and collaboration the students produced ten good IGL questions (see Table 3.2).

All of the IGL questions require students to formulate a testable hypothesis. A majority of the questions require students to design a typical experiment with independent and dependent variables, replication, and field data collection. All of the questions require students to collect data and then spend time working on data analysis, interpretation, and presentation.

In addition, these research projects require students to find resources, including peer-reviewed journal articles, and then compare their results to previously published studies. There is not a single "correct" way for students

Table 3.2. IGL Questions Created by Students for Use in ENSC 1000 Labs

1. How does water quality differ between surface water and groundwater?
2. Is the SteriPen, activated carbon Brita filter, or chlorine tablet the most effective method of drinking water purification?
3. How does the rate of flow affect water quality?
4. Using the sun's energy, what type of plastic water bottle most effectively reduces bacteria in water?
5. What is your edible water footprint?
6. How does the water quality of tap and filtered water on campus compare to bottled water?
7. How does the quality of lake water change after being processed at the drinking water treatment plant?
8. How can I have clean drinking water while backpacking?
9. Plastic microbeads—What products are they in and can we avoid them?
10. Are there any differences in the macroinvertebrate communities of urbanized vs. reference streams?

to approach these questions; there are multiple right answers (and wrong answers too). All of the questions require students to make decisions about the type of information that they are going to collect and then to critically analyze this information. This encourages students to engage with their research projects and feel ownership over the results.

The five students who worked on this project learned about IGL and had the opportunity to work collaboratively with their peers to create new lab activities for ENSC 1000. When asked what they had learned from this experience, these students provided some very insightful observations:

> I realized that there is a lot more that goes into writing a lab than I originally thought. Most importantly, taking into account the way that students learn is a huge part of creating a lab that is effective and efficient.

> This opportunity helped me gain experience in lab design which is an essential aspect of any field in environmental science. Taking part in this course revision allowed me to gain better comprehension of the process that goes into creating a lab manual which really illustrates why there is such particular content in these manuals.

> Creating inquiry guided labs with my peers allowed me to share the knowledge I have been acquiring here at Georgia College with incoming classes. It was a great idea to allow students who have been through this particular class and program to create and edit the labs.

> I enjoyed working collaboratively to create new labs based on what we thought was important to know about environmental science. For example, we made labs that related to their everyday lives, like how much water they use from the foods they eat, and if drinking bottled water is any better than the tap water on campus.

TRIAL RUN FOR OUR INQUIRY-GUIDED LEARNING QUESTIONS

One ENSC faculty piloted these IGL questions in a general education, global perspectives course: Water & Society, in spring 2015. All GC sophomores are required to take one global perspectives course, and they are able to select among dozens of course topics. In the ENSC program's Water & Society class, students examine issues surrounding global water use, management, and needs, and they investigate diverse responses of societies to contemporary water issues.

This class includes a large amount of group work. Throughout the semester, students worked in groups of four—there were six groups in this class—on a variety of assignments and activities. The IGL questions were presented to the class approximately six weeks before the end of the semester. Please see boxes 3.1 and 3.2 for examples of the prompts and background information that groups received.

Box 3.1

One example of a question and background information provided to students for their IGL research projects

Plastic microbeads—What products are they in and can we avoid them?

Plastic microbeads from face wash are polluting river sediment

By Rachel Feltman

September 29, 2014

Published in *The Washington Post*

http://www.washingtonpost.com/news/speaking-of-science/wp/2014/09/29/plastic-microbeads-from-face-wash-are-polluting-river-sediment/

Tiny balls of plastic from cosmetic products are showing up in river sediment for the first time, mixing with the rocks and dirt that line the bed of the Saint Lawrence River. Because scientists have mostly been looking for these plastic pollutants in the surface water instead of in the dirt, it means that their build-up could be even worse than previously imagined—and fish and other animals could be in serious trouble because of them.

You've probably heard of these dastardly microbeads by now: The tiny pieces of plastic, billed as miraculous exfoliators in facial wash and whitening scrubbers in tooth paste, are basically impossible to get rid of. They're too small for waste water processing plants to filter out, so they're ending up in the sea—building up in the water and posing risks to marine life and water quality.

In recent years, researchers have reported finding the microbeads in the Great Lakes. Further research has found them in the Saint Lawrence River, which connects those lakes with the Atlantic Ocean and flows from eastern Canada to the midwestern United States.

Previous research pulled the microbeads from the water itself, but in a study published recently in the *Canadian Journal of Fisheries and Aquatic Sciences*, researchers went digging in the dirt. "The more we looked, the more we found. That was definitely really worrisome," Suncica Avlijas, a graduate student at McGill University, told CBC News Montreal. In some areas, Avlijas and her colleagues found over 1,000 microbeads per liter of sediment.

The researchers only looked at the microbeads on the slightly larger end of the spectrum; so they suspect that smaller ones may have gone uncounted. This is worst in areas of slow river flow, where solids like these beads aren't being moved quickly enough to stay buoyant. In slow water, they sink—and build up—until the sediment is heavily polluted.

Now, these researchers will dissect fish that live on the polluted riverbed to see if they've been eating the plastic particles. If the microbead build-up is getting into the fish food chain, it could be endangering their health. In the meantime, look for toothpaste without any beads in it (dentists say they're useless, anyway) and make sure your exfoliating scrubs use particles that are safe and biodegradable.

Are students at Georgia College using products that contain microbeads? Design an experiment to answer this question.

> **Box 3.2**
>
> **One example of a question and background information provided to students for their IGL research projects**
>
> Are there any differences in the macroinvertebrate communities of urbanized vs. reference streams?
>
> The aquatic macroinvertebrate community is extremely diverse, represented by thousands of different species with different feeding strategies. Many insects, including dragonflies, damselflies, mayflies, caddis flies, stoneflies, midges, and mosquitoes have aquatic larvae. In addition, other invertebrates such as mollusks (snails, mussels, and clams), crustaceans (crayfish), and worms call rivers and streams home. The structure of the resident aquatic macroinvertebrate community is a direct measure of water quality. Aquatic macroinvertebrates are good indicators of contamination because they are resident monitors of pollution and are less able to migrate from the impairment. Since macroinvertebrates must persist in the contaminant field, they indicate past conditions as well as current conditions.
>
> Streams and rivers are constantly changing, and water quality measurements, such as pH, dissolved oxygen, or nitrate concentration, taken one day may be radically different the next day. For example, a stream may be turbid with fast-moving, well-oxygenated flood waters one day, and slow-flowing, deoxygenated, and clear the next. Because rivers and streams are so dynamic, biologists often use the presence and abundance of animal species as indicators of stream health. Because animals must live in the stream for a long time, their numbers indicate the health of the stream over the long term.
>
> Bioindicators are species whose presence and abundance can be used to quantify stream quality. Some animals are very sensitive to water quality, and their populations tend to fall as water quality declines. Sediment pollution and low oxygen levels are particularly influential in suppressing these populations. Thus, an abundance of these sensitive species in a stream is a good indication that the stream is in good health. Other animals are less sensitive to declines in water quality, and these species tend to persist when water quality declines. In some cases populations of these less-sensitive species can increase as water quality declines because the populations of their competitors decline.
>
> Are there any differences in the macroinvertebrate communities of urbanized vs. reference streams? Design an experiment that answers this question.
>
> Resources:
> Georgia Adopt-a-Stream: http://www.georgiaadoptastream.com/db/Macros.asp

Groups were allowed to choose their own question, and the class discussed the expectations surrounding this research project (see table 3.3). In addition, the class reviewed a handout that presented aspects of a good experiment (testable hypothesis, replication, control group, reducing confounding variables), and groups had time to work on preparing their proposals.

Over the next four weeks, all class time was focused on the IGL research projects. The instructor met with each group after they submitted their research proposal and after they submitted a rough draft of their lab report. Students indicated that this feedback was important to them. It gave students

Table 3.3. Research Project Deadlines and Point Values for the IGL Research Projects

	Due date	Points
Proposal (1 per group)	3/29	10
Lab report rough draft	4/11	10
Peer review	4/14	10
Presentations	4/21	50
Lab report (final)	4/26	80
Group member evaluations (everyone submits one)	4/26	30

an assigned time to meet with the instructor, to ask questions about their project and to discuss the feedback on the written assignments. This also helped to reduce student grade anxiety, since the IGL research projects were worth a substantial portion of their final grade. This was especially important for the "high achievers," some of whom expressed some anxiety about the group work and the unstructured nature of this project.

In the research proposals, each group had to state their hypothesis, describe the methods they would use to test their hypothesis, indicate a timeline for accomplishing the project, and also designate roles for all group members. The instructor used these research proposals to help organize equipment and supplies, which were already on hand based on the likely ways that students approach these projects. In addition, some groups needed to be encouraged to think more creatively about their questions while others needed to be reined in.

Students were able to sign out equipment to take into the field, and the instructor was available at set times in the lab to assist students with analyzing water samples and using equipment. It was chaotic and crazy at times, but all the students were engaged with their research projects and many of them were very enthusiastic and excited about their results.

Prior to designing and implementing their own experiments, these students had collected water samples from a local stream and analyzed these as a class; so they knew a little bit about some of the possible methods, but most of them had not actually done sampling like this before. And, while there were a few science majors within the class (five out of twenty-four), most of the students had no prior experiences with this type of work.

ASSESSMENT

Assessment of student learning was an important part of the IPLA workshop. Obviously, a standard multiple choice exam will not adequately assess the type of learning that occurs in IGL. At the IPLA workshop, faculty were presented with multiple examples of assessment instruments and had the opportunity to question the facilitators about the best ways to implement assessment and how to interpret assessment results.

The skills and aptitudes that IGL develops, such as critical thinking and problem solving, can be difficult to measure, particularly when students are in the early stages of developing these skills. As an instructor, it is much easier to show that students have learned if all you require them to do is memorize terms and definitions. However, this rote memorization will not lead to enduring understanding nor will it help students develop into critical thinkers who can act independently.

The assessment results from the new IGL labs come from the Water & Society course. For these projects, each group had to write a formal lab report and give an eleven- to twelve-minute oral presentation. The lab reports were assessed using a rubric that included sections on project creativity, background information, methods, data presentation, data interpretation, and references as well as organization and mechanics (see table 3.4).

In the future, faculty are going to add a section on "experimental design quality" so that the projects are evaluated based on how well designed the experiments are. They will also require students to include their predictions in their original research proposal. However, they will also explain that it is okay for these predictions to be wrong and that in the final lab report it will be very important for them to go back and discuss how well their data supported the original predictions.

The oral presentations were assessed using a rubric that focused on presentation skills: organization, delivery, visual presentation, and ability to answer questions (see table 3.5). Both oral and written communication skills are commonly developed by students who complete IGL projects (Justice et al., 2007). Students did quite well on these graded aspects of the IGL research projects. The average group grade on the oral presentation was 89.1 percent and the average grade on the lab report was an 88 percent. The lab reports benefitted greatly from instructor feedback on the rough drafts and being able to discuss the lab reports with each group after the rough drafts had been "graded." In addition, each group peer reviewed two other lab reports which gave the students experience with the lab report rubric and provided them with practice evaluating the sections of the lab report.

Students completed an ungraded pretest at the beginning of the semester and then similar questions were on their final exam. These questions were all aligned with the learning outcome of applying the scientific method and interpreting data. Because of their work in this course, a significant portion

Table 3.4. Lab Report grading Rubric Used to Evaluate Group Reports

Category Score	Exemplary (5)	Well done (4)	Accomplished (3)	Developing (2)	Beginning or Incomplete (1)
Project creativity *5 pts*	Creative approach to answering the inquiry question. Project includes multiple lines of evidence addressing the question.		A solid project, but not very creative. Project includes only one line of evidence to address the inquiry question.		Project lacks creativity. Group does the bare minimum required to answer the question.
Introduction Background information *10 points*	Uses scientific sources to provide context for the experiment and explain the relevant scientific principles.	Uses scientific sources to provide some context for the experiment and explain the relevant scientific principles.	Some introductory information, but missing some major points or some of the information provided is irrelevant.	Very little background information provided. Or information provided is incorrect.	Very poor. Little to no correct background information is provided.
Introduction Organization *5 points*	Starts out broad and gradually focuses in on the specific experiment. Section is cohesive. Ends with a clearly stated hypothesis.	Starts out broad and gradually focuses in on the specific experiment. Section is not always cohesive.	Introduction is not cohesive. No connections between paragraphs or ideas. Hypothesis is at end of introduction but is unclear or unscientific.	Organization needs work. Individual paragraphs contain multiple, disjointed ideas. Or hypothesis is stated in the beginning or middle of the introduction.	Very poorly organized. Or no clearly stated hypothesis.

(continued)

Table 3.4 (continued)

Category Score	Exemplary (5)	Well done (4)	Accomplished (3)	Developing (2)	Beginning or Incomplete (1)
Methods 15 points	Provides enough details that someone not familiar with the experiment could repeat the experiment. Includes information on dates, locations, equipment used, and replication. Written in paragraph form and in the past tense. Does not include unnecessary details.	Provides enough details that someone not familiar with the experiment could repeat the experiment. Includes information on dates, locations, equipment used, and replication. Written in paragraph form and in the past tense. Includes some unnecessary details.	Provides most of the information necessary to repeat the experiment, but one or two minor details are missing.	Missing a lot of important information. It would be very difficult for someone to repeat this experiment based on the information provided.	No methods section.
Results Text 10 points	A single paragraph at the beginning of the results section that correctly states the data trends and statistics (if appropriate).			Explains or interprets data in the results section.	No text.

Table 3.4 (continued)

Category Score	Exemplary (5)	Well done (4)	Accomplished (3)	Developing (2)	Beginning or Incomplete (1)
Results Figures and tables 10 points	All data are correctly presented in an appropriate figure or table. Figures and tables have captions.	One or two minor mistakes in the figures or tables.	Multiple mistakes in figures or tables.	Redundant figures and tables. Or raw data presented instead of averages. Or a figure includes multiple variables that shouldn't be together.	No figures or tables.
Discussion Interpretation of results 10 points	All important trends and data comparisons are interpreted correctly and discussed. Good understanding of results is conveyed. Includes a strong discussion of original hypothesis and why it was or was not supported.	All results correctly interpreted with one minor mistake. Good understanding of results is conveyed. Includes a discussion of original hypothesis and why it was or was not supported.	One major mistake in interpreting results. Or two minor mistakes. Weak understanding of results is conveyed. Weak discussion of original hypothesis and why it was or was not supported.	Two or more major mistakes in interpreting results. Weak understanding of results is conveyed.	Very incomplete or incorrect interpretation of trends and comparison of data indicating a lack of understanding of results. Little or no discussion of original hypothesis and why it was or was not supported.

(continued)

Table 3.4 (continued)

Category Score	Exemplary (5)	Well done (4)	Accomplished (3)	Developing (2)	Beginning or Incomplete (1)
Discussion Connections 5 points	Connections made to similar research and underlying principles and theory explaining the work.		Weak connections made to similar research. Or weak connections to underlying theory explaining the work.		Little or no connection to similar research. Or little or no connection to underlying theory.
Conclusion 5 points	Strong review of key conclusions. Insightful discussion of the main ideas presented.	Strong review of key conclusions. Good discussion of the main ideas presented.	Weak review of key conclusions. Some discussion of the main ideas presented.	Does not review main ideas.	No conclusion.
References 5 points Minimum three scholarly sources	All sources are accurately cited and references following ESA format. Includes at least three scholarly sources.	All sources are accurately documented, but one or two are not in the correct format. Includes at least three scholarly sources.	All sources are accurately documented, but three or more are not in the correct format. Or Only 2 scholarly sources.	References are not directly cited in text.	Contains no scholarly or peer-reviewed sources.

Table 3.4 (continued)

Category Score	Exemplary (5)	Well done (4)	Accomplished (3)	Developing (2)	Beginning or Incomplete (1)
Style 5 pts	Chooses words for their precise meaning and uses an appropriate level of specificity. Sentences are varied, yet clearly structured and carefully focused, not long and rambling.	Generally uses words accurately and effectively, but may sometimes be too general. Sentences generally clear, well structured, and focused, though some may be awkward or ineffective.	Uses relatively vague and general words, may use some inappropriate language. Sentence structure is generally correct, but sentences may be wordy, unfocused, repetitive, or confusing.	Too vague and abstract. Multiple awkward sentences; structure is simple or monotonous.	Many awkward sentences, misuses words, uses inappropriate language.
Mechanics 10 pts	Almost entirely free of spelling, punctuation, and grammatical errors.	Fewer than five grammar, spelling, or punctuation errors.	Fewer than six to twelve grammar, spelling, or punctuation errors.	Occasional grammar, spelling, or punctuation errors.	Frequent grammar, spelling, or punctuation errors.
Appearance and formatting 5 points	All sections in order, well formatted, and labeled. Formatting enhances readability. Succinct, descriptive title. No title page.	All sections in order, well formatted, and labeled. Formatting enhances readability. No title page. Title is vague.	No title or includes a title page. Sections correctly labelled.	Sections are not labelled.	No evidence of formatting.

Implementing Inquiry-Guided Labs   63

Table 3.5. Grading rubric for group oral presentations

	Exemplary (4)	Accomplished (3)	Developing (2)	Beginning (1)
Organization 10 percent	*Concise and clear* (1) Clear introduction, body, and conclusion; (2) Logical order of content; (3) Transitions effectively link topics of presentation.	Demonstrates competence in two of the three listed criteria for organization of an exemplary presentation.	Demonstrates competence in two of the three listed criteria for organization of an exemplary presentation.	(1) No introduction, body, or conclusion; (2) Content presented in no clear, logical order; (3) Transitions absent.
Use of visuals in communication 30 percent	*Text and graphics* enhance presentation of topics: (1) Text and graphics balanced; (2) Graphics have clear connection with content; (3) No mistakes in spelling and grammar; (4) Appropriate number of powerpoint slides.	Demonstrates competence in three of the four listed criteria for exemplary use of visuals in the presentation.	Demonstrates competence in two of the four listed criteria for exemplary use of visuals in the presentation.	(1) Amount of text used with graphic excessive; (2) Graphic has no clear connection with content of presentation; (3) Spelling and grammar mistakes in text; (4) Too many or too few slides used.
Delivery 30 percent	*Delivery mechanics* (1) Speech void of grammatical errors; (2) Volume is appropriate; (3) Speaker makes eye contact with the audience; (4) Good pace; (5) No distracting movements.	Demonstrates competence in four of the five listed criteria for an exemplary delivery.	Demonstrates competence in one or two or three of the five listed criteria for an exemplary delivery.	(1) Speech with numerous grammatical errors; (2) Volume too loud or too soft; (3) Fails to make eye contact with the audience; (4) Speaks to slowly or too quickly; (5) Speaker paces or has other distracting motions.
Timing 20 percent	Within thirty seconds of the allotted time.	Thirty-one to fifty-nine seconds over or under the allotted time.	One or two minutes over or under the allotted time.	More than two minutes over or under the allotted time.
Question and Answers 10 percent	*Prepared to address questions* (1) Anticipates and is prepared for questions; (2) Clearly listens to question from audience member; (3) Provides an appropriate response.	Demonstrates competence in two of the three listed criteria for addressing questions from the audience in an exemplary fashion.	Demonstrates competence in one of the three listed criteria for addressing questions from the audience in an exemplary fashion.	(1) Questions avoided or uninvited; Is not prepared for questions from the audience; (2) Does not listen to the audience member's question; (3) Does not answer the audience member's question.

of which was focused on their inquiry-guided projects, students made important gains in their ability to apply the scientific method and interpret data. On the pretest only 50 percent of the students correctly answered a question on applying the scientific method while 72 percent of the students answered this question correctly on the final. On three open-ended exam questions, students showed that they met the learning objectives of the inquiry labs with average scores of 89.6 percent, 98.3 percent and 75 percent on the final exam.

In addition to quantitatively measuring student learning based on exam results and lab reports, the instructor also gathered student feedback on the IGL project by asking each student, "What did you learn from completing your inquiry-guided research project?" While some students wrote about the specific content that they learned about, many others commented on the development of critical inquiry skills and collaborative skills including:

> I learned a great deal of information about my topic. I also learned a lot about the research process and analysis of a research idea.
>
> How to work well with others.
>
> I learned a lot about the accurate process of a scientific experiment and how to use several instruments in the lab.
>
> I learned how to go about forming an experiment and the different variables that could possibly skew the results.
>
> I learned how to better work well with a group and evenly distribute work load.
>
> How to properly do experiments and write reports.
>
> How to collect data in the field.
>
> I learned a lot about designing your own experiment.
>
> That there is a lot of uncontrollable error that can emerge when doing an experiment and good care must be taken to avoid error.
>
> How to conduct a well done experiment and produce a good lab report.

These comments show that this IGL research project gave students the opportunity to actually practice science and that these research projects are well aligned with the course student-learning outcome 1: *Students will be able to make critical observations, develop hypotheses, and test these hypotheses using the scientific method.*

FUTURE WORK

In fall 2015, faculty implemented the inquiry-guided labs in all ten sections of ENSC 1000L. In addition, they developed training material for the graduate teaching assistants who are the ENSC 1000 lab instructors. The graduate teaching assistants play a crucial role in the implementation of IGL in ENSC 1000L. And, there is hope that the teaching assistants will benefit from this IGL experience as much as the undergraduates do (Hughes and Ellefson, 2013).

Faculty will continue to revise the labs based on student and instructor feedback, and they will continue to improve the assessment instruments. In addition, they want to examine how inquiry is presented in ENSC 1000L, using Table III (in Lee, 2011), and determine if students have multiple opportunities to experience IGL in this class before the large group IGL research project. Currently, there are two labs earlier in the semester where students have a chance to test hypotheses and design their own experiments within very structured boundaries. Based on student feedback and assessment data, they will revise the semester pattern if necessary.

In fall 2016, and in subsequent semesters, faculty examined the impact of these revised labs on student learning, measured by post-test grades and by student self-assessment at the end of the course. During previous semesters, they collected student performance data using a similar pretest-post-test format and students also self-assessed their learning using the SALG (salgsite.org). Faculty will compare student performance in ENSC 1000L before and after these revisions in order to measure the effectiveness of these changes on student learning. These data will also contribute to the annual ENSC program assessment because ENSC 1000L is a required course for the major and one that is regularly used in program assessment reports.

For most scientists, research is a collaborative endeavor which is why students work in groups when they complete their IGL research projects, and being able to work collaboratively is an important skill that students need to develop. Also, it would be logistically impossible for an instructor to facilitate twenty-four individual IGL projects. Since group work is such a large part of ENSC 1000L, the ENSC faculty want to revise the ENSC 1000L SLO to include an outcome on working collaboratively. This outcome could be assessed by the "group member evaluation" that each student completes where they grade their other group members.

However, group work can be a challenge, and it is something that many students frequently complain about. Therefore, the instructors want to implement classroom activities that help students develop into good team members, and they also want to review how the IGL research project is implemented so that the instructors encourage collaboration and reduce frustration.

SUPPORT AT GEORGIA COLLEGE

At the IPLA workshop, one activity that all groups participated in was a listing of institutional "enablers" and "constraints" that would help or hinder progress (Spronken-Smith et al., 2011a). Faculty at GC are fortunate to have multiple institutional enablers that have supported the work on this project and on other related projects within the ENSC program, including the GC Undergraduate Research and Creative Endeavors (URACE) program (http://www.gcsu.edu/urace/) and the Science Education STEM mini-grant program (http://www.gcsu.edu/stem/stemmini-grantsprogram.htm).

In January 2013, the Environmental Science program received a URACE planning grant to support their work in redesigning the ENSC curriculum with a focus on undergraduate research. This grant paid for the team to attend the IPLA workshop in May 2014. In the summer of 2014, they received a Georgia College STEM mini-grant program to support the ENSC 1000L course redesign work. This grant provided three faculty with a small summer stipend to work on the course redesign. In addition, they were able to provide the undergraduate assistants with $500 each for their help and participation. Having this institutional support was very important for this project because it allowed the team to quickly move forward on a major course redesign.

CONCLUSIONS

The major benefits of using IGL in this context include the following.

1. Students develop problem solving and critical thinking skills as they complete their IGL projects.
2. The IGL projects contribute to high levels of faculty-student interaction in class.
3. The IGL projects contribute to high levels of student and professor engagement.

In sum, the IGL module helped cement knowledge of the scientific process in the nonscience major students because they actually got to apply the scientific method first-hand. Students' critical thinking, problem solving, and data collection skills were significantly increased because they were able to spend so much time thinking, planning, and working on research projects.

As evident in the students' feedback above, this group of students is now more equipped to design, carry out a project, analyze data, and present their work to others. These are the skills that employers and graduate schools are looking for when hiring new employees. The ENSC faculty believe that these students will have an added advantage over their counterparts who did not go through this IGL process when looking for employment, trying to find undergraduate research opportunities, or applying to graduate schools.

Another major benefit of our IGL module was the feedback system and interaction with the faculty that is built in the module. Having that personal or small group interaction with faculty is a key component of GC's liberal arts mission, and one of the reasons why most of these students choose GC over larger institutions. The activities in this IGL module also gave some of the students an opportunity to interact with graduate students and faculty in their research labs as they looked for extra help and equipment for their projects. This was a great networking opportunity for these students as some of them have remained in contact with these labs and can contact or use them as a resource in the future.

In addition, from the professor's perspective, facilitating these IGL projects was exciting and fun. Students seemed more engaged with their projects than in a typical course assignment. A majority of the groups were excited about being able to decide which variables to focus on and on collecting their own data. The students definitely felt a sense of ownership and pride toward their projects—which was motivating for both the instructor and the students.

The faculty who completed this work are passionate about giving non-science majors the opportunity to participate in the process of science and learn how to think critically and evaluate evidence. They also are working to assess these course-level changes and to develop assessment instruments appropriate for IGL activities. This process has been time consuming, and they are still working to overcome challenges associated with large class size and high teaching loads. Thankfully, they have been well supported within their department, and they have taken a collaborative approach to embarking on this long-term project. They are excited about the student feedback concerning the IGL module in this course and are looking forward to implementing these IGL group research projects on a larger scale.

NOTE

1. The 2014 Institute on Inquiry as a Way of Learning in Colleges and Universities was a special workshop within the IPLA. The workshop was facilitated by leading experts on IGL including: Virginia S. Lee of Virginia S. Lee and Associates, the United States; Philippa Levy, deputy chief executive of The Higher Education Academy, the United Kingdom; Rachel Spronken-Smith, professor in higher education and geography and dean of graduate research, University of Otago,

New Zealand; Catherine Chiappetta Swanson, educational consultant, McMaster Institute for Innovation and Excellence in Teaching and Learning, and Instructor, Faculty of Social Sciences, McMaster University, Canada.

REFERENCES

Beck, C. W. and Blumer, L. S. (2012). Inquiry-based ecology laboratory courses improve student confidence and scientific reasoning skills. *Ecosphere, 3(12)*, Art.112.

Bonnstetter, R. J. (1998). Inquiry: Learning from the past with an eye on the future. *Electronic Journal of Science Education, 3(1).* Retrieved on May 2015 from http://www.scholarlyexchange.org/ojs/index.php/EJSE/article/viewArticle/7595/5362.

Brewer, C. A. and Smith, D. (2011). Vision and change in undergraduate biology education: A call to action. *American Association for the Advancement of Science, Washington, DC.*

Hmelo-Silver, C. E., Duncan, R. G., and Chinn, C. A. (2007). Scaffolding and achievement in problem-based and inquiry learning: A response to Kirschner, Sweller, and Clark (2006). *Educational Psychologist, 42(2),* 99–107.

Hughes, P. W. and Ellefson, M. R. (2013). Inquiry-based training improves teaching effectiveness of biology teaching assistants. *PloS One, 8(10)*, e78540.

Hyatt, L. A. (2012). Personal plants: Making botany meaningful by experimentation. *Science, 337(6102)*, 1620–1621.

Jenkins, A. and Healey, M. (1995). Linking the geography curriculum to the worlds of industry, commerce and public authorities. *Journal of Geography in Higher Education, 19(2)*, 177–181.

Justice, C., Rice, J., Warry, W., Inglis, S., Miller, S., and Sammon, S. (2007). Inquiry in higher education: Reflections and directions on course design and teaching methods. *Innovative Higher Education, 31(4)*, 201–214.

Justice, C., Warry, W., Cuneo, C., Inglis, S., Miller, S., Rice, J., and Sammon, S. (2002). A grammar for inquiry: Linking goals and methods in a collaboratively taught social sciences inquiry course. *The Alan Blizzard Award paper: The award winning papers.* Society for Teaching and Learning in Higher Education: Toronto.

Lee, V. S. (2004). *Teaching and learning through inquiry: A guidebook for institutions and instructors.* Sterling, VA: Stylus.

Lee, V. S. (2011). The power of inquiry as a way of learning. *Innovative Higher Education, 36(3),* 149–160.

Lee, V. S. (2012). What is inquiry-guided learning? *New Directions for Teaching and Learning, (129)*, 5–14.

Lee, V. S. and Ash, S. (2010). Unifying the undergraduate curriculum through inquiry-guided learning. *New Directions for Teaching and Learning, (121)*, 35–46.

Luckie, D. B., Smith, J. J., Cheruvelil, K. S., Fata-Hartley, C., Murphy, C. A., and Urquhart, G. R. (2013). The "Anti-cookbook laboratory": Converting "canned" introductory biology laboratories to multi-week independent investigations. *Proceedings of the Association for Biology Laboratory Education, 34*, 196–213.

Olson, S. and Riordan, D. G. (2012). Engage to excel: Producing one million additional college graduates with degrees in science, technology, engineering, and mathematics. Report to the President. *Executive Office of the President.*

Prince, M. J. and Felder, R. M. (2006). Inductive teaching and learning methods: Definitions, comparisons, and research bases. *Journal of Engineering Education, 95(2)*, 123.

Spronken-Smith, R. and Walker, R. (2010). Can inquiry-based learning strengthen the links between teaching and disciplinary research? *Studies in Higher Education, 35(6)*, 723–740.

Spronken-Smith, R., Walker, R., Batchelor, J., O'Steen, B., and Angelo, T. (2011a). Enablers and constraints to the use of inquiry-based learning in undergraduate education. *Teaching in Higher Education, 16(1)*, 15–28.

Spronken-Smith, R., Walker, R., Dickinson, K., Closs, G., Lord, J., and Harland, T. (2011b). Redesigning a curriculum for inquiry: An ecology case study. *Instructional Science, 39(5)*, 721–735.

Staver, J. R. and Bay, M. (1987). Analysis of the project synthesis goal cluster orientation and inquiry emphasis of elementary science textbooks. *Journal of Research in Science Teaching, 24(7)*, 629–643.

Wiggins, G. P. and McTighe, J. (2005). *Understanding by design.* Ascd. Alexandria: VA.

Zehnder, C. B., Manoylov, K., Mutiti, C., Mutiti, S., and VandeVoort, A. R. (2016). Applying the process of backward design in revising an environmental science program. *Journal of Environmental Studies and Sciences*, 1–10.

Chapter Four

Resolving Early Career Paradoxes at the IPLA

Lia Schraeder

For many freshly minted PhDs graduating from research universities, paradoxes related to the craft of teaching emerge in the first few years after graduation. One paradox is evident in the keen words of Derek Bok (2013), who wrote that "the most glaring defect of our graduate programs ... is how little they do to prepare their students to teach." At research universities, graduate study typically involves years of rumination in a subject area to pass exams, followed by years of research and writing to complete a dissertation. Though the teaching assistantships available to graduate students are intended to serve as teaching apprenticeships, in reality most teaching assistants receive little dedicated pedagogical training or systematic observation and feedback on their teaching.[1]

Considering that a high percentage of new PhDs will accept jobs at public colleges and community colleges with teaching loads of three or more courses each semester, the limits of teacher training are more surprising. As they start out in teaching intensive positions, new faculty will likely experience new demands in managing the sheer number of courses and students in their classes. They will also experience challenges related to teaching in our rapidly changing times: connecting with students from more "nontraditional" backgrounds, defending education in a society increasingly skeptical about the value of liberal arts education, and using technology as a tool for learning and not distraction.[2] As teaching professors, new faculty will typically confront the realization that their advanced expertise in a field of study is not enough to help them succeed in teaching. They must quickly build the pedagogical, technological, and social knowledge needed to assume the role of effective college teachers today.

Yet another paradox for new faculty in college teaching positions lies in the contradictions they may face between the "instruction-centered" approach they often observed as graduate students, and the growing emphasis on "learner-centered" higher education. In what Robert Barr and John Tagg (1995) label the "Instruction Paradigm," instructors rely heavily on lectures in order to cover course material. In the "Learning Paradigm," by contrast, instructors guide students to learn through a variety of teaching methods in order to achieve more specific learning outcomes (Barr and Tagg, 1995).

New instructors may begin to work from the instructor-centered paradigm because it is what most often dominated in their teaching apprenticeships in graduate school, but they may also recognize limits of the approach as they enter the classroom.[3] Though new instructors may desire to shift paradigms, this transition can be difficult given the lack of models or experience with the latter approach.

One way new faculty may attempt to understand and address the challenges they face in the classroom is by seeking conversation and collaboration with colleagues. But an additional paradox of early career development often emerges within faculty cultures at teaching colleges. That is, though instructors of the same discipline share similar training and teaching assignments, and though they have much to gain from conversations about teaching, they are often remarkably isolated in their teaching practice. The combined demands on their time—service, scholarship, and teaching—along with anxieties, such as the fear of losing individual autonomy to a group agenda, may limit their ability or willingness to collaborate on teaching, or even to discuss it. The lack of discourse and community among college educators is a lost opportunity for all faculty, but it is especially lamentable for new faculty, who would benefit the most from conversation with more experienced faculty in their challenging first few years of college teaching.

In addition to turning to colleagues, new faculty may attempt to resolve the many paradoxes they encounter as college instructors through participation in faculty development workshops, organized on their campuses and beyond. New faculty seeking to grow as teachers would be fortunate to discover the faculty development program held annually at Emory's Oxford College, and known as the Institute for Pedagogy in the Liberal Arts (IPLA). This chapter outlines the ways the IPLA conference is a model faculty development program in the ways it effectively supports faculty in their efforts to address the paradoxes of early career development.

This chapter is written from the perspective of a history instructor who benefitted from attending the IPLA conference between 2012 and 2016 in the first few years of teaching at a public liberal arts college with a highly diverse student body. It describes the ways the conference workshops on inquiry (2012 and 2014), the Scholarship of Teaching and Learning (SoTL) (2014), and team-based learning (TBL) (2016) offered highly valuable ideas and methods for faculty to integrate into their own vision for effective teaching.[4] It explains how each of the sessions inspired significant shifts in the instructor's research activities, course design, and teaching methods. Finally, it analyzes the outcomes of IPLA-inspired changes in terms of improved learning outcomes among students and increased career satisfaction among faculty.

SIGNIFICANT PEDAGOGIES OF THE IPLA

The IPLA's two-day sessions each focus on a significant pedagogy. Of the many pedagogies discussed at the conference, one that is most regularly scheduled, and one that contributes to some of the most profound changes in how faculty think about teaching, is on the topic of inquiry-guided learning (IGL). Dr. Virginia Lee, a pioneer in the field of IGL, regularly leads workshops on the inquiry approach at the conference. She defines IGL as a pedagogy that "promotes the acquisition of new knowledge, abilities, and attitudes through students' increasingly independent investigation of questions, problems, and issues, for which there is no single answer" (Lee, 2012b, p. 6).

Lee began the first of a two-day session on "The Power of Inquiry as a Way of Learning in Undergraduate Education" with a short introduction to IGL pedagogy. For Lee, IGL is a method with roots in the scientific method—in which questions and discovery lie at the core of investigation and learning—as well as in constructivism—a theory of learning emphasizing the need for learners to construct their own meaning. Lee makes clear that IGL does not boil down to one simple technique; rather, it "comprises a suite of teaching practices that defies a simple prescription for practice" (2012b, p. 13).

In guiding faculty to think about inquiry, Lee encouraged not just a shift in practices, but also a shift in self-conceptualization for instructors. From the traditional view of instructor as the content expert sharing knowledge, she encouraged faculty to view the instructor as a guide to their discipline and its questions and methods. As guides, faculty support student learning by actively *doing* the discipline and not just learning its facts. The common ingredient of all the different manifestations of IGL lies in the "collective effort to define inquiry as a site of student learning rather than faculty scholarship" (Lee, 2012b, p. 13).

As the pedagogy placed value on active learning, so Lee used a variety of activities to help faculty process IGL and its significance to their teaching. Lee first encouraged active learning through multiple metacognitive writing exercises that encouraged faculty to reflect on how inquiry informed their scholarship and teaching. The exercises helped reveal not only assumptions but also shifts in thinking that emerged over the course of the workshop. In another exercise, she asked faculty teams to choose and interpret an image fragment. The activity increased faculty awareness about both the excitement and discomfort involved in open-ended exploration of any topic. In a third activity, faculty worked as teams to review a number of syllabi from different disciplines and to analyze their various levels of inquiry integration.

An article written by Lee guided faculty discussions in the second day of the conference. It defined faculty commitment to inquiry on a spectrum from "experimenting" to "developing" to "committed" to inquiry as the "dominant mode of learning and the primary stimulus for knowledge acquisition" and noted ways these different levels of commitment play out in course design and activities (Lee, 2012b, p. 11). The activity helped faculty to visualize the variety of ways inquiry is implemented as well as to reflect on their own commitment to integrating IGL. Lee also provided participants with pedagogy readings, rubrics, course planning worksheets, and references to support instructors who so wished to continue to pursue its integration into their courses after the workshop.

Beyond her call to shift the focus to student-centered and active learning, Lee encouraged faculty to consider deep questions of meaning through the inquiry methodology. In a keynote talk over lunch, "Bridging the Self and the Academic Disciplines through Inquiry," Lee communicated the potential of the inquiry approach for promoting not only cognitive learning outcomes, but affective learning outcomes among students.

She acknowledged that in higher education today, the climate is not always conducive to faculty asking questions of purpose and meaning such as "Who am I?" "What and whom do I care about?" and "How shall I live? (Daloz Parks, 2000).[5] Yet Lee insisted that these questions are essential to faculty and student lives alike, and so it is the responsibility of faculty to ask the "meaning-based" questions that will help students grow in holistic ways in their college years.

Another profoundly valuable pedagogy, also driven by questions and also a common IPLA workshop theme, is SoTL. Dr. Nancy Chick of Vanderbilt introduced this holistic approach to scholarship and teaching in the session "It Begins with a Question: Student Learning and the Scholarship of Teaching & Learning (SoTL)." Chick appropriately began the session with questions, by asking participants to identify examples of "narratives of constraint" and "narratives of growth."

For constraint narratives, participants cited common faculty complaints about student underpreparedness and disengagement, classroom overcrowding, and budget pressures. For growth narratives, participants brainstormed on the motivations that drive instructors to be their best, despite problems, such as when connecting with their highest ideals of education such as its potential to inspire and empower. The conversation helped faculty to grow in their awareness of their experience of both narratives, as well as to see growth narratives as the healthy and more constructive alternative to complaining about problems.

Chick then positioned SoTL as an avenue to scholarly teaching rooted in "narratives of growth." From a growth narrative approach, the problems, which inevitably arise in teaching are reframed as questions for faculty to research. Citing Randy Bass (1999), Chick encouraged faculty to connect with their scholarly curiosity about teaching problems, their origins, and their solutions. She then explicitly linked SoTL to IGL, noting that both place a central emphasis on the scholarly pursuit of answers to open-ended questions about problems. In an informative introduction, Chick discussed the full history of SoTL and its origins in the "paradigm shift" from "instruction" to "learning" as described by Barr and Tagg (1995).

As the session progressed, Chick introduced four different categories of SoTL, defined by Patricia Hutchings (2000) as: "What works? What is? What's possible? and Theory-building." She provided participants with models of SoTL scholarship in the four areas and asked faculty to identify the question and category for each form of scholarship. From these models of SoTL, she led faculty into conversations about the application of the literature to their own teaching problems, questions, and developing SoTL projects.

As with the IGL session, SoTL session encouraged faculty to shift their thinking about what it means to be a teacher. Chick first challenged faculty to expand their view of teaching to include scholarship and to identify as "scholarly teachers." Rather than simply guiding students toward the inquiry methodology, SoTL approach invites faculty to actively conduct inquiry-based research within their classrooms.

Beyond their roles as scholars of learning in their own classes, Chick cited the work of Brookfield (1995) as she called on faculty to think of their teaching in a more "critically reflective" and social way. For Chick, this included reflection on the experience of scholarly teaching but also on the views expressed by students, by colleagues in their field, and by the relevant scholarly literature. In rethinking their roles as scholars of learning in their discipline, in dialogue with a community, Chick encouraged faculty to think of SoTL as a path to deeper meaning and personal fulfillment.

While the inquiry and SoTL approaches helped faculty participants to envision a general structure for exploring questions in a course, other IPLA sessions focused more specifically on ways to integrate aspects of the inquiry methodology in class meetings. The IPLA session, "Team-Based Learning: Students Taking Charge of Their Own Learning" led by Oxford College professor, Dr. Henry Bayerle, introduced a highly systematic way to integrate inquiry in class by placing questions at the center of team-based discussions. To implement TBL, its advocates encourage a "flipped classroom" approach that pays attention to Bloom's Revised Taxonomy of Learning Objectives and "backward design," as discussed in Michael Sweet and Larry Michaelson (2012, pp. 11–18).

The prescribed method for TBL begins with a five-part "readiness assurance process" as follows: (1) students read and perhaps watch videos before class to gain understanding of foundational concepts; (2) students take an "individual readiness assurance test" of about 15–20 questions before class begins; (3) students then work as teams and retake the same test that they took individually, using a scratch off scoring card; (4) students may make appeals about any question they perceive to be unclear or unfair; and (5) instructors may conclude the session with a mini-lecture on concepts that students struggled with more in the team test (Sibley and Spiridonoff, 2014, p. 2).

Once student readiness is established, the majority of class time in TBL is dedicated to guiding students through more challenging "application activities," designed around "significant problems" (Sibley and Spiridonoff, 2014, p. 3). In the application stage, TBL provides a framework for implementing inquiry by using questions to drive analysis and dialogue both within teams (collaboration) and across teams (competition).

TBL advises a "4s framework" for designing TBL activities as follows: (1) students work on a *significant* problem as a team, ideally one students find interesting and relevant; (2) all teams work on the *same* problems, so that teams will be set up to dialogue with each other on the same content; (3) teams must make a *specific* choice, ideally selecting one from a list of options, to facilitate dialogue and debate within groups; and (4) all teams report their answers *simultaneously* to encourage dialogue across teams about how they reached a given conclusion (Sibley and Spiridonoff, 2014, p. 3).

As with previous sessions, Bayerle regularly asked faculty to apply their learning actively, analyzing questions as teams to determine what makes a good question for TBL, and testing out TBL-based lesson plans in the second session. The activities helped faculty participants to experience the inherent excitement engendered by the TBL approach and to move from the theory of the approach to the pragmatic reality of integrating TBL.

RESEARCH POST-IPLA

A testament to the power of the IPLA is the way it inspires faculty to continue to research signature pedagogies in the aftermath of the conference. So, in considering how to implement an inquiry-based framework in the world history survey at Georgia Gwinnett College (GGC), a history professor's research after the IPLA sessions focused on how historians construct knowledge. The scholarship on history and inquiry integration conveyed in a more concrete way how the inquiry model can move a history course away from a course framework based on covering "the facts" toward a richer pedagogical approach aimed at guiding students toward "thinking historically" and actually "doing history."[6]

One example of an influential scholarly work on history pedagogy, by Sam Wineburg (2001), elaborates on the role of "historical thinking" in an inquiry approach to history. For Wineburg, the dominant history curriculum at the K-12 level focuses on "the facts," while it lacks awareness about its own biases and its failure to teach students to actually think in the methods of historians. For Wineburg, history teachers should help learners to move toward more thoughtful engagement with both the differences and similarities of the past and present, by asking learners to mentally grapple with the past in all its foreignness and familiarity, messiness, and diversity.

Teaching "historical thinking" is accomplished only by asking rich inquiry questions and by guiding students to interpret answers for themselves, using primary sources from the past. Working with the Stanford History Education Group, Wineburg created a world history curriculum for K-12, driven by questions and curated primary sources. Though aimed at a K-12 teaching audience, Wineburg's approach provides a model for education led by questions and primary sources with application to the college level.

The work by Joseph Gonzalez on IGL, or what he refers to as "Inquiry-Based Learning" (2013), provided another useful example of inquiry integration more specific to "doing history" in higher education.[7] The author begins by conveying how his frustration with low student engagement and his refusal to blame students led him to seek help with his teaching at conferences. He ultimately experimented with the inquiry-based approach because he hoped "if [he] turned [his] classroom into a place where students answered questions, rather than memorized answers ... they would become more engaged in the learning process and learn more deeply" (Gonzalez, 2013, pp. 33–34).

Gonzalez explains how his inquiry-based course design includes three forms of instruction: (1) cognitive apprenticeship, (2) group work answering questions, and (3) inquiry projects drawing from project-based and active learning techniques. He also explains how he divides the course into two parts with distinctive teaching approaches.

In the first half of the semester, he plays a stronger role in structuring the course: introducing and guiding discussion, clarifying and reinforcing connections made by students, and bringing closure to lessons. In the second half of the semester, he takes a more open approach: helping students work on projects, encouraging them to journal their reflections, and coaching students through "the difficult process of integration" (Gonzalez, 2013, p. 37).

He celebrates how the inquiry approach more effectively "move(s) students toward increased independence, competence, and cognitive sophistication" (p. 46). His discussion of teaching methods and organization in two parts proved to be highly influential on the ongoing redesign of the world history survey at Georgia Gwinnett College.

INTEGRATING NEW PEDAGOGIES IN A WORLD HISTORY SURVEY COURSE

Beyond the challenges of a general education course, the scope of the modern world history survey course is daunting, covering 500 years of human history around the globe. The more "traditional" approach to the course prioritized coverage of as much content as possible, relied on a textbook to convey the broad narrative, and reinforced select themes from the textbook in lecture-heavy class meetings.

Although the class included some time for brief discussions, the effort to "cover" history left little time in class for deep discussions about any given topic or for much work on skills. Assessments, including exams and writing assignments, showed disappointingly low levels of comprehension. Most students approached the course as a superficial practice in memorization, and beyond the grade they earned, the course lacked relevance to their lives. Student evaluations often expressed dissatisfaction with the fast paced nature of the course, the amount of content and reading, and the lack of variety in class activities.

The IPLA sessions on IGL, in tandem with pedagogy readings on inquiry-integration in history, inspired a significant shift in course design toward inquiry-oriented approaches. The first change to the course design involved reflection on and refinement of course learning outcomes on the syllabus. In refining learning outcomes, the course continued to place value on historical literacy as one primary goal. But more than in pre-IPLA iterations of the course, the additional course outcomes made explicit statements about "historical thinking" and the skills related to "doing history."[8]

Gradually, the course also narrowed its overall focus in a way that brought many benefits. In the place of a popular fifteen-chapter textbook, covering a wide variety of themes, it adopted a more concise textbook consisting of five chapters.[9] To supplement the textbook, and to enable deeper discussion of a few events and questions, the instructor next moved to assign additional readings based on a single theme that would be of interest to students. After some trial and error with different themes, the theme of "rights struggles and revolutions" resonated the most with students and instructor alike and ultimately became the central focus in the course. Additional readings in primary and secondary sources were then assigned based on selected "case studies" in rights and revolutions, such as the specific revolutions that unfolded in France, Haiti, Japan, Russia, Iran, and South Africa. More recently, the course is taking a regional approach in the form of even fewer "spotlight units" in an effort to bring more depth of understanding about transforming conceptions of rights.

One advantage of the thematic approach was that it moved students to higher levels of learning, according to the well-known taxonomy established by Benjamin Bloom.[10] That is, rather than simply remember or understand facts about the revolutions, the course more consistently began to encourage students to apply, to analyze, and to evaluate factual information. The role of inquiry was fundamental in the new approach as questions gradually began to frame the course.[11]

Another benefit of the thematic approach was that by streamlining course content, more time opened up in class to discuss the questions above and to help students practice and build both the critical reading and interpretation skills they need to answer questions. As students engaged with questions and higher-order thinking skills in class, they were encouraged to see history as more of a discipline than a list of names and dates, and to see themselves as practitioners of the discipline.

Perhaps the most significant impact of consciously covering less with a thematic approach is that new space emerged in the course to pursue the highest level of "Bloom's taxonomy": "to create" projects through inquiry-driven research. After midterm, the course significantly shifts direction from exploring macro questions about world history as a group, to exploring a fundamental question about human agency in world history as individuals: "how did individuals contribute to rights struggles and revolutions?" Assignments guide students from easier to more challenging tasks related to the craft of history including choosing a manageable topic; asking historical research questions; locating sources and making discerning choices about credibility, context, and relevance; annotating sources; and ultimately, reporting on their findings in both an essay and a presentation.

Class meetings post midterm aim to support student efforts to successfully complete a project in which they do the work of historians. Early in the process, classes go the library to meet with librarians and to clarify expectations for the project. Later in the process, classes are designed around skill building, peer review, and instructor feedback on drafts of work. In moving from the content phase of the course to the project phase, student interest in the course improves as they begin to embrace the role of a historian and take greater ownership in their work. In both the essay and presentations, students now produce their best work of the semester.

In the first couple of semesters of teaching the revised course, change unfolded slowly. In initial iterations, for example, the learning outcomes on the syllabus did not always correspond to actual class activities, assessments, or learning outcomes. Even as the course integrated more questions and aspired to build history, discipline-based skills and old instruction-centered habits continued in class meetings based primarily on lecture. Even efforts to include "inquiry" sometimes revealed a tendency by the instructor to default back to the instruction paradigm and to ask closed-ended questions with "correct" answers, or to ask and then attempt to answer questions for students. Instructor discomfort with change and the lack of concrete models for inquiry integration in history both contributed to the slow pace of change. The end of each semester afforded some reflection on needed adjustments, but a significant influence on ongoing course transformation was continued attendance at IPLA.

FINDING SUPPORT AT THE INSTITUTE FOR PEDAGOGY IN THE LIBERAL ARTS 2014

IPLA 2014, and the IGL session in particular, helped to reinforce successful changes and to guide refinement of course design at a crucial time in course development. The IPLA session, "Course Design for Inquiry-Guided Learning," led by Dr. Beverly Taylor and Dr. Marjorie Nadler of Miami University, offered a highly structured workshop that helped participants reflect on and advance the role of inquiry in their courses.[12] First, Taylor and Nadler reinforced the importance of working from the "backward design" model, in which faculty start their course design by first clarifying the "enduring understanding," "big ideas," and "essential questions" they hope will result from their courses (Wiggins and McTighe, 2006).

With the overarching learning outcomes established, they next recommended that instructors determine what evidence would be necessary to show they achieved their desired outcomes. Lastly, they advised that instructors should plan their learning experiences and instruction methods. The session that followed guided participants through reflection on their own path of inquiry integration and provided concrete examples of inquiry courses with well-aligned assignments, objectives, and outcomes from various fields, including history.[13]

The inquiry session in 2014 influenced the ongoing world history redesign in a number of ways. First, it helped the instructor to appreciate the successes of the course in integrating inquiry in the previous two years, both in its focus on a core theme and big questions, as well as in its incorporation of an inquiry-based research project. Taking stock of the progress of the course improved instructor morale and inspired further efforts to fine-tune the course to be more effective.

The workshop also helped to inspire ongoing revisions of the course. In thinking through the goal of producing evidence of learning, for example, it became clear that students were not yet demonstrating strong historical thinking skills, especially in their research essays and presentations. Taylor and Nadler imparted specific strategies for how to improve learning outcomes. One strategy the course embraced more fully was to include scaffolding of all history skills by first modeling the skill, then allowing time for students to practice the skill as teams and individually in formative assessments before the summative assessment, as in the essay.

Another strategy to improve student work was to add more detail to the rubrics to guide student preparation on research-based assessments. Taylor and Nadler provided sample rubrics on reading, analysis, critical thinking, and writing, created by the Association of American Colleges and Universities, that proved invaluable for honing the grading criteria.[14] Refined rubrics more clearly conveyed expectations to students, and this in turn resulted in notable improvements in the quality of student work in subsequent semesters.

The IPLA 2014 session also helped to raise instructor awareness about the need for a greater openness in course design in order to more effectively place students and questions at the center of the course. It was after IPLA that the organization of class meetings gradually became driven by the more open-ended and interesting questions, more consistent with effective inquiry.[15]

As the questions became more engaging, students participated more actively in discussion. As students grew more involved, the instructor grew more dynamic in creating lesson plans to allow more time for discussion, especially about issues in which students conveyed greater interest. Before IPLA 2014, losing content time to discussion was sometimes a cause of concern. But a greater awareness of the value of discussions as inquiry exercises helped guide gradual and mostly organic cuts to lecture content and helped facilitate an increase in the rewarding moments of heightened student engagement.

ACTIVE LEARNING AND INQUIRY INTEGRATION

Though student discussions have always been a mainstay in the course, the integration of inquiry in class activities beyond discussion is increasingly a pedagogical priority for course design. Participation in campus workshops on active learning, a new assignment to teach the world history course as a hybrid course, and IPLA 2016 all helped inspire the instructor's drive to expand and diversify active learning methods.[16]

Some activities in the course now integrate technology tools. One activity, for example, encourages understanding of the revolution in Meiji Japan and the skill of researching online. Students are asked to consider the question of whether or not post–Meiji era modernization was more beneficial or problematic for everyday Japanese people. To answer the question, they are asked to work as teams to consult an online database of primary source images and to select and curate a presentation on one image, sharing it in Google Slides. This activity helps prepare students to find and analyze primary sources when they conduct their research later in the semester.

In-class debates and role-play are also now common activities in the course. In one assignment, combining debate and role-play, students are asked to become Russians on the ground before the popular revolution against the Tsar in 1905. They must respond to the question, in which political direction should Russia go? In answering the question, they embrace a political ideology of the time: monarchism, liberalism, socialism, or communism. Teams then work together to define their ideology and to explain its appeal to specific segments of the Russian population. Then one spokesperson in the group must try to sell the ideology to classmates, attempting to appeal to Russians of different social strata.

Students can be hesitant with role-play at first, but with some encouragement most will get into character. More heated debate sometimes ensues across the different groups in this exercise, as students are more willing to disagree with each other's ideas as characters than as classmates. Role-play activities in history help students to achieve important historical thinking outcomes, including considering multiple perspectives on events and practicing historical empathy.[17] Future iterations of the course will expand use of the method in the form of role-play games.[18]

In recent semesters, the course is also beginning to integrate more of the techniques of TBL. An initial team-based quizzing experiment, before attending the IPLA session, was informed by the work of Burkholder (2014). It involved asking students to take a quiz on the campus Learning Management System before coming to class, then asking them to retake the same quiz in class as a team. From the initial experiment, the pedagogy seemed promising, with high levels of student engagement. But there was lingering uncertainty about how to better integrate the team quizzes into the course and how to refine the questions for optimum results.

The recent IPLA TBL session (2016) addressed earlier concerns and influenced a second attempt at integration of TBL methods, which proved to be more successful. The more recent iteration of the approach more carefully incorporated the TBL "readiness assurance process," asking students to read a chapter and to complete a short written response to the question, "which Atlantic world revolution or rights struggle was the most revolutionary and why?"[19]

Students then worked as teams to rank the revolutions of the United States, France, Haiti, South America, as well as the rights struggles of abolitionism and feminism, from 1 (most revolutionary) to 6 (least revolutionary). After all teams achieved consensus, they revealed their answers. Debate then ensued between groups as they defended their positions with historical evidence and logic. The activity generated both enthusiasm and depth of analysis that is uncommon in typical discussions and greater integration of the technique in future semesters is likely.[20]

IMPACTS OF THE INSTITUTE FOR PEDAGOGY IN THE LIBERAL ARTS–INSPIRED AND SUPPORTED CHANGE

Transformations to the world history course, both inspired and supported by the IPLA, brought tangible improvements to the course over a number of years. One indicator of improvement in the course is evident in the lower numbers of students who drop out or fail the course. These regularly improving pass and retention numbers suggest a correlation to course redesign and the increasingly student-centered approach.[21]

Another change observed by the instructor, though difficult to measure, was higher levels of student engagement in the course. From the instructor's perspective, students responded to questions more attentively and demonstrated greater command in higher-order thinking skills in class and in their research. They also seemed to enjoy history more as a discipline and not just a list of names and dates, as they did in the course before its revisions.

Course evaluations from students in the world history survey likewise reflect improved ratings of the course and instructor and a growing number of positive comments. Students now regularly describe the course as "very interesting and inspiring" (Faculty Evaluations, 2015–2016). In the words of one student, "even though the majority of the class consists of non-majors," it was "worthwhile and exciting for everyone who is a part of it" (Faculty Evaluations, 2014–2015).

Students also often remark on their awareness that they are learning more because of the skill-building activities and research project in the course. In the words of another student, the course "taught us the best ways to complete research projects/papers and how to use critical thinking/application skills" (Faculty Evaluations, 2014–2015). Students also comment that course methods help them in learning the material more deeply: "not memorizing but actually learning it" (Faculty Evaluations, 2014–2015). Lastly, students now regularly report a sense that the course is useful to them personally: "I was able to take what I learned in history to apply it to other classes and life" (Faculty Evaluations, 2015–2016).

The inquiry-based course redesign also improved the instructor experience in the course. As course design expanded the time allotted to explore and discuss less content in more depth, each class meeting began to feel less rushed and the possibility of more fulfilling interactions with students increased. Noting improvements in student success in the course, in their engagement, in their higher pass and retention rates, and in their historical thinking and research skills also increased instructor satisfaction with the practice of teaching history as a scholarly discipline, and not just a set of facts to be memorized. The inquiry-based and SoTL approaches to teaching influence a holistic connection of identities as both teacher and scholar and contribute to supporting sustainable career satisfaction.

Currently, the research question that drives evolutions in course design and SoTL research is that of how to engage student interest beyond the classroom to achieve not only cognitive but also affective learning outcomes.[22] Most recently, literature readings and classroom-based experimentation focuses on active learning through role-play and through highly interactive role-play games. One especially promising form of role-play is emerging in games designed by faculty in the liberal arts and sciences, collectively known as "Reacting to the Past" (RTTP) games. In RTTP games, students spend about a month assuming historical roles based on texts and acting out those roles within a game, with benefits evident for both student engagement and learning. Future research will test the claim of Mark Carnes and the growing RTTP community that role-immersion games are powerful tools to promote more engaging classroom experience for students and faculty alike (2014).

SIGNIFICANCE OF THE INSTITUTE FOR PEDAGOGY IN THE LIBERAL ARTS FOR FACULTY DEVELOPMENT

At the most obvious level, the impact of the IPLA sessions is to better inform faculty about deeply impactful pedagogical approaches. Among the many pedagogies introduced at the conference, IBL, SoTL, and TBL are examples of approaches with profound significance for faculty development. The conference is also effective at helping faculty to integrate new pedagogies in their classrooms because of its highly professional and engaging presenters and because of their regular use of active learning strategies and peer review to support faculty-driven changes.

But more than just promoting innovative pedagogy, the conference drives faculty connections to a community in a way that is essential to faculty development, even though it is often neglected in the higher education context. The conference attracts a diverse faculty of international, national, and local origins, from a variety of campus environments, and from a variety of disciplines tied to the liberal arts and sciences. It is highly valuable for a diverse group of instructors to be around others who are passionate about the common work they do as teachers.

The conference creates a friendly environment for faculty interaction at its sessions, breaks, and meals that contribute to easy flowing and collegial conversation. The conference is successful at creating a community, if only for a few days. Sometimes connections made at the conference continue in the wake of the conference, in informal conversations and the more formal dialogue enabled by SoTL. In revitalizing and connecting participants, the IPLA conference leaves an impact on faculty that draws many back to the conference year after year.

Perhaps the most significant aspect of the IPLA is the way the conference helps participants to take the time to reflect on and reinvigorate their own commitment to personal growth as teacher-instructors. The fact that the conference is held less than a week after the end of the spring semester for most faculty, when responsibilities are generally lower, creates a well-timed opportunity for thoughtful reflection.

For those who attend the IPLA year after year, the conference enables faculty to check in on ongoing issues and to build from sessions they attended the previous years, accruing more benefits over time. The intensity of the events may, at times, be fatiguing for participants, but in the aftermath of the conference, they often note more energy and drive to transform their teaching. As described in this chapter, the IPLA conference continues to inspire and guide faculty development well after the conference ends.

In summation, the IPLA conference is highly beneficial for all who attend, but especially for college instructors who are new to teaching and who may benefit the most from pedagogical developmental support. The conference offers a wellspring of ideas to help instructors answer their questions about teaching and to inspire new approaches to their courses. It also guides faculty through ways of implementing desired changes in course design, practice, and teaching-related scholarship. Its workshops integrate practices of active learning and help faculty to experience and test out and receive feedback on their plans and their use of new pedagogies and methods.

Most significant for early career faculty development is the way the IPLA conference provides a comfortable, safe, and supportive setting for addressing teaching problems within a community framework, and at the same time, it creates the time for in-depth exploration and reflection instructors need for their personal growth. The conference, thus, leaves instructors rejuvenated as pedagogues and members of a larger community of teachers-scholars invested in SoTL. In these ways, the IPLA supports instructors to improve not only student engagement and learning outcomes but also their own career satisfaction.

NOTES

1. Bok (2013) notes that "some improvement has occurred in recent years with the spread of centers to help graduate students learn to be teaching assistants" but it is still "far from adequate to prepare aspiring professors for the challenges they are likely to face once they embark upon an academic career."

2. The term "nontraditional" here refers to the greater diversity of social backgrounds, ages, and non–school related responsibilities of students today, as compared to the past. Societal expectations about college have always varied but a stronger consumer mentality permeates, as compared to the past. On the changing landscape of higher education as it relates to technology, see McCluskey and Wright (2013).

3. Limits may include their own frustration with the rush to cover all the content, their students' apathy in relation to the content emphasis and the broad scope, and the low performance of students in assessments that measure critical understanding and skills.

4. "Effective teaching" for the author includes student-centered practice using active learning strategies and a scholarly approach to teaching.

5. To explain why it is both controversial and difficult to discuss questions about meaning in higher education, Lee cited the "research agenda, its attending epistemology and ethics of objectivism (Palmer & Zojonc, 2010; Kronman, 2007)" as well as the career emphasis in higher education today (Lee, 2012a).

6. The literature in K-12 history education and inquiry appears to be more robust than in that of higher education, though hopefully this is changing as IGL spreads through conferences and SoTL.

7. This article was assigned reading at IPLA 2014 session entitled "Course Design for Inquiry-Guided Learning."

8. The more specific learning outcomes are now stated on the syllabus as follows:

Students should be able to demonstrate:

a) *Accurate factual knowledge about modern world history, including the ability to answer questions about select historical geography, concepts, and terms.*

b) *Historical thinking skills, including the ability to: critically read primary and secondary sources, analyze cause and effect, compare/contrast diverse historical perspectives and/or historical interpretations.*

c) *Historical research skills including the ability to: choose a research topic and craft a historical question, create a relevant bibliography on the topic, annotate tertiary, secondary, and primary sources on the topic, and report on tentative findings as well as future research directions.*

d) *Historical communication skills, including the ability to: communicate historical interpretations in oral form and in short writing assignments in class, as well as to write a formal interpretive essay in clear, evidence-based, and professional writing, using formal citation.*

9. The concise narrative in the textbook by Robert B. Marks (2015) highlights two general themes: (1) the rise of western power in which it challenges a "west is best" narrative, and (2) the environmental impact of modernization.

10. See one explanation of the revised taxonomy at the Vanderbilt Center for Teaching website: https://cft.vanderbilt.edu/guides-sub-pages/blooms-taxonomy.

11. Since IPLA 2014, questions include: How do we define a political revolution? How do we measure the impacts of revolution? How do we compare/contrast the impacts across different case studies? What role did ideas play in revolutions? Do you think the gains of revolutions and rights struggles worth their costs?

12. Taylor and Nadler used thoughtfully designed worksheets to systematically guide faculty through careful reflection on their own courses. In addition to the detailed workshop, they invited faculty to share materials from their classes for peer review of clarity and alignment.

13. Taylor and Nadler assigned the Gonzalez article on IGL in history and discussed specific examples of history instructors implementing inquiry.

14. The Association of American Colleges and Universities VALUE rubrics attempt "to determine whether and how well students are meeting graduation level achievement in learning outcomes that both employers and faculty consider essential" (http://www.aacu.org/value).

15. After IPLA 2014, the courses began to include the more open-ended questions referenced in note 10.

16. The "hybrid course" embraces the "flipped classroom" model in which screencasted lecture, along with multimedia resources are viewed before class to prepare students for applying their learning in class.

17. On the value of "historical empathy" and other core learning outcomes of the history discipline, see the American Historical Association, Tuning Project website: https://www.historians.org/teaching-and-learning/tuning/history-discipline-core.

18. Carnes (2014) provides an excellent overview of "Reacting to the Past" (RTTP) games and their potential for student and faculty engagement.

19. TBL encourages a multiple-choice quiz but the writing assignment of a paragraph in length worked well.

20. TBL advises that a significant part of a student's grade should be a team-based grade with some peer review component to insure student willingness to participate. Future iterations of the course will include a teamwork grade, which was not included in the summer.

21. The instructor estimates failure rates above 20 percent in each section before attending the IPLA, while current failure rates in the course are closer to 5 percent.

22. See Bloom for explanation of learning domains: cognitive, affective, and psychomotor.

REFERENCES

Association of American Colleges and Universities. (2014). VALUE (Valid Assessment of Learning in Undergraduate Education). Retrieved July 14, 2016, from http://www.aacu.org/value.

Barr, R. and Tagg, J. From teaching to learning: A new paradigm for undergraduate education. *Change, 27(6)*, 12–25.

Bass, R. (1999). The scholarship of teaching: What's the problem? *Inventio, 1(1)*.

Bok, D. (2013, November 11). We must prepare Ph.D. students for the complicated art of teaching. *The Chronicle of Higher Education.* Retrieved on May 2015 from http://chronicle.com/article/We-Must-Prepare-PhD-Students/142893/.

Brookfield, S. (1995). *Becoming a critically reflective teacher,* 1st ed. San Francisco: Jossey-Bass.

Burkholder, P. (2014). A content means to a critical thinking end: Group quizzing in history surveys. *The History Teacher, 47(4),* 551–578.

Carnes, M. (2014). *Minds on fire: How role-immersion games transform college.* Cambridge, Massachusetts: Harvard University Press.

Gonzalez, J. (2013). My journey with Inquiry-Based Learning. *Journal on Excellence in College Teaching, 24(2),* 33–50.

Hutchings, P. (2000). Introduction. *Opening lines: Approaches to the Scholarship of Teaching and Learning.* San Francisco: Jossey-Bass.

Lee, V. S. (2004). *Teaching and learning through inquiry: A guidebook for institutions and instructors.* Sterling, VA: Stylus Publishing.

Lee, V. S. (2012a). Bridging the self and the academic disciplines through inquiry. Keynote remarks at the IPLA Conference, May 15, 2012.

Lee, V. S. (2012b). What is inquiry-guided learning? *Inquiry-guided learning: New directions for teaching and learning, Number 129,* 1st ed. San Francisco, CA: Jossey-Bass.

Marks, R. B. (2015). *The origins of the modern world: A global and environmental narrative from the fifteenth to the twenty-first century.* Lanham, MD: Rowman & Littlefield.

McCluskey, F. and Winter, M. (2013). *The idea of the digital university: Ancient traditions, disruptive technologies and the battle for the soul of higher education.* Seattle, WA: CreateSpace Independent Publishing Platform.

Parks, D. (2000). *Big questions, worthy dreams: Mentoring young adults in their search for meaning, purpose, and faith.* Hoboken, NJ: Wiley.

Sibley, J. and Spiridonoff, S. (2014). Introduction to team-based learning. Retrieved June 26 from https://c.ymcdn.com/sites/teambasedlearning.site-ym.com/resource/resmgr/Docs/TBL-handout_February_2014_le.pdf.

Sweet, M., and Michaelsen, L. K. (Eds.). (2012). *Team-Based Learning in the social sciences and humanities: Group work that works to generate critical thinking and engagement.* Sterling, VA: Stylus Publishing.

Wiggins, G., and McTighe, J. (1998). *Understanding by design.* Alexandria, VA: Association for Supervision & Curriculum Development.

Wineburg, S. (2001). *Historical thinking and other unnatural acts: Charting the future of teaching the past.* Philadelphia: Temple University Press.

Part II

PEDAGOGIES OF COMMUNITY

Foreword

Catherine Chiappetta Swanson

As an instructor and educational consultant, my education is grounded in the inquiry-based approach to learning. Through the years, I have come to realize the importance of reflecting on my own practice. At my institution, McMaster University in Ontario, Canada, we are fortunate to have a number of pioneers of the inquiry-based learning (IBL) model who both teach and mentor others. I have had the privilege of being mentored by these expert teachers who are sought out by educational institutions globally to share their expertise, strategies, and methods they have honed individually and as a team over many years. This mentorship has been invaluable to me in teaching my inquiry based courses and supporting other instructors in their own development and teaching practice. Now, as I have the opportunity to guide others, I appreciate that learning is a two-way street between the learner and the educator.

As educators, we recognize that faculty need pioneering, supportive contexts within which to conceive, develop, revise, and publish innovative teaching models using the same foundational principles of learning for student success; active learning and experiential learning, two such models, are the focus of the chapters in this section. In addition, applying the inquiry-based approach to learning while engaging in community and service-learning provides opportunities for students and teachers to experience a deeper learning through guidance and reflection.

The following three chapters look both outward and inward, charting how IBL and innovative strategies developed at IPLA are applied in classrooms and local communities. Each of the narratives spotlights the authors' work from conception, through implementation, to revision as they apply and reflect on novel approaches to facilitate meaningful community and service-learning experiences for their students, grounded in inquiry-guided learning (IGL).

In their analysis, Rebecca L. Harrison, Angela Insenga, and Heather Giebeig highlight the effects of using IBL in secondary classrooms to build meaningful pedagogical bridges between collegiate and K-12 faculty through a community project. Patricia Owen-Smith describes how through service-learning initiatives learners can become more contemplative, mindful, and aware of the world around them and their responsibility to it. The third chapter challenges common assumptions about community-based learning through the use of IGL. In this chapter, Emily R. Yowonske and C. Aiden Downey discuss how reflective practice can help students to understand what meaningful service can be and, importantly, that it is a two-way street, benefiting all involved. Together the chapters illustrate how grounding outreach and collaboration in the IBL approach can increase the learning potential for both learners and teachers.

Chapter Five

Inquiry-Based Learning
Partnering to Increase Student Engagement
Rebecca L. Harrison, Angela
Suzanne Insenga, and Heather Giebeig

> The time has come for rethinking education, making it evidence based from the ground up, beginning with the child and the conditions under which children thrive. ... [and] actually learn.
>
> —Angeline Stoll Lillard

> Students learn best when they are actively engaged in using their critical faculties to take ownership of their intellectual journeys and in seeing the practical benefits of their endeavors. ... Inquiry-guided learning can confer, then, not simply a dynamic way to acquire and harness knowledge, but habits of intellectual discipline that transform the individual from pupil to a life-long independent thinker and learner.
>
> —Ana Kennedy and Susan Navey-Davis

In the wake of recent calls to reform public educational practices in Georgia and increased performance standards prescribed to teachers with little support for implementation, our research team began to consider how and to what end we could bring our experience with inquiry-based learning (IBL),[1] garnered from attending multiple Institute for Pedagogy in the Liberal Arts (IPLA) conferences and practiced in our own collegiate classrooms, to public school educators and students in our local community. Much of IBL's scholarly literature critiques models of traditional schooling, focusing the call to (re)awaken student curiosity and love of learning long stifled in American K-12 environments almost exclusively on university educators. Even Virginia Lee's germinal text *Teaching and Learning through Inquiry* voices the sentiment: "The challenge ... becomes taking undergraduate students, many of whom have become accustomed to the numbing passivity bred by years of traditional schooling, and trying to reignite in them a spirit of curiosity, will, and purpose that manifests itself in independent questioning and inquiry" (2004, p. 5).

Such Balkanizing of IBL initiatives is ineffectual. It does little to build meaningful bridges for student success across grade levels that can nurture our children's cognitive and moral needs and, in turn, feed our university classrooms. If the hallmark of a successful college student is active questioning and independent engagement, should not educator efforts with IBL center more squarely the transformational potential of such pedagogies and curriculums in public school settings? And, should not discipline experts and IBL practitioners play a meaningful role in such efforts?

Our trio quickly found that many of IBL's advocates naively see it as a movement almost wholly appropriate for collegiate learning.[2] A false skepticism exists concerning the capabilities of younger students with self-directed, robust inquiry, despite established and growing research to the contrary. While these camps generally support using IBL heuristics in public schools, such support is typically confined to isolated activities and exercises rather than more sweeping overhauls of curricula and "best classroom practice" discussions.

In the wake of these realizations, we targeted IPLA 2014—a year focused predominantly on inquiry—as an ideal opportunity to found a partnership with a local gifted elementary teacher and full-format IBL practitioner, Heather Giebeig, to study the potential for infusing IBL practices in our local secondary community. This effort sought to innovate dissemination practices and improve student engagement and learning in Carroll County, GA, via the introduction of IBL methodology across a sampling of grade levels that spanned the gamut of traditional, public education: elementary, middle, and high school environments. This chapter details the implementation and subsequent outcomes of our team's project; reveals the untapped potential of IBL in traditional public school settings; and makes a case for the vital role that collegiate IBL faculty can play in collaborations aimed at bridging the gap between our intrinsically linked educational spaces.

INQUIRY-BASED LEARNING AND THE COMMON CORE

As hybrid faculty in a discipline department who share the responsibility for observing and administering field work for student teachers, two-thirds of the investigators in this study saw IBL's applicability to the secondary school system early on in our tenure at the IPLA. The methods learned from visiting scholars over the last five years and now utilized in our literature and pedagogy-centered classrooms became strategies that we encouraged student teachers to infuse into their own planning and teaching. Our own experience evinced that IBL is not the sole province of higher education. Instead, IBL can work against the "numbing passivity" (Lee, 2004, p. 5) existent in traditional school models and in tandem with state standards to create educationally charged spaces in which student-led interaction with material is an ultimate goal.

The Common Core standards, adopted by Georgia and forty-five other states in 2012, charge all secondary instructors with ensuring that "students graduate from high school prepared with the skills that that they will need in college, careers[,] and life" ("Common Core Georgia Performance Standards," 2008, para. 3).[3] Each Performance Standard offers detailed expectations "for assessment, instruction, and student work," and "they isolate and identify the skills needed to use the knowledge and skills to problem-solve, reason, communicate, and make connections with other information" ("Curriculum and Instruction," 2015, para. 1). English Language Arts (ELA) Common Core standards under these directives include systematic reference to active verbs—analyze, determine, identify, and explain—all of which connect to inquiry practice.

In the ubiquitous deductive models seemingly necessitated in public schools in the era of the standardized test, teachers inevitably have trouble helping students achieve the higher-order thinking skills referenced by the aforementioned verbs. Mastery of these cognitive tasks requires recursive practice in an environment that recognizes students' Vygotskian "zone[s] of proximal development" (as cited in Cole et al., 1978, p. 84) by asking them to perceive phenomena from their existing knowledge base before connecting with new knowledge accessed under the guidance of a trained instructor.

As students are asked to respond experientially to the text or idea at hand in IBL classrooms, teachers can diagnose proficiency and work with greater ease to guide students toward more complex methods of questioning. And, since all questions formulated about the subject at hand are viable in an IBL classroom, students who would not typically engage begin to participate, their reluctance about providing a wrong answer eradicated.

Another challenge faced by public school educators at all experience levels is differentiation of material in inclusion classrooms. Faculty working with student teachers in the English Department at the University of West Georgia found that IBL could serve as an instrument of differentiation. In landmark work on the subject, Carol Ann Tomlinson and scholars in the field of educational leadership recommend that teachers striving to include all learners

- Focus on the essential ideas and skills of the content area, eliminating ancillary tasks and activities.
- Respond to individual student differences (such as learning style, prior knowledge, interests, and level of engagement).
- Group students flexibly by shared interest, topic, or ability.
- Integrate ongoing and meaningful assessments with instruction.
- Continually assess; reflect; and adjust content, process, and product to meet student needs (as cited in Huebner, 2010, p. 79).

Though these talking points are now well-known, they can be difficult to accomplish in a multifaceted classroom, especially for teachers who primarily work in the deductive mode.

In fact, these guidelines often raise more questions than answers for educators. How, after all, can we truly assess what thinking skills students possess—not facts or scholarly interpretations memorized by rote—without hearing them talk through the content we seek to teach? Can we truly focus on all students in a traditional top-down classroom space where ability levels differ greatly? And, finally, do tenets of IBL work to encourage all students to enter discussions from their existing vantage points and learn from others' talking points as well as our own?

Literacy Today: Teacher Inspired ELA Resources reports that IBL "provides a context for differentiated instruction" ("Inquiry Based Learning," n.d., para. 2) with four key student and instructor characteristics: readiness, interest, respectful tasks, and assessment for learning. In each area, IBL can encourage behavior that allows students to build on existing knowledge via authentic engagement with new ideas.

Our answers to questions about the difficulties of differentiated instruction bring us back to endemic IBL practices, especially since both share a foundation in constructivist philosophy that asks teachers to honor student ability before proceeding to more difficult tasks born out of increasingly complex questioning and the exchange of ideas. Where the two differ greatly is in the amount of deduction—or guidance—a teacher utilizes to bring his or her students to the same point in any given instructional unit.

Even the most "at risk" student can formulate questions about basic terms, as one of our team members observed in the collaborative mixed-abilities classroom in which one study participant employed IBL. And teachers can assess student progress through listening to the caliber of questions posed. For instance, should a single student in an IBL classroom ask only plot-related questions about Charlotte Perkins Gilman's "The Yellow Wallpaper"

(1997) while all others have moved on to characterization, the instructor-guide may assume that the language features of the piece are not too difficult for most students and can encourage them to move onward, listening to students discuss questions related to nuances of characterization.

The teacher-learner can also rely on other members of the discourse community to answer elementary questions about plot or interject at opportune moments to tie together such questions with one that moves into more complex arenas. Higher ability students, then, model for others who struggle with the kind of questions to ask, and, over time, they learn from each other's ideas alongside their instructor's in the consistent IBL classroom. Likewise, should a teacher-learner note that several students are formulating questions related to plotline or language features, s/he can interject to discuss syntax or context, providing a blend of IBL formats.[4]

IBL offers the possibility for some *natural* differentiation that relies on the organic unfolding of conversation between participants who have been exposed to various modes of querying and have been trained by peer and teacher modeling. Students can inquire about a text from their current vantage point and hear others' questions before answering, refuting, or noting the rhetorical structure of them. Repeated class periods in which students create, answer, and debate questions related to readings begin to solidify the appropriate methods of formulating investigative questions for a challenged student.

INQUIRY-BASED LEARNING IN THE CONTEXT OF ENGLISH STUDIES

Our introduction to IBL compelled an expedition in which we learned from scholars, pondered implementation in our courses, and formed interstitial connections between new ideas and our own content-specific precepts. The trek toward implementation of IBL in the context of English studies required first the recognition of the typical definitions but then consideration of how commonly recognized activities of scientists—the group most often associated with inquiry—apply also to the study of literary and cultural artifacts.

Alan Colburn, a Professor of Science Education, distinguishes two types of inquiry, both applicable in the hard sciences. He writes, "Scientific inquiry refers to the diverse ways in which scientists study the natural world and propose explanations based on the evidence derived from their work." Inquiry, he continues, "*also* refers to the activities of students in which they develop knowledge and understanding of scientific ideas, as well as an understanding of how scientists study the natural world" (n.d., para. 5).

The steps of the scientific method, we reflected, are embedded in the pursuits of English practitioners for whom "extensive and intensive debates have taken place ... concerning the intellectual and philosophical bases of critical engagement with literature" (Hutchings and O'Rourke, 2002, p. 73). Learners and scholars in the hard sciences observe, question, test, and report findings before questioning again in a more complex manner. Academic quests in English and the Language Arts mirror this process, though the foci involve sustained research and study of various art objects in verbal and written modes.

Much like scientists in their scholarly pursuits, practitioners in English conduct thought experiments with the written word to foment active learning, "confront[ing] the dichotomy between research and teaching" (Baker, Le Heron, and McEwen, 2006, p. 77). Deploying inquiry to study literature or composition, then, required us to dismantle the extant model in which knowledge is delivered by the scholar-teacher *to* the student, and, instead, set up conditions under which students become burgeoning scholars engaged *with* research and investigation.

Rather than reserving scholarly pursuit for professionalizing work, instructors can choose to enlist students in the vital work of hypothesizing about the texts within their discipline. Adopting this new positionality affords "research-teaching linkages in communities of inquiry in which staff and students are 'co-learners' engaged in exploratory ventures" (Healey, 2005, p. 7). IBL increases investment since students tasked with the responsibility of asking questions about a difficult subject become "motivated when they can see the usefulness and relevance of what they are learning—especially in their local community" (Spronken-Smith, n.d., p. 7). Here, we found, the instructor fosters a community of learners by providing a framework for questioning in the arena where students of all abilities can enter and engage.

William Hutchings and Karen O'Rourke (2002) provide a blueprint for instructors in English at the college level, indicating that teachers who provide students with a discipline-specific framework for inquiry facilitate productive investigation. As instructors of eighteenth-century literature, they created a class in which second-year university students heard a set of plenary lectures encompassing satire, the work of Samuel Johnson, lyric poetry, and the novel. Each of these talks preceded a seminar in which students in groups of five were given primary texts from the literary period and a question related to them. They could use their notes from plenary talks or research to understand new elements before presenting findings to the class.

Students in these college classes, Hutchings and O'Rourke contend, became larger stakeholders in their education as they engaged in informed interpretation constructed from their IBL interactions with material and each other. Alongside teacher-scholars who guided from time to time, they began to "take their cue from this demonstration of the vitality and *open-endedness* [emphasis added] of [English studies]" (2002, p. 73). Rather than learning meaning already constructed by scholars, students experienced the intricacies involved in making meaning of their own through the vital activities of research, questioning, and reportage.

Research that connects inquiry to our discipline strengthened our classroom deployment and functioned as preplanning, providing a foray into our study of IBL at work in public school classrooms. Importantly, because we experienced positive outcomes in our own college classrooms and observed IBL in action during our visits to student teacher demonstrations at their secondary site schools, we became convinced that it could fortify the bridge between K-12 and collegiate spaces that we navigate in our hybridized professional endeavors.[5]

CONNECTION TO THE INSTITUTE FOR PEDAGOGY IN THE LIBERAL ARTS 2014

The germ of this project began with a combination of end-of-year funds and the local Montessori school. We received a University Presidential grant allocated for community partnership efforts, which our department matched, along with an opportunity to join a delegation of West Georgia faculty attending IPLA 2014. At the time, we had only a vague sense of what we wanted to do with local school partners, but we were certain that our efforts would foreground pedagogical innovation via inquiry.

Heather Giebeig's use and advocacy of IBL in elementary schools was familiar to us through our mutual dealings with the local Montessori school, and she, too, had studied inquiry at Oxford College of Emory University in a summer 2009 seminar hosted by the Oxford Institute for Environmental Education (OIEE). When we approached her about attending IPLA 2014 with us and our collegiate delegation, none of us was certain what final direction our initiative would take. The nebulous nature of this enterprise proved serendipitous as it allowed our own studies and reflections at IPLA to inspire this venture.

Between the three of us, we attended workshops on engaging students in research and inquiry, building IBL assessment plans, and bringing meaningful off-campus components to the undergraduate curriculum. We workshopped our ideas with IBL experts and participated in a lunch roundtable with Virginia Lee who helped strategize our crystallizing initiative. Each evening, we gathered around a dinner table, debriefed what we learned that day, and followed the inquiry process itself as we questioned, reflected, questioned again, and finalized our study preparations that focused on the potential for IBL in English studies with a K-12 audience.

THE STUDY

In Carroll County, educational reform efforts are commonly piloted on a small, targeted scale with approval from the County Board office. Our project with IBL was unique in its use of nontraditional pedagogy, but also because we were collegiate, *discipline* faculty requesting permission for a multischool collaboration.[6] We targeted three volunteer teachers across the Mt. Zion cluster, a school system located at the doorstep of our university, to test IBL strategies in a variety of grade levels within one school system.[7] We also included one teacher from Temple High School, a county school in the nearby Villa Rica cluster, to measure the applicability of the model in a different school venue. In the end, our participants' instructional loads provided us with broad coverage across fourth, seventh, tenth, and eleventh grade, spanning student audiences that contained special education, general education, honors, and self-selected AP students.

After a rigorous Institutional Research Board (IRB) approval process, the team trained four volunteer teachers on the concepts inherent in inquiry pedagogy across two training workshops in the summer of 2014.[8] The training focused on orienting the participants to full-format and hybridized inquiry models and appropriate assessment methods for K-12. In addition to using the IBL principles we learned at IPLA 2014, we designed the two-part workshop itself following a similar paradigm; the volunteer teachers learned the theoretical and definitional principles and then practiced applications. The first training seminar illuminated the tenets of the method—defining and learning a range of IBL theories and strategies—while the second focused on workshopping participant ideas and plans for implementation.

One challenge we anticipated was that our teacher volunteers came into the study believing that they already practiced inquiry in their classrooms. They assumed that any activity that involved student participation met IBL standards. The expectation failure they experienced on the first day of training was challenging for them as they immediately had to wrestle with their own understanding of inquiry pedagogy and how to mesh the principles of this approach with the Common Core standards and assessment structures in which they work; it was also key to their growth and success with the method.

To facilitate our participants' journeys with IBL, we provided them with a small stipend and two texts to orient them to both collegiate and secondary inquiry practices: Virginia Lee's edited collection *Teaching and Learning*

Through Inquiry (2004) and John Barell's *Problem-Based Learning: An Inquiry Approach* (2007), a text geared toward pragmatic K-12 applications of IBL transferable across grade levels.

TRAINING DAY ONE

Our dual goal on the first day involved sharing theoretical concepts before transitioning to one practitioner's implementation of full-format inquiry in her elementary education courses. To begin, we discussed the problematic yet typical lesson plan structures found in the surrounding public schools in which we observe student teachers and school partners. Often constructed with time constraints or desired results in mind, instructors implement the deductive mode. They provide expected outcomes prior to lecturing or conducting brief discussion about goals, and then assign group or individual practice. Standardized pre/post-test results too often act as the sole measure of student learning and privilege deduction, since students must arrive at the right answers instead of the most complex questions for investigation.

Even the most well-meaning teachers in our area announce, dictate, and evaluate without providing opportunities for exploration crucial for adolescent intellectual development. A temporary type of memorized learning does occur in such deductive classrooms but self-led critical endeavor—a competency prescribed by the Common Core standards—is not often a lasting outcome.

We shared with our study participants an understanding of their plight: how teachers are under more pressure to meet annual benchmarks for their institutions, and that some must achieve base scores in order to receive merit pay raises.[9] This mutual understanding of their working environments set-up needed common ground for us to address that the achievement of high test scores does not have to rely on deductive pedagogies since, in the long run, they fail to empower students to create knowledge as they encounter increasingly complex situations.

The next section of our first training day involved presenting evidence that IBL fosters skill sets that increase student learning globally as it builds critical frameworks that promote educational goals instituted as far back as No Child Left Behind in 2001, which ushered in an era of standardized testing. To that end, we talked with our participants about a plethora of IBL classroom studies that demonstrate success in concrete learning and beginning theorizing.

Richard Felder and Michael Prince, they learned, provide a primer of quantitative data from IBL use resulting "from 81 experimental studies involving thousands of students," which "found that inquiry learning produced significant positive gains for academic achievement, student perceptions, process skills and analytic abilities" (2003, pp. 10–11). They also contemplated the five-year study of Justice et al. who saw "students' writing improve" via "writing in [an] Inquiry Notebook" (2002, p. 10) alongside other inquiry practitioners writing of better engagement and "[enthusiasm] for more inquiry courses" (Spronken-Smith, n.d., p. 12). Finally, the team shared Alan Colburn's conclusion that IBL is best suited for learning "observable ideas" (n.d., para. 11) rather than theoretical precepts.[10]

These findings indicate that teacher implementation of IBL almost always results in increased performance with skill sets standards prescribe. As Heather Giebeig's elementary classroom results fall in line with these positive results, the next section of Workshop One provided our team members with granular detail of her personal journey with the method in a traditional public school, where she grappled with connecting IBL to classroom practice.

Ms. Giebeig noted that early in her career as an elementary gifted facilitator she established a more traditional gifted curriculum focused on Latin, advanced math, and various in-depth social studies and science units. Though the parents and administrators seemed pleased with her design, she always questioned how and to what end the lessons elicited thought distinct from that evoked in regular classrooms. At this juncture, she laid bare for our participants how she stumbled by accident into IBL practices through a Junior Great Books lesson on Beatrix Potter's *The Tale of Squirrel Nutkin* (2002) in which she deployed activities requiring students to elicit and answer their own critical queries using textual evidence. This lesson was so impactful that she decided to receive formal IBL training in science disciplines at the 2009 OIEE.[11] These experiences culminated in her pedagogical transformation and commitment to engage students in critical thinking skills across her curricula via inquiry practices.

To make this technique pragmatic for our teacher volunteers, Ms. Giebeig walked them through an inquiry science experiment surrounding the buoyancy of leaves, designed from start to finish by her third graders. In so doing, she equated the inquiry methodology with steps of the Scientific Method, what she considers IBL in its purest form. Our teacher participants came to understand how each phase in the full-format process requires students to use higher-order thinking. Authentic examples of students' observations, questions, thoughts, and conversations from this experiment illustrated for trainees how an immersion in analysis, synthesis, and evaluation throughout the entire process are unique benefits of IBL stratagem.

Ms. Giebeig underscored the integral role that both observation and questioning, the first two steps of full-format IBL, play in placing the responsibility for learning into the students' hands, as well as empowering them to access their own environment for ideas and inspiration. To differentiate between induction and deduction, she showed a visual contrasting the inquiry-based, student-initiated experiment with a traditional format for teaching the same lesson.

This chart depicted how lower-level thinking dominated the teacher-guided method, and, instead of students devising questions and conducting an experiment derived from their own observations, how the instructor would be inserting an exercise aimed at higher-level thinking into a format that would not support it. Reiterated was the argument that full-format inquiry, like the Scientific Method, immerses the student in independent higher-level thinking throughout the process. She then showed a series of visuals correlating a literary discussion to the steps of the Scientific Method.

Ultimately, Ms. Giebeig posited the idea that a theory is the "experiment" which a student designs during a literary discussion. This theory undergoes testing via student debate where textual evidence either serves to support or disprove the idea via discussion of it. Ms. Giebeig addressed each step of the Scientific Method along with its application to literature, and, cognizant of state mandates for measurable outcomes, she shared an IBL assessment tool designed to gauge the level of student engagement with the inquiry process (see appendix 5.1). This instrument, shared with students, aids in the enhancement and quality of responses they provide, and it offers her a clear method for assessing critical skill set development during a dynamic discussion.[12]

Mick Healey and Martin Jenkins's inquiry-based workshop at IPLA 2014 inspired the last planned activity on this opening day of training. This exercise would require study participants to come up with ten specific ways that they could imagine themselves making use of IBL in their respective classrooms, writing each item on separate Post-It notes. After this independent activity, they would pair up and share their ideas, sticking each to a poster on the wall. Finally, all pairs would present the most interesting ideas from their collaboration. Such an inductive activity, we postulated, would stimulate early thinking concerning IBL potential in the English classroom. But we never got to this activity.

Instead, our group began the organic process of questioning and responding to what we had just shared with them. One participant formulated verbally ways she might use IBL as a method to teach Lois Lowry's *The Giver* (2002), comparing some of what we had shared to protagonist Jonas's plight to learn about his culture's practices. Another discussed ways to set up "experiments" in her Advanced Placement (AP) language class before a third participant shared how Ms. Giebeig's "leaf exercise" could be modified to teach connotative language. They began, then, the epistemological process of coming into understanding via interrogatives followed by discussion, throwing out their own gossamer threads of knowledge to connect with the new.

TRAINING DAY TWO

Our design for the second workshop strategically provided participants with a month between seminars to read and study the primary IBL materials we provided, to prepare questions they had after digesting the materials, and to design their own ideas and plans for instituting inquiry into their classes. We opened this session with a brief review of the inquiry process and time to answer questions generated by their summer reading. In this section, participants reported difficulty engaging with Lee's collection *Teaching and Learning through Inquiry* (2004) given its more theoretical bent and focus on collegiate learning, but they found Barell's (2007) practical text useful and could draw from it a plethora of ideas applicable to their classrooms.

After addressing their follow-up questions, we spent the first half of the session deploying the Post-It activity described above, using it as an activating strategy for our subsequent discussion of the method. We deviated from our original planned activity in two ways. First, the leadership team opted to participate in the activity with them. Doing so gave us a more intimate look at their engagement with the process and developing understanding of true IBL approaches, and it allowed us to begin to formulate how to better support them in their unique classroom environs.

Each group then had to arrange and consolidate the wealth of generated ideas and come to some consensus concerning which ones worked best with IBL practices before presenting them to the larger group. This exercise was fruitful for all of us. Our volunteer teachers produced insightful design ideas in this exercise, some we even borrowed and adapted to our college classrooms, and the follow-up discussion generated even more practical applications in and among the schools represented in the group.

Though a successful activity, the group remained unsure about how their students, accustomed only to traditional school models, would adjust to IBL practices. To illustrate student engagement, we followed this exercise with footage of Heather Giebeig's second and third grade classes participating in a self-directed IBL literature unit. Our teaching volunteers were surprised by the level of engagement, risk taking, debate, and self-correction of which this young student population was capable. This classroom footage served as the most compelling evidence for their own application of the method, and it provided Ms. Giebeig with another opportunity to discuss inquiry assessment, stemming from a real classroom scenario.

The second half of this seminar gave our cooperating partners an opportunity to present their IBL classroom implementation plans to the group for workshopping. This structure—one we had practiced in IPLA sessions—provided them a space to explore IBL in the context of their subject and grade levels with a support structure in place for immediate feedback and revision. Further, it allowed us to collaborate with them on devising some common assessment markers to measure student progress quantitatively in ELA while implementing IBL across the represented grade levels. The participants, thus, departed armed with a better understanding of IBL and concrete strategies for deploying it in a self-selected unit of study, which they were to implement during a nine-week period of their 2014/2015 school year.

CHALLENGES OF THE STUDY

One flaw with our study design concerned participant numbers. Two of our four participants withdrew due to personal circumstances within the first four weeks of the fall term. Our remaining two participants still afforded us with middle and high school sites across three grade levels, but this turn of events left the study with a gap at the elementary level. To fill in this knowledge set, Drs. Harrison and Insenga observed Ms. Giebeig twice across her combined second/third grade and fourth/fifth grade classes—classes that utilized full-format IBL—to get a better sense of IBL's application potential at the elementary school level.[13] Replicate studies would be better served by garnering two to three teachers at each level to ensure appropriate coverage should a participant withdraw. Further, such a model would provide them with a built-in site support system throughout the implementation timeframe. [14]

Our limited budget presented several challenges as well. While we did offer small stipends to our participants to attend summer training, these sums were miniscule given the curriculum and assignment overhauls the method dictates. Our insufficient study budget contributed to our small numbers as we could not afford to include more than four teacher participants in the initial design. It also reduced the number of times we could observe them in the field and the amount of support materials we could provide. Most importantly, the lack of funds and institutional support available for this work has stalled our efforts with furthering the initiative with a larger sample of public educators in the coming academic years.[15]

ASSESSMENT

The two participants who completed the study—covering seventh and tenth/eleventh grade respectively—were each observed three times by the leadership team over a nine-week period at weeks three, six, and nine. The observations were teacher/classroom centered, focusing on the teacher's deployment of IBL pedagogy in the context of the discipline and

104 Chapter Five

subsequent student reception. Each observation was scored quantitatively using a Likert scale, and, each observer wrote a narrative letter to the participant that discussed the observation and offered suggestions for revising practices.

In addition to our observations of their classroom spaces, our volunteer teachers collected quantitative student achievement data via a pre/post-test that measured each student's ability to pose critical questions about, analyze, and synthesize a text. They also agreed to keep a log of their journey—challenges and successes—throughout the nine-week process, which they shared during the culminating focus group session.

THE DATA

Our participant from Temple High School, Ms. Jessica Bohlen, elected to institute IBL across all six of her courses: three tenth-grade classes, of which two were inclusion sections containing eleven special education students, and three eleventh-grade self-select AP classes. Her data, shown in figures 5.1 and 5.3, represent the results of inquiry practices amongst 125 students.[16] Ms. Bohlen's point-based pre/post-test was divided into three areas that measured her students' ability to formulate critical questions about, analyze, and synthesize Silvia Plath's poem "Mirror" (1971) by connecting it to another text within a thirty-minute timeframe. The tenth and eleventh graders were given identical tests, and neither class studied Plath or poetry during the nine-week inquiry unit.

Ms. Bohlen's student data evidences the impact that IBL methods can have on secondary student populations when implemented at the curricular level, as opposed to just isolated IBL exercises more commonly seen in public

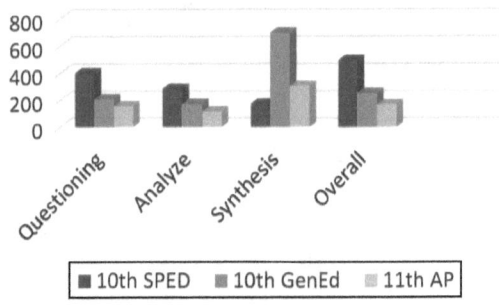

Figure 5.1. Percent Improvement by Test Area

schools (figure 5.1). The three tenth-grade classes improved by an average of 250 percent on the post-test with triple digit improvement percentages in each test area: 209 percent (Questioning), 172 percent (Analysis), and 695 percent (Synthesis).

The transformational data for this teacher participant, however, concerned the performance of her eleven tenth grade special education students, many of whom, she reported, had not accessed full conceptual understanding of analysis and synthesis. This student population improved by an average of 492 percent globally on the post-test with an equally impressive improvement average in each test area: 400 percent (Questioning), 283 percent (Analysis), and 172 percent (Synthesis).

The positive reception of this method by the students combined with their scores drew the attention of her colleagues, department chair, and administration.[17] Ms. Bohlen was subsequently asked to do an in-service on IBL for the full department, whose members adopted IBL across the board as of fall 2015. This pedagogical shift at Temple High School, an outcome of this study and IPLA 2014, means that five English teachers across twenty-seven sections of English and one section of psychology are now utilizing IBL, impacting approximately five hundred students per year.

Our middle school participant elected to test IBL in one of her seventh grade honors ELA classes composed of twenty-two students. She used the same three-part pre/post-test structure as our high school volunteer, but centered it on an excerpt from Gary Soto's *A Summer Life* (1991). Her seventh graders achieved a 320 percent average improvement rate on the post-test, an equally impressive data set given the younger student group: twelve- and thirteen-year olds (see figure 5.2). Given IBL's impact on her students, she

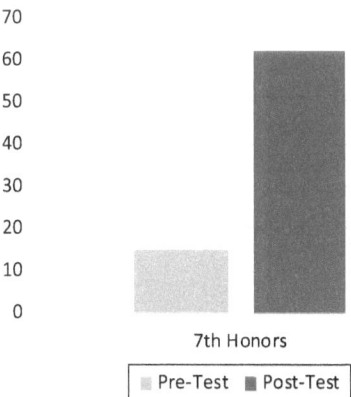

Figure 5.2. Average Test Score

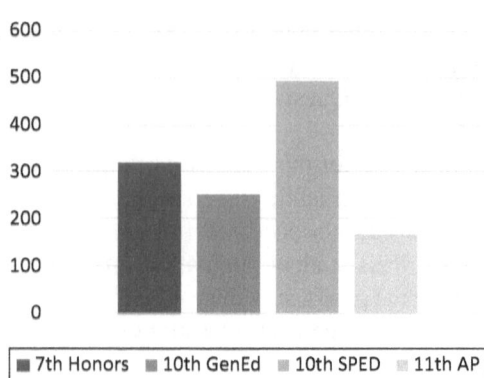

Figure 5.3. Pre/Post-test Percent Improved

plans on continuing its use across all of her classes, broadening the reach of the method in our community.

Though some IBL advocates believe that inquiry is most appropriate with older, more advanced students, our participants' uniform experiences suggest that this is not the case. The comparative data, in fact, evidences a greater percentage increase in the essential skill set tested with the seventh graders and tenth grade special education students as opposed to the eleventh grade advanced students (see figure 5.3). These results are consistent with Ms. Giebeig's historical data using the method with elementary students, a population spanning children seven through ten years of age. These outcomes support our assertion concerning the potential of IBL to impact student learning across K-12 environments.

The leadership team monitored the teacher participants at three strategic points throughout the nine-week study. These observations gave us a first-hand account of their challenges and successes utilizing the method. Generally, observation reports show initial struggles with falling into traditional patterns of instruction intervention, especially when students gave a "wrong" answer, and difficulty with letting the students guide the discussion away from instructor interests and comfort zones. Writing instruction proved problematic as well, and participants struggled with IBL's application in this area throughout the nine weeks.[18] By the third observation, however, both volunteer teachers demonstrated exceptional competency with the method and assessment practices in literary analysis with one participant devising an IBL approach to her school's required Daily Grammar Practice exercise, an area of application we never anticipated. It is of note that no member of the leadership team observed any student reluctance to IBL practices, even in the first weeks of the study. Regardless of age or ability, the students gravitated to this form of learning, progressing to an engagement and focus level rarely seen in our first-year college classrooms.

Though we find the cumulative quantitative data compelling, the most poignant evidence of IBL's application potential in public schools derives from a participant's phenomenological experience. Below, we open an uninterrupted space for her qualitative feedback, which speaks directly to our secondary school partners, many of whom may still not see a clear pathway toward implementation of IBL with their pupils. She writes:[19]

> When asked if I would participate in an inquiry-based teaching study, I felt confident that the experience would not be that different from my typical instruction. My pedagogy methods already included discussion-based learning and real-world applications that many of my colleagues rarely utilize, as it is less comfortable and familiar than traditional lecture models. Admittedly, my *supposed* familiarity with IBL was one of the reasons I accepted the challenge of utilizing this new method in my classroom.
>
> Once I became educated about how inquiry works, I realized it would require relinquishing more control than I was accustomed to and allowing students to guide the learning in a direction meaningful to them. These differences were not discouraging, but they were intimidating, especially when I thought about my courses with students who have specialized learning needs. When it came to accomplishing the goals of IBL, I was concerned and doubtful of my students' ability, as well as my own.
>
> Pressing forward in the face of reservations, I immersed my classrooms into the inquiry method from the onset of the 2014 school year. I included general IBL guidelines and expectations in my syllabi and adorned my walls with posters of specific techniques and strategies I wanted the students to utilize within the lessons, such as the inquiry step-by-step process: observe, think, question, interpret, evaluate, and synthesize. I knew with state tests and standards that I would not be able to perform inquiry with every lesson, but I wanted it to be a habitual activity in the learning environment.
>
> I think this commitment not only helped hold the students accountable for their own learning, but it helped me remember to give up control at times and move away from mere discussion to a truly inquiry-based approach where I became a guide to promote the student's process in grappling with the material. Rather than facilitating the discussion *I* felt the students needed to have, I helped them explore areas they felt interested in and/or confused by. I expected students to resist this responsibility of determining the direction of critical engagement with inquiry. However, most students accepted this innovation without opposition.
>
> In addition to modifying my classroom environment and syllabi to reflect inquiry goals and expectations, I began the term with an inquiry pretest the second day of class that would enable me to assess student progress at the end of the unit and determine the impact of IBL. The pretest involved three activities with the poem "Mirror" by Sylvia Plath. Students were to compose questions

that demonstrate critical engagement with the text, explain what they thought the text meant, and thematically synthesize it with something outside of the text. The students were given thirty minutes to complete these tasks and told that it was purely effort based. I stressed that no one would receive less than full credit if they were putting forth effort to do what the test requested.

My efforts to prevent the discouragement I knew was going to occur failed; the students were frustrated, confused, and, in some cases, angry. Some students called me over and asked me questions, such as "what questions do you want me to ask?" or "what do you need me to explain?" The most frustrating word in these questions was the resounding "you."

It became obvious that teachers, like me, had made these students dependent on our singular opinions of what needed to be learned and comprehended, as if it existed as an absolute. The students were unable to form their own reactions to the text because their time in public education and around standardized tests had made them ill-prepared to think independently. This reaction made me feel confident in my choice to alter my teaching methods.

As I began the process of planning and modifying lessons to facilitate inquiry pedagogy, I was insecure. Regardless of how much IBL literature and sample lessons I studied, clear models for implementation into a public school environment were nearly nonexistent.

My first few lessons focused on their summer reading. Implementing inquiry with reading facilitated engagement in the collaborative process, allowing students to follow individual interests and, thus, make more meaningful and critical connections. Students were enthusiastic taking ownership of our textual discussions and were quickly holding one another accountable for staying focused on the text for their questions and responses.

My inquiry "Ah ha" moment, if you will, came almost half way through the nine weeks in my tenth-grade classroom. While teaching one of my favorite short stories, "Desiree's Baby" by Kate Chopin [2013], I realized the true potential of IBL. Though I had been using inquiry for a few weeks, I had not used it with a text I loved to teach.

"Desiree's Baby" discusses miscegenation in Louisiana. Desiree, a deserted child adopted by an affluent family, marries a plantation owner. They are happy until she gives birth to a child who appears to be partially black. Her husband assumes she is responsible due to her ambiguous genealogy (though he later finds out about his own black ancestry), leading her to despair; she walks into the bayou with her child, never to be seen again.

My pre-IBL lesson leads the class towards exploring what gender implications exist among the racial themes in the text. However, with IBL, students in one class had a very different interest. In this classroom, students became fixated on whether Armand, Desiree's husband, was acting racist or just reflecting the expectations of his time. Students wanted to discuss if an individual is responsible for following social expectations or traditions.

While this is not a theme I would have brought up, what followed was a fervent debate over the role of the individual in perpetuating stereotypes that was related to gay rights. IBL practices allowed my students to pursue an intellectual avenue that was engaging for them. It was obvious the students felt strongly about this topic, and by using the expectations of inquiry discussions in my classroom, they had a respectful and purposeful conversation about an important social issue.

Even though what *I* like to discuss did not happen in that class period, those students made their own relevant meaning out of the text, rather than merely acquiring mine. I understood in this moment how inquiry transforms the classroom into an environment where students learn not simply what I teach them but what they can teach one another.

Some skeptics of the inquiry method may deny that it has potential to work in a public school environment. I too was unsure of the efficacy once implemented, especially with my tenth graders. However, I found my classrooms operating much smoother than in the past. One large difference I noticed was a decrease in moderate behavioral issues. Many students known for acting out or even sleeping in other classes were engaged in my class. Unlike in traditional classrooms, they were allowed and encouraged to participate in the lesson. In addition, 83 percent of my special education students earned higher grades on tests and/or writing assignments with IBL practices than their past academic records show. Most started shy and unsure, but throughout the process they grew more confident, impacting their participation and overall performance.

The general education students seemed empowered by the process—no longer afraid of being wrong because their idea is not identical to what I was thinking—while my AP Language classes needed longer to accept the freedom and responsibility of inquiry. Overall, each class engaged well with the process, gifting me with the fewest behavior issues I have ever had and some of the most interactive lessons of my instructional career.

When the time came for me to judge the efficacy of my inquiry incorporation, my expectations were that everyone would improve on task one, the questioning of the text, but I was unsure how many students would comprehend the postmodern poem, much less synthesize it with a text or event outside of it. Once I sat down to go through the post-tests, I was overwhelmed by how well all students did across all three tasks. Both tenth and AP improved greatly with regards to idea generation and articulation. Their scores improved so much that I suspected I had been too harsh at the beginning of the nine weeks.

After viewing the pretests via a side by side comparison, the incredibly high post-results were confirmed. The results are especially impressive given that I never taught a unit on poetry analysis during the first nine weeks of school, much less Silva Plath; yet, students were understanding themes and meanings within the poem that had completely eluded them nine weeks prior. Students who initially thought ideas were literal used their own close reading to discover that those ideas were more metaphorical. Inquiry taught them the *skills* to grapple with difficult texts and do it well: their high marks had nothing to do with regurgitation of knowledge, but evidenced intellectual achievement.

Once the study ended, I not only chose to continue the practice of inquiry in my classroom, but I also shared my experience with other teachers at my school. A few faculty members even requested to observe how I use IBL so they can begin the implementation themselves. Skeptics may feel that inquiry would "waste" valuable instructional time where teachers need to be instructing and lecturing students about specific terminology on high-stakes tests. I have found myself more confident with my students' ability to perform on exams since beginning the inquiry-based learning study.

Teachers never know what information will be included on our course's state test. We have a general idea, but the specifics remain obscure. To combat that frustration, inquiry prepares students to tackle the unknown without the panic and dependency I observed when I administered the inquiry pretest. In fact, with the new focus on "college and career readiness" and the CCGPS standards, where students are required to connect reading and writing skills to various texts and engage in critical thinking on various levels, inquiry allows instructors to teach students how to perform confidently in regards to those challenging standards.

This professional's account speaks to the value of IBL methods, even when they are implemented in a hitherto calcified, top-down pedagogical environment. Her sustained reflection also indicates that IBL meshes with state standards and appeals to learners in challenging classroom environs.

IBL worked for this participant because its inductive impulse harnessed the innate but suppressed student desire for independent and self-guided learning. The installment of the method allowed students to explore without persistent teacher intervention. Students came to see that learning is more about asking good questions, not coming up with correct answers, and they transferred this practice to the post-test in which they independently theorized about Plath in advanced ways hitherto undemonstrated.

The positive data achieved by these students after a nine-week encounter allay fears that the introduction of this model would disadvantage them on state-mandated tests. On the contrary, quantitative data paired with vital analytical reflections like the complete one we share above provide an effective prototype for achieving an increase in student performance and offer a path toward fulfilling the stringent standards formulated for the Common Core.

While our study was a small one, it gleans remarkable data which supports the use of IBL at all learning levels in the public school environment. We found that IBL foregrounds critical processes vital in English Studies and invites students to discover alongside teachers and better prepares them for the sort of complex questioning of texts that state literary and informational Common Core standards require. We also deployed IBL parallel to the study, observing that our own students began to move beyond mere accession of material to the assimilation of it into their expanding horizons of experience.

Traversing the space between the university, Ms. Giebeig's classroom, and participating site schools spurred us onward, as we began to see how IBL could affect reluctant readers and could temper response from the most vociferous in our classrooms to open spaces for reticent students. Our observations of a single student in one IBL classroom also illustrated that a student taught how to ask questions in a discourse community early on in his or her educational experience will remember how to do so again *if the teacher provides the framework*.[20] Such an observation points to the sustaining qualities IBL has beyond single classrooms, intimating how larger deployment may effect the elusive goal of "lifelong learning" via questioning.

As we had the benefit of seeing others teach using IBL methods tailored for their specific learners, we could also reflect upon our own practices, modifying or enriching when necessary. These interactions illustrate a crucial aspect of this study: IBL begets IBL. That is, our commitment to observing, questioning, reporting, and questioning yet again meant that we too underwent constant revision as we integrated new techniques and notions about student learning into our own work. We, along with our participants, built a micro-network of instructors connected by a commitment to using a pedagogical mode to improve student mastery of state-required standards.

This inward glance notwithstanding, the data from our small cadre of public school participants is not just the proverbial pebble thrown into a large pond; rather, it is a boulder disrupting an established current and indicates the sort of educational ownership possible in classrooms that shift focus to the development of interrogative skills. The measurable outcomes from our small study demonstrate that this inductive learning model works in gifted, general education, *and* university English classrooms.

We find ourselves, as a result, even more invested in following the concentric ripples of our work outward, broadening our scope and continuing to tout the benefits of inquiry. Part of this ongoing effort involves returning to IPLA, where our journey started, as it motivates and bolsters our continuing goal to bridge the gaps—perceived and real—between elementary, secondary, and collegiate teachers. Thus, we aim to effect larger understanding of how IBL meshes with Common Core standards (GSE), engendering student achievement inside the classroom and beyond.

INQUIRY ASSESSMENT CHART

Fifth Grade

Subject: _____   Date: _____

Name	Response	Theory	Opinion	Solicit	Question	Higher Level	Comment

A = answer
com = comment
dis = disagree
Ag = agree
E = evidence

P = prediction
cl = clarified
pix = pictorial clue
O = observation
au = author's intent

ac = comment related to author
M = relating movie/TV/ Video Game to
H = relating history to a passage/story
S = relating another story to a passage/story
Exp = relating personal experience to a passage/story

Tally marks = The number of responses for all categories, except "Response." In the "Response" column, the type of response is recorded according to the above key.

Opinion: Level I Thought—Equate to a first impression when meeting someone new. Does not take much evidence to form.

Theory: Level II Thought—Takes considerably more evidence, possibly pulled from different excepts of the text.

Perceptive Well-Developed Connection: (Rated as "Higher-Level Thinking.") Level III Thought—Symbolism; Hidden Meaning; Theme; Author's Intent; Linking of Fine Threads of Evidence, etc. Takes a great deal of evidence or very convincingly-linked evidence.

NOTES

1. IBL, a method whereby students work independently from inception to end of any given course or project, is an overarching goal for instructors, we contend, though the process toward this goal can require deployment of inquiry-guided learning (IGL) wherein an instructor demonstrates the method prior to student-initiated and led work. This distinction is outlined in Lee (2004). Ms. Giebeig refers

to IBL as "full-format" in this piece, and we, while cognizant of the difference between IBL and IGL, utilize the phrase IBL also, as increased student performance and investment acted as an impetus for navigating classes toward increasingly independent student investigation.

2. Such perceptions arise from discipline-specific faculty having limited knowledge of public school practice and adolescent development. Further, many derive their K-12 experiences anecdotally or personally, as parents of public school children.

3. Common Core standards were renamed the Georgia Standards of Excellence (GSE) in 2015.

4. Full-format inquiry is defined in this chapter as a cyclical process that uses all steps of the Scientific Method and alternately employs logic and creativity. The role of the instructor during this process is that of a facilitator who enters pupil-led debate *only* through a question, placing the responsibility for learning into the hands of the students. Guided inquiry involves the tenets of full-format but includes more teacher input at key places in the question and answer process. In guided inquiry, teachers are more than facilitators in the learning process. They can steer instruction if necessary or highlight student ideas for more class focus.

5. For more on the role and benefits of discipline faculty participating in teacher training programs, see Harrison and Insenga (2015).

6. Generally, our board office deals with initiative requests from faculty housed in Colleges of Education; we are English faculty located in a College of Arts and Humanities.

7. The Mt. Zion cluster comprises Mt. Zion Elementary, Mt. Zion Middle School, and Mt. Zion High School.

8. The lengthy approval process for the study involved IRB training, review, and local board and principal approval.

9. These issues partially explain the dearth of investigative models in public schools and are why a large instructional focus on answers instead of questions is an imperative in these frameworks.

10. Alan Colburn states that "inquiry-based instruction is likely to be effective for showing many students that chemical reaction rates depend on the concentrations of reactants." Conversely, Colburn reports that some studies record increased accountability as stressful for students ("What Teacher Educators," n.d., para.11).

11. For more on the Oxford Institute for Environment Education see http://oxford.emory.edu/oiee/about-us/oiee-program/.

12. The IBL discussion assessment instrument is revealed as students learn and practice the process. They begin to hold themselves accountable for achieving marks in each area measured during literature discussions. Participants adopted this tool and reported similar positive results.

13. True to the full-format model, Ms. Giebeig even utilized IBL to teach the required state standards. Seeing this unexpected application of inquiry and student engagement with standards informed our thinking about our own pedagogy classes for pre-service secondary teachers.

14. We recommend that replicate studies include site visits during preplanning and in the first weeks of the study to increase the amount of help and support offered to teachers as they distill IBL for public school environments.

15. The English major with a concentration in secondary education represents over 40 percent of the English major at UWG. With only two tenured faculty assigned to administer the program, our ability to further these important community efforts is limited.

16. Ms. Bohlen consented to being named in this text. Self-selected AP classes, a current trend in both high school honors and AP courses, means that the students did not have to qualify to be in the course; they simply elected to take it.

17. Many of the students in her classes spoke about IBL methods to other teachers who also noticed better intellectual stewardship with this group in their classes.

18. We did not model IBL with writing instruction during participant training; we would include this ELA area in any subsequent professional development seminars.

19. This reflection was written by study participant Jessica Bohlen and is included here with her permission.

20. One of Ms. Giebeig's former elementary students happened to be in our middle school participant's seventh grade class. His engaged performance during the inquiry unit demonstrated the potential of inquiry as continuing practice.

REFERENCES

Baker, R., Le Heron, R., and McEwen, L. (2006). Co-learning: Re-linking research and teaching in geography. *Journal of Geography in Higher Education, 30(1)*, 77–87.

Barell, J. (2007). *Problem based learning: An inquiry approach.* Thousand Oaks, CA: Corwin Press.

Chopin, K. (2013). Desiree's baby. *The awakening and selected short stories* (pp. 110–114). Seattle, WA: CreateSpace Independent Publishing.

Colburn, A. (n.d.). What teacher educators need to know about inquiry-based instruction. *California State University.* Retrieved on May 2015 from http://web.csulb.edu/~acolburn/AETS.htm.

Cole, M., John-Steiner, V., Scribner, S., and Souberman, S. (Eds) (1978). *Mind in society: The development of higher psychological processes.* Cambridge, MA: Harvard University Press.

Common Core Georgia Performance Standards. (2008). *Atlanta Public Schools.* Retrieved on May 2015 from http://www.atlantapublicschools.us/commoncore.

Curriculum and instruction. (2015). *Georgia Department of Education.* Retrieved on May 2015 from http://www.gadoe.org/External-Affairs-and-Policy/AskDOE/Pages/Parents-Curriculum-and-Instruction.aspx.

English Language Arts Georgia Standards of Excellence. (2015). *Georgia Department of Education.* Retrieved on May 2015 from https://www.georgiastandards.org/Georgia-Standards/Pages/ELA.aspx.

Felder, R. and Prince, M. (2003). Inductive teaching and learning methods: Definitions, comparisons, and research bases. *Journal of Engineering Education, 95*, 123–138.

Harrison, R. and Insenga, A. (2015). Building robust teacher training programs within English departments. *South Atlantic Review, 78(12)*, 110–131.

Healey, M. (2005). Linking research and teaching: Exploring disciplinary spaces and the role of inquiry-based learning. In R. Barnatt (Ed.), *Reshaping the university: New relationships between research, scholarship, and teaching* (pp. 67–78). New York: McGraw-Hill/ Open University Press.

Huebner, T. A. (2010). What research says about differentiated learning. *Educational Leadership, 67(5)*, 79–81.

Hutchings, B. and O'Rourke, K. (2002). Problem-based learning in literary studies. *Arts and Humanities in Higher Education, 1*, 73–83.

Inquiry-Based Learning. (2015). *Literacy today: Teacher inspired ELA resources*. Retrieved on May 2015 from http://www.literacytoday.ca/differentiation/effective-teaching-strategies/article/inquiry-based-learning.

Justice, C., Warry, W., Cuneo, C., Inglis, S., Miller, S. Rice, J., and Sammon, S. (2002). A grammar for inquiry: Linking goals and methods in a collaboratively taught social sciences inquiry course. *The Alan Blizzard Award paper: Special edition of the Society for Teaching and Learning in Higher Education.* Retrieved on May 2015 from https://www.researchgate.net/publication/238498325_.

Kennedy, A. and Navey-Davis, S. (2004). Inquiry-guided learning and the foreign language classroom. In V. Lee (Ed.), *Teaching & learning through inquiry* (pp. 71–80). Sterling, VA: Stylus.

Lee, V. (Ed.). (2004). *Teaching & learning through inquiry.* Sterling, VA: Stylus.

Lillard, A. S. (2005). *Montessori: The science behind the genius.* New York: Oxford University Press.

Lowry, L. (2002). *The giver.* New York: Laurel Leaf.

Perkins, C. G. (1997). The yellow wallpaper. In P. Negri (Ed.), *The yellow wallpaper and other stories* (pp. 1–16). Mineola, NY: Dover Publications.

Plath, S. (1971). Mirror. In T. Hughes (Ed.), *Crossing the water* (p. 35). New York: Harper & Row.

Potter, B. (2002). *The tale of squirrel nutkin.* New York: Penguin Putnam.

Soto, G. (1991). *A summer life.* New York: Laurel Leaf.

Spronken-Smith, R. (n.d.). *Experiencing the process of knowledge creation: The nature and use of inquiry-based learning in higher education.* Retrieved on May 2015 from https://akoaotearoa.ac.nz/sites/default/files/u14/IBL%20-%20Report%20-%20Appendix%20A%20-%20Review.pdf.

Chapter Six

Constructing a Social Justice Pedagogy through Contemplative Service-Learning

Patricia Owen-Smith

Oxford College's Institute for Pedagogy in the Liberal Arts (IPLA) evolved from its enduring relationship with the Carnegie Academy for the Scholarship of Teaching and Learning. It was this relationship that facilitated the college's first Carnegie Scholar in teaching and learning, advanced the fruition of the service-learning program, and resulted in our college serving as a Carnegie national leadership site in cognitive-affective learning (CAL). The work of the CAL leadership team (which comprised six institutions around the country) was not only the result of a consciousness around affective dimensions of engaged learning and teaching, but it also led the author of this chapter to the Contemplative Mind in Higher Education movement.

Certainly, if one considers the history, theory, and practice of some of the pedagogies emphasized by IPLA, each emanates from similar ground. Collectively, they have their origins in a participatory and transformative epistemology, a vision of the student who has both an exterior and interior self, and a theoretical orientation that not only offers ways of understanding the cognitive aspects of development but also the affective, moral, and spiritual development of students.

Conceptions and practices of service-learning, social justice, and contemplation should dance effortlessly with one another. However, they often do not for a myriad of reasons. Much of our literature and research suggest that chief among these reasons is an ill-defined and poorly understood definition of these pedagogies, which, in turn, leads to practices that are fragmented, lacking evidence, and potentially deleterious to student learning, growth, and development.

The purpose of this chapter is to provide an overview of service-learning in terms of its evidence, pedagogical strengths and weaknesses, and its critical relationship to both a social justice and contemplative education. Three objectives are integral to this overview.

The first objective is to examine briefly the history of service-learning, definitions that have emerged from this history, and how this history informs the ways in which service-learning programs and courses contribute to citizenship, engagement, and both student and community development. (The service-learning literature and research are expansive, and it is not the goal of this chapter to restate in-depth histories and definitions which others have done so eloquently).

The second objective is to explore the meaning of a social justice education as it specifically relates to service-learning. Too often service-learning courses and programs have obscured rather than clarified concepts of social justice resulting in a superficial approach to meaning-making and social justice.

The final goal is to describe contemplative practices in higher education. Central to this description is a consideration of how the use of specific contemplative practices addresses problems that currently exist between the service-learning and social justice relationship and how they might deepen and bring integrity to this relationship.

SERVICE-LEARNING: PAST AND PRESENT

Among the many pedagogies of engagement that exist in higher education today, service-learning has the longest and most persuasive history. The concept of a "secular service" dates back to the early 1900s and to the work of early pioneer Jane Addams and others who conceptualized service-learning as a *practice*, not a theory, and as originating in the *community* among women with the university playing only a supportive role. This historical understanding, often marginalized or dismissed in the service-learning history, is particularly germane to the discussion that follows as it offers an essential reminder that the initial foundation of service-learning was in *community* and in *practice*.

The argument that service-learning began in the university is most often situated in the educational and social philosophy of John Dewey and his emphasis on an education grounded in experience, a democratic community, social service, reflective inquiry, and social transformation (Saltmarsh, 1996). Giles and Eyler (1994), among many other service-learning scholars, observe that Dewey's philosophy posits a theory of service-learning unparalleled by other educational theories and that "service learning reflects, either consciously or unconsciously, a Deweyian influence" (p. 78).

In spite of Addams's and Dewey's influence and enormous contributions to the concept of service-learning it was not until the 1980s that the pedagogy emerged on the educational scene as a viable solution to bridging the gap between academic achievement and service to community. Jane Kendall (1990) noted that by the early 1990s, 147 definitions of service-learning existed, and perhaps many more such definitions are present today. In some ways, this multiplicity of definitions problematizes our understanding of what service-learning is and also contributes to a number of the issues discussed below.

One of the most enduring definitions centers on service-learning as both a theory and practice. This definition assumes that practical, course-related experience outside the theory of the classroom is an imperative for engaged, meaningful learning and that the partnership with community organizations develops social responsibility and citizenry. Neururer and Rhoads (1998) deepen this definition by their emphasis on the social justice component. They observe that service-learning as a pedagogy "serves as a vehicle for connecting students and institutions to their communities and the larger social good, while at the same time instilling in students the values of community and social responsibility" (p. 321).

The current empirical evidence and theory supporting the impact of service-learning on student learning is compelling. A 2011 meta-analysis of 62 studies involving 11,837 students demonstrated that students participating in service-learning courses showed significant gains in five outcome areas: attitudes toward self, attitudes toward school and learning, civic engagement, social skills, and academic performance (Celio, Durlak, and Dymnicki, 2011). Of particular importance with this meta-analysis was the assessment of specific practices used in service-learning courses.

Celio, Durlak, and Dymnicki (2011) note that the practice of reflection in the classroom led to some of the more favorable outcomes. However, they also point out that reflection was the only practice used in over half of the studies suggesting that current service-learning programs might be overlooking other important practices associated with or undergirding reflection. Similarly, a 2012 meta-analysis on the influence of service-learning demonstrates that it has positive benefits for increased multicultural awareness and enhanced social responsibility as well as student-learning outcomes (Warren, 2012).

Each year the International Association for Research on Service-Learning and Community Engagement Conference highlights studies that both affirm and expand analyses such as the above. Service-learning, therefore, appears to be what Astin (2004) calls a "pedagogical panacea: almost all aspects of the student's academic, personal, and moral development are favorably influenced by participation in service learning, and the teachers themselves are also often transformed by teaching such courses" (p. 10).

SERVICE-LEARNING AS SOCIAL JUSTICE: POTENTIALITIES AND HURDLES

As suggested above in both theory and evidence, the service-learning pedagogy is a prototype of engaged learning, a potential venue for social responsibility and citizenry, and one supported by robust theoretical perspectives and evidence. Yet, as we celebrate the merits of service-learning and the progress made in its pedagogical development, we are reminded that the implementation of a service-learning pedagogy is not a method without difficulty.

Clayton and Ash (2004) observe that service-learning is a counternormative pedagogy and "... a teaching process that is messier, more self-critical, and more open-ended than most students—or most instructors—have been socialized into, creating an experience of dissonance that is all the more filled with learning potential because of these very differences" (p. 61).

Illeris (2014) refers to this counternormative pedagogy as a type of transformative learning that is "leading learners to the edge ... whereby learners come up against their limitations, go beyond the habitual, experience the unaccustomed, meet, split, or breakdown, face dilemmas, feel insecure, or must make incalculable decisions" (p. 11). These observations capture not only the extraordinary potentialities of service-learning but also several major hurdles that continue to haunt service-learning courses and programs.

The first of these hurdles centers on the potentially disturbing intensity of the service-learning experience juxtaposed against a classroom structure and an instructor that might marginalize or deny this intensity. Such conditions often occur when well-intentioned instructors experience anxiety with such emotion and are ill-prepared for guiding students through this disruptive terrain. Regardless of the instructor's intentions, students are left unaccompanied on this emotional journey and left "on the ledge."

A second difficulty plaguing the service-learning pedagogy is what Laura Rendon (2009) refers to as hegemonic "agreements" rooted in an academic culture that is based on a traditional pedagogy, one that fails to speak to the wholeness of human beings. These agreements privilege "intellectual/rational knowing, separation, competition, perfection, monoculturalism, outer work, and avoidance of self-examination" (p. 26). This outmoded pedagogical understanding also frames many service-learning courses across the country and, therefore, contributes to a service-learning course that fails to reach its transformative power.

A third major problem and one related to and derived from Rendon's hegemonic agreements is that service-learning can lead to a superficial approach to meaning-making and social justice. Furco (2011) reminds us that this type of issue in a service-learning course can reify stereotypes, lead to a poorly articulated understanding of social issues, and exacerbate power differentials between and among groups.

Pompa (2002) observes that in societies where patriarchal perspectives and hierarchies are dominant, "'service' can unwittingly become an exercise in patronization ... and service-learning's potential danger is for it to become the very thing it seeks to eschew" (p. 68). In fact, some critics suggest that the word *service*, in and of itself, is hierarchical and one that implies need and deficit on the part of the community.

Both Furco and Pompa speak to Mitchell's (2008) concern as it relates specifically to social justice and what she sees as the prevailing yet fallacious assumption that all service-learning is inherently "social justice." She differentiates between a *traditional* service-learning pedagogy that "... emphasizes service without attention to systems of inequality, and a *critical* approach that is unapologetic in its aim to dismantle structures of injustice" (p. 50). For Mitchell, a critical service-learning program is a political act in which students are required to become change agents, revolutionaries, and reformers for the goal of social justice.

Warren (1998) also conceptualizes social justice in service-learning as student understanding of "... the context of their service in the socio-political dimensions of social justice" (p. 134). In their seminal work on educating undergraduates for moral and civic responsibility, Colby et al. (2003) also address this relationship by defining social justice as systematic social responsibility and central goals of civic learning.

Drawing from numerous research studies, they point to the findings that while undergraduates are increasingly more involved in service activities, their involvement does not necessarily nurture a deeper insight into political and social issues.

Similarly, in Einfeld and Collins' (2008) research on the relationship between social justice and service-learning, many of their student participants increased such skills as empathy, patience, attachment, reciprocity, trust, and respect along with awareness of inequalities. However, only a few adopted a commitment to social justice. Einfeld and Collins discuss these results as emblematic of the complexity of service-learning experiences as they relate to social justice.

Each of these scholars recognizes that that the traditional service-learning paradigm is not adequate if we wish it to be linked to a social justice education. All call for a critical service-learning that privileges a social justice consciousness. Boyle-Baise and Langford (2004) summarize this notion in describing the components of a service-learning for social justice course as (1) assisting in self-understanding, deepening knowledge, and encouraging action; (2) attending to community; and (3) including substantive inquiry and analyses.

In practice, many instructors fail to emphasize these components preferring to rely on a narrow understanding of the service-learning pedagogy, one that separates experience from theory, confounds service with justice, and disregards interior ways of knowing. Therefore, this partial understanding of learning informs service-learning courses in such a way whereby service is an extracurricular aspect of the course with little attention given to the meaning-making necessary for a social justice perspective and accompanying practice.

Certainly the academy's commitment to social justice is one that is highlighted by the majority of today's institutions. An examination of college and university mission statements and/or presidential messages clearly reveal this commitment.

Harkavy (2006), however, observes that "disciplinary ethnocentrism, tribalism, and guildism strongly dominate American universities today and strongly work against their actually doing what they rhetorically promise to do" (p. 14). This "siloization" in universities, according to Harkavy, has disallowed the interdisciplinary and multilayered approaches necessary to resolve complex social problems.

Ironically and perhaps predictably, both large and small academic institutions often turn to their service-learning programs as one significant exemplar of their institutional commitment to social justice education. As Marullo (1996) suggests, the choice of the service-learning pedagogy "... asserts that universities have a role to play in solving the problems of the community and society around them, and that service (not just pure research or classroom education) is an appropriate method for universities to fulfill that obligation" (p. 2). If our service-learning programs are to reflect this social justice perspective (which many of our institutions say they do) and if as practitioners this is our goal, how might we address the current problems that consistently disrupt this pedagogy, weaken it, and jeopardize its integrity? How do we directly connect service-learning to social justice? Although there are institutional and community factors that may contribute to some of the difficulties in implementation (and these may be beyond the individual purview of instructors), there are some potential and substantive responses to these questions that can be found in how we, as teachers, structure our service-learning classrooms.

Virtually all of the impediments addressed above suggest a difficulty with and/or dismissal of the reflective process that is at the heart of a social justice–based, service-learning classroom. In an attempt to define service-learning, Giles and Eyler (1999) remark:

> We have embraced the position that service-learning should include a balance between service to the community and academic learning and that the hyphen in the phrase symbolizes the central role of reflection in the process of learning

through community experience. And indeed there is a considerable best practices literature of practitioner wisdom that stresses the importance of reflection as the vital link between service and learning. (p. 4)

Bringle and Hatcher (1999) support these observations by defining service-learning as the "intentional consideration of an experience...[with] the presumption that community service does not in and of itself produce learning" (p. 180). Bringle and Hatcher's point is an important one. The provision of an experience without consideration of its meaning is simply an experience which may or may not yield significance and worth.

Likewise, Mitchell et al. (2015) comment that "critical reflection during the service-learning experience allows students to expand initial, simplistic conceptions of the world into more complex and accurate representations of messy 'real world' problems" (p. 50). Therefore, the process of reflection is the *sine qua non* component of a well-constructed service-learning course, one that honors and integrates social justice.

Scholars of the service-learning pedagogy argue that student reflection must be at the core of and consistently integrated into all service-learning courses and must extend beyond a simple description or summary of the students' respective community placement. A "reflective" approach that is merely a commentary of what is "good" or "bad" about the community experience is an unprincipled and reductionist approach to a service-learning, social justice-based course. The transformative and revolutionary potential of the pedagogy is grounded in an analytic reflection of social systems that produce inequality, injustice, and oppression (Moore, 1990; Marullo, 1996).

Paradoxically, a fully developed understanding of what reflection is and how to introduce and structure it into the classroom is sorely missing. Many service-learning teachers report that they feel unprepared to facilitate students' deep analyses of their experiences and how these experiences relate to the development of social responsibility. There are also those who see the use of deep reflection as time consuming and difficult to include in their classroom hour and, therefore, are hesitant to embrace consistent and continuous reflection. Still others are uncomfortable with both the silence and the pauses that reflection and contemplation necessitate.

Many teachers are diligent in constructing their service-learning courses and in providing a well-crafted experience for the student, but they fail to insure that students make meaning of the experience and that they derive understanding of self and others. We often assume that students actually make the connections we as teachers make and see as significant. For all of these reasons, reflection is often absent, minimized, underdeveloped, misunderstood, or limited to a few venues such as journaling and discussions.

To ask students to reflect on the profound moments of community work without proper preparation for this reflection is a disservice to the student, the communities of which they are part, and social justice education. In fact, a recent study assessing reflective practices reports that the least helpful reflection activities reported by former service-learning students were journal writing and online discussion forums (Mitchell et al. 2015). However, one might question whether journals and discussions, in and of themselves, are ineffective reflection approaches or whether they are ineffective because students have very little understanding of *how to reflect* using these venues.

Many students point out that while they are expected "to reflect" in many of their classes, they do not know how to reflect or are unclear as to what the term actually means. One result of this fragmented use of reflection is an increase in student anxiety, sense of failure, and confusion around meaning-making in service-learning courses. Some of the tools for reflection can be effective if carefully explained by the instructor; however, many simply reproduce conventional practices in the classroom that are not always relevant to the service-learning, social justice experience. Consequently, they fail to deepen the type of knowledge and critical questioning that should emerge from the service-learning experience and one that leads to an emphasis on social justice.

A CONTEMPLATIVE APPROACH TO REFLECTION

Many such difficulties with service-learning classrooms may be due to our failure to attend to dimensions of thinking and learning that are the initial requisites for and components of reflection, dimensions located in contemplative practices. Contemplative methods can serve as models for service-learning reflection, specifically one leading to a social justice education.

A contemplative perspective is one which focuses on *particular practices* that draw upon the human capacity to know through stillness, awareness, attention, mindfulness, and reflection. The Center for Contemplative Mind in Society, the formative voice for the contemplative perspective in higher education, envisions these practices in the following manner:

> The experiential methods developed within the contemplative traditions offer a rich set of tools for exploring the mind, the heart, and the world. When they are combined with conventional practices, an enriched research methodology and pedagogy become available for deepening and enlarging perspectives, leading to lasting solutions to the problems we confront. (http://www.contemplative-mind.org/practices/tree)

Barbezat and Bush (2014) expand this articulation by noting that contemplative practices are those that "support mental stability" and by necessity allow for focus and attention development, inquiry into one's own interiority, exploration of personal meaning, and the deepening of compassion and connection to others. They state that all contemplative practices have "an inward or first-person focus. ... and place the student in the center of his or her learning so the student can connect his or her inner world to the outer world" (pp. 5–6).

Kanagala and Rendon (2013) delineate contemplative pedagogy in this way: "We define contemplative pedagogy as a teaching and learning experience that involves the learner in a participatory epistemology characterized by a deeply immersed, insightful learning experience fostered through carefully selected reflective practices that complement the learning assignment" (p. 40). Therefore, a contemplative learner is one who can quiet the habits of the mind, deepen attention, allow for the development of insight, cultivate compassion, appreciate the interconnectedness of living beings, and reflect intensely on experience.

While contemplative practices have been absent or marginalized in contemporary higher education, they nevertheless have deep roots in both our own individual development as well as the major theories of learning produced in the past four decades. Without hesitation, we begin our lives with the ability to perceive, feel, experience, and explore the world with a contemplative lens. Young children sit, stare, see, question, ponder, think, and wonder. They are knowledge builders and scientists.

Sadly, the majority of individuals begin to lose their contemplative selves as knowers and learners at a very specific juncture in their developmental and educational journeys. Just as contemplative selves emerge early in life, so do they leave early in life. Both developmental and educational psychologists argue that in most cases the loss occurs when formal schooling begins.

The rules of modern educational systems, from kindergarten through graduate school, impose a set of restrictions and mandates that disallow the flourishing of contemplation and, therefore, deep learning. We are no longer given time and space for that which leads to imagination, curiosity, creativity, and a consciousness of self and others. We lose access to that which we have always had. The stillness and quiet necessary for thought development and deep intellectual inquiry become nonproductive, a wasting of time, and a squandering of resources. Students learn clearly that they may not stand in the gap of their experiences, pause, and consider.

In learning these rules well, there is a loss in the ability to attend mindfully and to reflect. These losses result in costs that are profound for both the individual and the world inhabited by these individuals. The higher education known today seems to reflect this legacy of loss in spite of the fact that it did not always reflect such deficiencies.

Contemplative methods find expression in the words of many of our educational philosophers, poets, artists, and scientists all of whom held tightly to their contemplative lens of childhood. Some historians point out that the Greek philosophers were the first to acknowledge contemplation as a way of knowing. Contemplative modes were also central to the monastic schools and the ways of teaching and learning born in those schools.

Augustine, Seneca, and Montaigne relied on forms of contemplative reflection. Augustine and Seneca used the oral dialog for self-inquiry, and Montaigne's writing practice was a type of contemplative autobiography (Stock, 2012). Einstein clearly practiced a contemplative approach in his articulation of the stages of insight and imagination. Similarly, Isaac Newton often talked of truth as first requiring a commitment to contemplation.

Psychologist, philosopher, and educator William James (1890) noted the significance of contemplative awareness and attention in observing that *"Genius, in truth, means little more than the faculty of perceiving in an unhabitual way"* (p. 424). Rilke's (1903) poetry emerged from his distinct ability to look, attend, and see into the heart of something, perhaps best captured in what may be one of his most profound admonitions; *"Live the questions now, perhaps then, someday, you will gradually, without noticing, live into the answer."*

The integration of contemplative knowing into the American school system was born in the works of our educational innovators. Paulo Freire (1970), one of the most influential educational theorists in the twentieth century, stressed pedagogical contemplation as a requisite for deep reflection and for *liberation and the transformation* of the world. Our educational innovators, reformers, and theorists insist that access to interior faculties is necessary for reflection and learning and in understanding both the self and others.

The origins of experiential and service-learning echo the legacy of contemplative scholars. They are firmly grounded in Freire's notion of a critical pedagogy, Piaget's affective development model, Vygotsky's "tools of the mind," Mezirow's "alternate language," Kolb's experiential theory, and the participatory, feminist epistemology of both Belenky et al. and Gilligan. Each of these theorists has conceptualized education as focused on the mind, body, *and* spirit of the student in the context of relationship.

These epistemologies of knowing are clearly apparent in the current work of educators such as Parker Palmer, Alexander and Helen Astin, Art Zajonc, Mirabai Bush, Tobin Hart, Laura Rendon, and Mary Rose O'Reilley. Each has written eloquently about honoring interiority through contemplative knowing and all are careful examiners of the processes of teaching and learning.

CONTEMPLATIVE PRACTICES IN THE SERVICE-LEARNING CLASSROOM

Repetti (2010) defines contemplative practices as "… metacognitive exercises in which attention is focused on any element of conscious experience" (p. 7). The Center for Contemplative Mind in Society conceptualizes a tree of contemplative practices with its roots expressed in communion, communication, and awareness. The branches represent different groupings of practices (http://www.contemplativemind.org/practices/tree). While some of these practices might not be applicable for the service-learning classroom, many are useful and particularly necessary to a social justice education.

Palmer and Zajonc (2010) expand these conceptualizations of contemplative practices. They observe that experiential and transformative learning might be seen as the practice of "contemplative knowing" (p. 15). Certainly, this definition suggests that a well-implemented service-learning course should be a stunning exemplar of a contemplative practice.

ABirsch (2009) discusses the need for "creating spaces" in our classrooms whereby contemplative knowing can mature. Such spaces inspire "… reflection, contemplation, and introspection, processes which provide deep insight into lived experience, enhance intellectual development, and, in the best of cases, lead to civic engagement" (p. 2). Contemplative practices provide for and are deepened by such spaces.

It is only in the spaces of the heart and mind that a social justice–based service-learning course can emerge. Practices such as stillness and silence, mindfulness, music, deep listening, *lectio divina*, free-writing, and contemplative arts are those that are particularly relevant to service-learning courses and a social justice consciousness. They call us to attend to the world in a particular manner. Many of these spaces and practices serve as a road map in teaching and affirm the cultivation of habits of the heart and mind in both students and their instructors. Each of these allows access to inner knowing and interiority, a prerequisite for the type of reflection necessary for service-learning, social justice courses.

The choice of classroom practices is one unique to the instructor and derived from a relationship with students. O'Reilley (1998) holds that each instructor has her/his own "prayer hall." Each teacher brings a unique history, values, and perspectives to a class. Similarly, Grace (2011) asserts that the strength of a pedagogy rests not in its technique but in the teacher's "authentic congruence" with it. Kirsch (2009) reminds us to incorporate the contemplative in a manner that comes "from the depth of our own being, from our own traditions, from what is in our heart" (p. 3).

The following practices have as their central core the disruption of unproductive habits allowing for the development and maturation of awareness.

As such, they are critical to the service-learning pedagogy. All of these are grounded in introspection and self-reflection and serve as an important means for accessing interiority.

STILLNESS AND SILENCE

The speed, chatter, busyness, and anonymity of many of today's classrooms might contribute to a breadth of knowledge but at the expense of depth and meaning-making. These losses result in barriers to interior development, self-understanding, understanding of others, and deep learning. Powers (2010) refers to this as a "traffic jam" at the center of our lives producing "... a struggle *for* the center of our lives, for control of how we think and feel. When you're scrambling all the time, that's what your inner life becomes: scrambled" (p. 17).

This "traffic jam" has enormous implications for learning in general but specifically to service-learning classes. Silence interrupts the traffic jam. It facilitates the ability to ponder, wonder, consider, and allow for compassion to emerge, compassion for self and others. It is in silence that interiority and self-knowledge are located and that insights and analyses initially emerge. It is in silence that the work of social justice begins.

How might the requisite of silence be engaged if there is no space for stillness? How might the journey into self be forged without calm, a hush, a pause? How might the sense of interconnectedness and compassion develop in the midst of "scramble"? In a culture that fears silence, there is a comfortability with noise. As Grace (2011) observes, noise has an addictive quality whereby distractions are a welcome respite from our real lives.

Many teachers and their students are addicted to this noise. They enter the classroom distracted, rushed, anxious, and unfocused. Instructors are sometimes polysyllabic, concentrated on bestowing rote-type words to students. From this context, many service-learning courses emanate and simply resemble volunteerism with an occasional, poorly done reflection period.

Contemplative teachers often begin their classes with silence and relaxation, sometimes with meditative music and sometimes without. These teachers often report that the familiar sounds of clicking mobile phones and lap tops as well as the compulsive chattering that begins most classes can be replaced by silence and the sounds of a quiet space. Students who are often skeptical in the early few weeks of the semester seem to welcome and relax into this space as the semester progresses. These same instructors speak of a spirit of calmness, quiet, and respect that develop and that inevitably changed the ethos of the classroom.

Many contemplative teachers see music as providing both a context for and a hospitable way to introduce silence. Initially, students are more likely and prepared to sit in silence when contemplative music is playing. It is from the groundwork of music that a contemplative class might move toward longer minutes of silence, without music, throughout the sixty- to seventy-five-minute class.

While many would argue that stillness and silence are important for all learning environments, they are particularly significant in the service-learning classroom where social justice is the focus with its disorienting moments, disturbing realities, sociopolitical interrogations, and sometimes sorrow. These periods of silence can provide a brief respite from an intense moment, a time to sit with sadness and suffering, and a space where, paradoxically in silence, students find their voice through their inner conversation. It is this capacity that inevitably allows us to reflect upon and extend a "hospitality" to the voices of others (Parks Daloz, Keen, and Keen, 1996).

While a teacher might ask for minutes of silence in the classroom, the request for a moment of silence can be any class member's call. As the class progresses through the semester, students can often find their own comfort in calling for silence when they feel the need. The class might talk about why silence was needed, what was learned from it, and what might be done because of it. Sometimes students may write about it or merely let it go and move on. Just as the moment and spirit of the class determine the call for and welcoming of silence, so do they govern the nature of its ending. The practice of silence helps all members of the classroom both engage and disengage according to what the moment requires.

AWARENESS AND MINDFULNESS

Mindfulness is born and matures in silence. It begins with a quieting of the mind and practice in the cultivation of openness and receptivity (Lutz, Dunne, and Davidson, 2007). Roeser and Peck (2009) describe contemplative practices, such as silence, as those that lead to an "education in awareness" (p. 133). Mindfulness is an attention to and beholding of our interior selves, a noticing of what is present in that self. Bai et al. (2014) describe awareness as a "… capacity for witnessing what our mind does, seeing what is going on moment-to-moment in the field of consciousness" (p. 292). As such, awareness and mindfulness are a witnessing of our own subjectivity that leads to an interruption and transcendence of our habitual perspectives and freedom from our inflexible thought patterns.

In her 2014 address to the Mind & Life Conference, Sheryll Petty argues that our awareness, or what she calls "enlightenment," is a natural state.

However, she urges us to consider the ways in which we often detach from this enlightenment in our "subtle re-coiling" and how mindfulness of this brings greater presence and awareness of the moment. Roeser and Parks' review of research into mindfulness practices suggests that most human beings do not automatically develop this type of concentration and awareness unless they participate in some specific mental practice which they call "contemplative education" (p. 128).

The first step in the journey of a social justice education begins with this consistent attention to the practice of self-awareness. We cannot compassionately behold the other before beholding the self, a particularly important lesson in the service-learning classroom. Many of our students have moved away from their natural state of enlightenment. They are offered few practices, if any, that might rescue this enlightenment. For a variety of reasons, many of which are located in the structure of today's colleges and universities, students have lost their sense of self, their personal narrative, and their agency. They are confused as to where to place their attention in the "traffic jam" of their lives. As one student confidentially said to this author a number of years ago, "I think I might not have a self," a terrifying thought to her and a sobering one to hear from a student in a college that prides itself on teaching to the *whole* student.

The development of mindful attention can be cultivated in our classrooms. As noted above, sitting in silence, if only for a few minutes throughout the class hour, provides the first venue through which access to the moment and to the self is possible. In spite of the message often conveyed to students by their teachers "not to just sit there," momentary *just sitting and doing nothing* is crucial to deep learning and particularly salient in a service-learning course. Both the literature and evidence on teaching and learning support the significance of silent sitting.

Students might be invited to "check in" with their interior selves and to be present to what they may find there. They may be encouraged to notice and listen carefully to what they are experiencing in their heads and their hearts and to pay attention in what Kabat-Zinn (1994) calls a "... particular way: on purpose, in the present moment, and non-judgmentally" (p. 4). This leads to what Kabat-Zinn calls a deeper awareness and clarity. We cannot consider, interrupt, and challenge oppressive systems until we are first fully aware of them, pay attention to them, and reflect on them with a clarity of consciousness.

The practice of mindfulness is just that—a practice; it is a lifelong process. But the journey can begin in classrooms and in service-learning communities heightening an understanding of the place each student has in the social justice calling.

DIALOGIC LISTENING

Attention to and a mindfulness of experiences in each moment are central to communication and community with others. Scott (2014) refers to these as "dialogical virtues" suggesting that the dialogical encounter or turning to the other is grounded in mindful listening. It is in listening that we honor and care for ourselves and one another. Attentive listening to the self and to others brings a conscious lucidity, but it is a difficult process to acquire. Psychotherapists spend many years of their training in learning how to listen.

We are socialized away from listening just as we are socialized away from silence. So few of us take the time or know how to hear silence and to hear ourselves and others. However, there is another reason. As Fischer (2004) says, listening can be dangerous and risky. It is inherent in us not to wish to listen because "it might cause you to hear something that you don't like, to consider its validity, and therefore to think something you never thought before" (p. 44).

Fisher's words are particularly relevant to a social justice-based, service-learning course where students and their teachers both see and hear injustices that mandate attention. To choose not to listen and, therefore, not to see absolves us of our responsibility to act. O'Reilley (1998) points out that "people are dying in spirit for lack of it" (p. 19). The world's current problems clearly reflect this deficit in courageous and deep listening.

The voice of the classroom can be one of critique and criticism. Many students have grown accustomed to listening only to teacher censorship. They are distrustful of and, at times, devastated by honest communication; they are fearful of both hearing the other and being heard by the other. They are well conditioned to this paradigm.

In an effort to partner with students in more effective listening, some instructors choose an exercise called *Mindful Dyadic Dialogue* (see appendix 6.1). This exercise is particularly significant to service-learning courses as an intimate way to discuss community experiences. Central to the exercise is a full presence to the partner in a silent, nonjudgmental mode of listening carefully and intentionally for three minutes. Roles are then exchanged so that the listener becomes the speaker for the next three minutes.

It is in dialogue that individuals are called upon to be vulnerable with and trusting of the person who is listening. As the listener, students are required to practice acceptance, compassion, and care. This is not an easy method for students although it is not an easy task for their instructors also. Faculty meetings suggest such difficulty.

For many instructors the method of *wait time* in the classroom is an effective means for listening more intentionally. Wait time requires both a pause for three to five seconds after the instructor asks a question. This method is not new. Brown (2014) summarizes studies on wait time that have been done since the 1970s pointing out that this method demonstrates an increase in student response, deeper understanding of content, more flexible and sophisticated student-teacher interactions, more complex information processing, and improvement in academic achievement scores. Wait time is clearly a contemplative practice in that it affords a mindfulness about speech and a respect for the listener that can change the class atmosphere.

Just as with all other contemplative pedagogies, deep listening is cultivated slowly, particularly in today's busyness. Many instructors who choose to implement wait time report the generous willingness of students to engage in this exercise and then practice it with commitment. They also report that the class becomes a more thoughtful, respectful, and engaged community because of it.

LECTIO DIVINA

The tradition of *lectio divina* is an adaptation from early Judaism as a way to read and interpret the Hebrew bible. In the Christian tradition, it became known as contemplative reading having its origins in monasticism. Many of today's contemplative scholars, in both secular and faith-based institutions, point to the use of the *lectio divina* as not only a way to contest and interrupt the chaotic speed reading of today's college student but also as a method for deep reflection and personal connection.

The *lectio divina* can be a significant pedagogy in service-learning classes. Before students begin their community work and, in the first few weeks of the semester, the concept of a social justice-based, service-learning course can be introduced through selected readings about justice, care, activism, and service. For example, Paul Loeb's *The Impossible Will Take a Little While* (2007; 2014) and *Soul of a Citizen* (1999) offer a venue for group recitation of a specific selection with each member reading a few lines or a paragraph. It is then read again silently with each student choosing a specific paragraph of their choice that is important or resonates on a personal level. The personal selection is read again by the individual student.

It is incumbent on the instructor to choose carefully those sections that are directly related to both the community placements and justice issues embedded in these placements. This method might be used throughout the semester as a prologue to community service discussions and as a context for meaningful discourse.

Photographs might also be used in the same manner. While it is necessary to connect the community experience directly to the disciplinary material of the course, the *lectio divina* method allows for both a deeper understanding of course material and a thoughtful, contemplative discourse about social justice. Many contemplative teachers who use the method of *lectio divina* have adapted the traditional scriptural approach to one that is centered on social justice readings (see appendix 6.2).

FREE-WRITING

All classroom writing has the potential for being a contemplative practice. Like all contemplative pedagogies, writing involves the process of inquiry that reflects the content and nature of the mind, a communication with other, and the expression of self. Writing can both advance contemplative practices as well as benefit from these practices. Barbezat and Bush (2014) point out that contemplative writing might include journal writing, daily reflective writing, mindful writing, storytelling, and free-writing.

Free-writing adds an unparalleled dimension to service-learning courses. It provides an unmonitored space and place for students to spontaneously sit with, consider, and observe experiences derived from their partnership with the community. Popularized by Peter Elbow (1973), free-writing is a method of writing that is nonstop for a particular period of time. As Elbow points out, free-writing provides no feedback nor editing, a "writing without teachers."

In a review of contemplative methods used for his philosophy course, "Obligation, Compassion, and Global Justice," Kahane (2009) observed that free-writing as contemplative inquiry "… allows writing without so much scripting and conscious control; one gets into the flow of an idea or impulse, and writes things that one didn't know one had to say" (p. 10). Free-writing allows students the opportunity to observe their emotions and reactions to community experiences and reflect on the "rawness" of these experiences in the safe space of unmonitored writing.

Many contemplative, service-learning instructors see free-writing as an imperative. In spite of efforts to make the classroom a place of safety for all students, it is not always experienced as such, particularly when issues of gender and sexual orientation, ethnicity, race, and class are discussed which is often the case in a service-learning course. Free-writing provides an avenue for the expression of confusion, sadness, disagreement, shame, and frustration.

Free-writing assignments can be collected but do not need to be graded. Some instructors simply respond to them with a comment of appreciation when papers are returned. At times, this can be difficult for an instructor particularly if a student has expressed a misunderstanding, a blatant prejudice, or a reliance on a stereotype concerning the community in which they are placed. It often necessitates the development of patience with this process allowing the student to develop a social consciousness in her/his own time.

Students might be asked to choose several of their free-writes for inclusion in their final service-learning portfolio which is graded. The instructor might remind them that they do not need to submit a free-write if for some reason they are uncomfortable with its contents and that they may remove a part of a free-write should they so choose prior to submission. However, many instructors who use free-writes note that rarely has this occurred in the many years of doing these exercises.

CONTEMPLATIVE ARTS

Kanagala and Rendon (2013) speak of "birthing internal images" through what they call the "*cajita* project" (p. 7). Designed by Alberto Pulido at the University of San Diego, a *cajita* is a personal reflective box that students create through the use of artifacts that might symbolize identity journeys, life stories, political and philosophical commentaries, and the like. In her IPLA 2015 workshop, Rendon described the *cajita* as a "creative knowledge canvas" and "a cultural autobiographical story." Rendon argues that if students are to participate in the world in a socially conscious manner, they need to appreciate who they are and, therefore, become "reflective scholar-practitioners" (2015, p. 43).

The *cajita* becomes a means for self-reflection and for moving more deeply into internal and external learning. For Rendon (2009), this type of examined experience creates a place that values "… inner knowing (deep wisdom, wonder, sense of the sacred, intuition, and emotions) as well as outer knowing (intellectual reasoning, rationality, and objectivity" (p. 27). The *cajita* offers possibilities for service-learning and social justice–reflection.

Systemic injustices as depicted in artifacts from the community allow for a deeper consciousness about these systems. Students might bring to class such artifacts from their community placements (i.e., drawings from elementary school children, autobiographies written by residents in a local prison, letters to students from occupants in half-way houses and group homes, etc.). Each of these could be used in a *cajita* with an accompanying reflective narrative and presentation to class members. As Pulido (2002) says, such hands-on experiences allow students to move from abstractions in course theory to their own personal lives and the lives of others.[1]

Similar to Rendon's and Pulido's work with the *cajita* is the Talisman exercise. Students bring an object that is representative in some way of their community experience and share its story with class members. The object might in some way communicate or symbolize what is of significance to the student. Each student tells a story and leaves their object on the "table of inspiration."[2]

Students in service-learning classes, when permitted by the school or agency, can be urged to bring photos of children who they are tutoring or residents in an assisted living facility with whom they have developed an important relationship. Some might bring brochures about their particular nonprofit agency or small drawings or other gifts presented to them by preschool children.

One instructor describes a student, engaged to be married, who brought a wedding quilt made by women in a senior citizens retirement center and presented to her as a memory of them. The student talked at length about this great act of generosity on the part of women who had very little power by societal standards but had great power in terms of their wisdom. The class covered their "table of inspiration" with this quilt.

The list of examples is exhaustive, but each is centered on how the object is related to both the community experience and to a particular social justice issue. The construction of these objects, whether in a *cajita* or on the "table of inspiration," provides an important method for substantive, contemplative thinking about a community experience and one's own place in producing social justice.

The literature and research on contemplative practices in higher education are beginning to burgeon in both peer-reviewed journals and in books. Shapiro, Brown, and Astin's (2008) report reflects those contemplative approaches in teaching and learning that are firmly grounded in research and yield specific outcomes. Chief among these findings are the reduction of distractive thoughts and capacity to focus attention, development of internal technologies (i.e., perceptual and cognitive abilities), increased thought patterns and flexibility, and enhanced emotional awareness, management, and psychological well-being.

Several recent studies have focused on social justice components such as the place of multiculturalism and contemplative practice in facilitating students identities as social change agents (Rendon, 2009), mindfulness as a method to access and understand community engagement experiences (Stewart, 2011), and deep reflection and exploration of identity as venues for understanding positionality and privilege (Mitchell et al., 2015).

As more contemplative scholars engage in service-learning research and justice mindfulness, a heightened consciousness supportive of the integration of a contemplative pedagogy within a service-learning, social justice education is anticipated. However, it will take a radical bravery on the part of both teachers and students. Dianna Chapman Walsh (2014), past president of Wellesley College, makes the observation that we as a society are in a crisis of caring (2014) and former Harvard dean Harry Lewis (2006) describes today's university as one "without a soul." Bush (2008) states that in today's world we are faced with one central question: "What does it mean to be human? What is the unique and appropriate role on this planet for us and the seven generations that follow? Contemplative awakening through practice in academic settings is helping us ask that question in a way that could lead us to the essence of what it is to be human" (p. 82).

The type of pedagogy envisioned in this chapter is offered at a period in time when our institutions are becoming more corporatized and less hospitable to social change. Our students are frantic, frightened, and blinded by a societal value system that is at odds with much of what we hold dear as service-learning contemplatives and social justice educators. Instructors are alienated from one another, exhausted, and sometimes reproved for teaching in a counternormative manner.

It is in this context that we must do work unfamiliar to academic culture, take risks, endure the angst that is always a part of social justice work, breathe deeply, contemplate, think, and forge ahead always carrying with us the question: "What does it mean to be human," and what is our responsibility to answering this question?

As I move toward the end of my teaching career, I am reminded of what I wrote in my service-learning teaching journal over two decades ago:

> Certainly, I want my students to understand the concepts of my courses and how they may or may not be manifested in their service placements. Of course, I want to offer them a firm foundation in the basic tenets of my discipline. However, I hope that they will gain far more. I want to create both space and time for students to pause, sit with contradictions and moral dilemmas, and to consider the narratives we each bring to the world. I want them to listen intentionally and speak carefully, and I want them to understand what it means to go within for the important questions and to trust the answers they find to those questions. I want them to appreciate their responsibility to and connections with other human beings and all living things. I want them to understand the fragile relationship between community organizations and the university. I want them to develop a sense of how class, race, ethnicity, sexual orientation and gender inform our responses to social problems. Finally, I want them to build a saner and a more loving, peaceful world.

I do not know whether my students and I have accomplished any of these heartfelt wishes made so long ago, but I do know that I have found my path toward these wishes, a path that rests in the contemplative, in a social justice-based, service-learning pedagogy. I am reminded of Rainer Maria Rilke's (1914) compelling words: *"The work of the eyes is done. Go now and do the heart-work on the images imprisoned within you."*

Appendix 6.1

MINDFUL DYADIC DIALOGUE

> Mindful dialogue calls us to practice acceptance and trust, acceptance of ourselves and each other just as we are, and trust that we can speak our truth and respond mindfully and compassionately to our partner. Trusting that, beneath the ego-driven fears that make us feel vulnerable, the natural interconnection of heart and mind that we share with all people will tend to prevail. (Mark Knickelbine, 2013)

In our class we will regularly practice mindful listening and mindful dialogue. Listening is a type of dialogue in that we are fully present to the other and in communication with this person through our silence and shared space. This mindfulness practice seems easy to understand, but it is very difficult to do. Therefore, we will practice intentionally during the course of this semester with no judgment of the other or the self. If our minds wander as we are listening to another person, simply acknowledge it and return to being fully present to the other. When we speak, notice the difference from that which might come from ego and that which comes from the heart. In dialogue we are called upon to be vulnerable with, humble, and trusting of the person who is listening. If we find that our speech is grounded in defensiveness and/or inauthenticity, simply acknowledge it and return to your authentic self.

The steps below will be helpful as we practice listening and speaking:

- Pause in silence.
- Be aware of your breath and begin to breathe deeply.
- Cultivate attention to self and to the other. In the words of Simone Weil, "*attention is the rarest and purest form of generosity.*"
- We will have a specific amount of time to discuss our community placements related in our dyads.
- Typically one student (the speaker) will spend three minutes talking freely about a meaningful moment in their community placement.
- The other student (the listener) will be attentive and fully present to the speaker but remain silent.
- The listener then takes three minutes to reflect back on what she/he heard the speaker saying with no judgment nor interpretation.
- The speaker then takes a minute to reflect back on how it felt to be heard.
- Roles are then reversed.

If at any time you experience anxiety, anger, sadness, or any emotion that interrupts the dialogue, you may ask your partner for a pause, return to your breath, and proceed when you feel ready.

Appendix 6.2

WHAT IS LECTIO DIVINA?

The tradition of *lectio divina* is an adaptation from early Judaism as a way to read and interpret the Hebrew bible. In the Christian tradition it became known as contemplative reading having its origins in monasticism. In our class we will use an adaptation of the traditional *lectio divina* as a method of "slow reading" a specific paragraph that allows for deep reflection with and a personal connection to this material and to those issues that we will engage in our community placements.

Our method—We first read through the entire selection in its entirety, then read and reread one short passage in the manner of *Lectio*[3]:

1. Sit quietly and relax our minds and bodies for one minute.
2. We will read aloud, slowly, the entire text, each of us reading one or two sentences, "passing along" the reading to the left to the next reader.
3. One minute of silence and reflection.
4. Choose a paragraph or passage that is important or resonates for you personally (you might mark it in your book if you so desire so as to return to it).
5. Reread this paragraph again silently.
6. One minute of silence and reflection.
7. One of us reads aloud this passage that we have marked.
8. Another minute of silence and reflection.
9. We each share a word or short phrase in response to the reading—just give voice to the word without explanation or discussion.
10. One minute of silence and reflection.
11. We share longer responses to the passage—a sentence or two. We listen attentively to one another without correcting or disputing, just hearing all our responses.
12. One minute of silence and reflection.

NOTES

1. For a more complete description of the implementation of the *cajita*, see Kanagala and Rendon, (2013).
2. This exercise was retrieved from the Center for Contemplative Mind in Society Archives.
3. Modified from the syllabus of David Haskell, Professor of Biology, Sewanee: University of the South, entitled *Food and Hunger: Contemplation and Action* (by permission of the author).

REFERENCES

Addams, J. (1892). The subjective necessity of social settlements. Retrieved on May 2015 from TeachingAmericanHistory.org.

Astin, A. (2004). Why spirituality deserves a central place in higher education. *Spirituality in Higher Education Newsletter, 1(1),* 1–13.

Bai, H., Cohen, A., Culham, T. Park, S. Rabi, S., Scott, C., and Tait, Saskia. (2014). A call for wisdom in higher education: Contemplative voices from the *dao*-field. In O. Gunnlaugson, E. W. Sarath, C. Scott, and Heesoon Bai (Eds.), *Contemplative learning and inquiry across disciplines* (pp. 287–302). Albany: State University of New York Press.

Barbezat, D. P. and Bush, M. (2014). *Contemplative practices in higher education.* San Francisco, CA: Jossey-Bass.

Boyle-Baise, M. and Langford, J. (2004). There are children here: Service learning for social justice. *Equity & Excellence in Education, 37(1)*, 55–66.

Bringle, Robert G. and Hatcher, J. A. (1999, Summer). Reflection in service learning: Making meaning or experience, *Educational Horizons,* 179–185.

Brown, R. C. (2014). Transitions: Teaching from the spaces between. In O. Gunnlaugson, E. W. Sarath, C. Scott and Heesoon Bai (Eds.), *Contemplative learning and inquiry across disciplines* (pp. 271–286). Albany: State University of New York Press.

Bush, M. (2008). Compassion practices in higher education. In *Contemplative practices in higher education: A handbook of classroom practices.* Center for Contemplative Mind in Society. Northampton: MASS.

Celio, C., Durlak, J., and Dymnicki, A. (2011). A meta-analysis of the impact of service-learning on students. *Journal of Experiential Education, 34(2),* 164–181.

Clayton, P. H. and Ash, S. L. (2004). Shifts in perspective: Capitalizing on the counter-normative nature of service-learning. *Michigan Journal of Community Service Learning, 1(1)*, 59–70.

Colby, A. Ehrlich, T. Beaumont, E., and Stephens, J. (2003). *Educating citizens: Preparing America's undergraduates for lives of moral and civic responsibility.* San Francisco: Jossey-Bass.

Daynes, Gary and Longo, Nicholas V. (2004). Jane Addams and the origins of service-learning practice in the United States. *Michigan Journal of Community Service Learning, 11(1),* 5–13.

Einfeld, A. and Collins, D. (2008). The relationships between service-learning, social justice, multicultural competence, and civic engagement. *Journal of College Student Development, 49(2)*, 95–109.

Elbow, P. (1973). *Writing without teachers.* Oxford: Oxford University Press.

Fischer, N. (2004). *Taking our places: The Buddhist path to truly growing up.* New York: Harper Collins.

Furco, A. (2010). Foreword. In T. Stewart and N. Webster (Eds.), *Problematizing service learning.* Charlotte, NC: Information Age. ix-xii.

Giles, D. E. and Eyler, J. (1994). The theoretical roots of service-learning in John Dewey: Toward a theory of service learning. *Michigan Journal of Community Service Learning 1(1)*, 77–85.

Giles, D. E. and Eyler, J. (1999). *Where's the learning in service learning?* San Francisco: Jossey-Bass.

Grace, F. (2011). Learning as a path, not a goal: Contemplative pedagogy—Its principles and practices. *Teaching Theology and Religion, 14(2)*, 99–124.

Harkavy, I. (2006). The role of universities in advancing citizenship and social justice in the 21st century. *Education, Citizenship, and Social Justice, 1(1)*, 5–37.

Illeris, K. (2014). *Transformative learning and identity.* Abingdon, UK: Routledge.

James, W. (1890). *The principles of psychology: Volume 1.* New York: Holt.

Kabat-Zinn, J. (1994). *Wherever you go there you are: Mindfulness meditation in every life.* New York: Hyperion.

Kahane, David. (2009). Learning about obligation, compassion, and global justice: The place of contemplative pedagogy, *New Directions for Teaching and Learning, 118*, 49–60.

Kanagala, V. and Rendon, L. (2013). Birthing internal images: Employing the cajita project as a contemplative activity in a college classroom. *New Directions for Teaching and Learning, 134*, 41–51.

Kendall, J. (1990) *Combining service and learning: A resource book for community and public service.* Michigan: National Society for Internships and Experiential Education (U.S.), University of Michigan.

Kirsch, G. E. (2009). Creating spaces for listening, learning, and sustaining the inner lives of students. *The Journal of the Assembly for Expanded Perspectives on Learning, 14,* 56–67.

Knickelbine, M. (2013). Some notes on mindful dialogue. Received on May 2015 from: http://secularbuddhism.org/2013/10/09/some-notes-on-mindful-dialogue/.

Loeb, P. (1999/2010). *The soul of a citizen: Living with conviction in challenging times.* New York: St Martins.

Loeb, P. (2004). *The impossible will take a little while.* New York: Basic Books.

Lewis, H. R. (2006). *Excellence without a soul: Does liberal education have a future?* Philadelphia, PA: Perseus Book Groups.

Lutz, A. Dunne, J. D., and Davidson, R. J. (2007). Meditation and the neuroscience of consciousness. In P. E. Zelazo, M. M. Moscovitch, and E. Thompson (Eds.), *Cambridge handbook of consciousness.* New York: Cambridge University Press.

Marullo, S. (1996). Sociological imagination. The service learning movement in higher education: An academic response to troubled times. Retrieved on 2015 from comm-org.wisc.edu/si/marullo.htm.

Mitchell, T. D. (2008). Traditional vs. critical service-learning: Engaging the literature to differentiate two models. *Michigan Journal of Community Service Learning, 14(1)*, 50–65.

Mitchell, T. D., Richard, F. D., Battistoni, R. M., Rost-Banik, C., Netz, R., and Zakoske, C. (2015). Reflective practice that persists: Connections between reflection in service-learning programs and in current life. *Michigan Journal of Community Service Learning, 21(2),* 49–63.

Moore, D. T. (1990). Experiential education as critical discourse. In J. Kendall and Associates (Eds.), *Combining service and learning,* Raleigh, NC: National Society for Internships and Experiential Education.

Neururer, J. and Rhoads, R. A. (1998). Community service: Panacea, paradox, or potentiation. *Journal of College Student Development, 39(4),* 321–330.

O'Reilley, M. R. (1998). *Radical presence.* Portsmouth, NH: Bounton/Cook Publishers.

Palmer, P. J. and Zajonc, A. (2010). Introduction. In P. J. Palmer and A. Zajonc (Eds.), *The heart of higher education: A call to renewal.* San Francisco, CA: Jossey-Bass. 1–18.

Parks Daloz, L. A., Keen, C. H., Keen, J. P, and Daloz Parks, S. (1996). *Common fire: Leading lives of commitment in a complex world.* Boston: Beacon Press.

Pompa, L. (2002) Service-learning as crucible: Reflections on immersion, context, power, and transformation. *Michigan Journal of Community Service Learning, 9(1),* 67–76.

Rendon, L. (2009). *Sentipensante (sensing/thinking) pedagogy: Educating for wholeness, social justice and liberation.* Sterling, VA: Stylus Press.

Rendon, L. (2015, May). *Contemplative Engagement: Teaching and learning for wholeness and social change. Presentation to the Institute for Pedagogy in the Liberal Arts.* Oxford, GA: Oxford College.

Repetti, R. (2010). The case for a contemplative philosophy of Education (Special Issue). *New Directions for Community Colleges: Contemplative Teaching and Learning, 151,* 5–15.

Rilke, R. M. (1903). *Letters to a young poet—#4,* Trans. 1934, New York: W. W. Norton, pp. 1–59.

Rilke, R. M. (1914). *Turning Point.* New Poems. Trans. 2003. Vancouver, Canada: Anvil Press.

Roeser, R. W. and Peck, S. C. (2009). An education in awareness: Self, motivation, and self-regulated learning in contemplative perspective. *Educational Psychologist 44(2),* 119–136.

Saltmarsh, J. (1996). Education for critical citizenship: John Dewey's contribution to the pedagogy of community service learning. *Michigan Journal of Community Service Learning, 3(1),* 13–21.

Scott, C. (2014). Buberian dialogue as an intersubjective contemplative praxis. In O. Gunnlaugson, E. W. Sarath, C. Scott, and H. Bai (Eds.), *Contemplative learning and inquiry across disciplines* (pp. 325–340). Albany: State University of New York Press.

Shapiro, S. L., Brown, K. W., and Astin, J. A. (2008). Toward the integration of meditation into higher education: A review of research. Prepared for the Center for Contemplative Mind in Society. Retrieved from http://www.colorado.edu/ftep/events/eventdocs.documents/ShapiroResearchReport.pdf.

Stewart, T., & Webster, N. S. (2011). *Exploring cultural dynamics and tensions within service-learning.* Charlotte, NC: Information Age.

Stock, B. (2012, April). *Western contemplative tradition in higher education.* Presentation to the International Symposia for Contemplative Studies, Denver, CO.

Walsh, D. C. (2014, October). *Education for ethical and compassionate leadership.* Presentation to the Mind and Life International Symposium for Contemplative Studies, Boston, MA.

Warren, K. (1998). Educating students for social justice in service learning. *The Journal of Experiential Education, 21(3)*, 134–139.

Warren, J. L. (2012). Does service-learning increase student learning?: A meta-analysis *Michigan Journal of Community Service Learning, 18(2)*, 56–61.

Chapter Seven

Common, yet Uncertain, Ground

Listening as Service-Learning

Emily R. Yowonske and C. Aiden Downey

> I expected this to be more about service, but I realized I have so much to learn from these students instead of just trying to impart knowledge on them.
>
> —College Undergraduate

This chapter spotlights a faculty/student service-learning partnership, The Clarkston Roving Listener Project, developed in a community-based undergraduate course. Drawing on the stories, experiences, and reflections of the professor and seventeen undergraduates who participated in the course titled "Education and Culture," the chapter explores how adopting an inquiry-guided learning (IGL) framework (Lee, 2012) helped to challenge misconceptions about community-based service-learning and open a space for counterconventional learning. It argues that inquiring into the unavoidable uncertainty endemic to community-based service-learning courses can help students and professors alike reconsider their assumptions about community, service, teaching, and learning. Participant experiences suggest that an inquiry-based learning (IBL) framework, ultimately, builds common, yet uncertain, ground that fosters relationships and meaningful learning.

COMING TO INQUIRY-GUIDED LEARNING

During his second year of teaching at Emory University, the lead professor taught an undergraduate course in a local middle school that involved Emory undergraduates working with middle school students to understand their experiences in and ideas about education. While the undergraduates enjoyed working with the middle school students and reported learning a great deal from the experience, the professor struggled with the workload of the course, mostly trying to tame the uncertainty produced by unforeseen circumstances and situations related to working across two institutions.

Challenges unique to community-based learning, like the logistics of transporting students and arranging snacks and classroom space in the middle school, consumed an inordinate amount of the professor's time and interfered with other professorial responsibilities. In comparison to "regular" courses, the course required twice the amount of work. Despite the extra workload, the professor felt the course had been a valuable learning experience and was worth trying again. He reached out to fellow professors about how to make the community-based course more manageable.

During the early phases of planning the course in Clarkston, Jeff Galle at the Emory Oxford Campus advised inviting the students into the course design process. IPLA's 2012 session on "The Power of Inquiry as a Way of Learning in Undergraduate Education: Designing Courses and Curricula through Inquiry-guided Learning," led by Virginia Lee, encouraged professors to use the model of inquiry they employed in research as an approach for teaching. In other words, a professor's methodology for learning could become part of their methodology for teaching.

Methodologies of narrative inquiry (Clandinin and Connelly, 2000) center around a narrative understanding of experience that involves "attending to and acting on experience by co-inquiring with people who interact in and with classrooms, schools, or in other contexts into living, telling, retelling, and reliving stories of experience" (Huber et al., 2013, p. 213). This method, when combined with IGL pedagogical practices, served as a course framework that sought to build an inquiry-based course. In fact, several investigators in Canada have outlined how to use narrative inquiry as a form of pedagogy (Huber et al., 2013).

Another important reason for using narrative inquiry to guide student learning was that the undergraduate course would be based in the Clarkston community and centered on listening to and sharing the stories of its vibrant community. Beyond the methodology's ability to draw out the community's stories, narrative inquiry would elicit Emory students' stories about who they were in relation to the Clarkston community. Previous community-based courses had unearthed a common conception among Emory students that service-learning involved helping those less fortunate. Narrative inquiry provided a means for constructing a counterstory (Nelson, 1995) to this larger narrative about service-learning that took a deficit-approach to interacting with communities.

The course took place in the community of Clarkston, a small city (population 8,000) located just outside of Atlanta, Georgia. Since becoming a refugee-resettlement location in the 1990s, Clarkston has gained a reputation as one of the most diverse cities in the country, if not the world. Students from over fifty countries attend its high school, and the massive influx of refugees put a strain on the local schools, which struggle to address the language learning and interrupted education issues many of their students face.

Several Emory University community-based initiatives target the Clarkston community. Undergraduate volunteers serve as academic tutors in several of the schools with large refugee populations. In fact, several undergraduates in the course had already tutored Clarkston youth.

The professor had been part of a coalition of Clarkston community members interested in creating better educational opportunities for Clarkston youth. This coalition provided an introduction to Ms. Kim Ault, a community activist and parent, who shared her desire to develop a Roving Listener Project. DeAmon Harges, the original Roving Listener, started listening to the stories and passions of the community in Indianapolis, Indiana, to build community and the economy in 2004. Ault's conception of a listener project meshed with the tenants of narrative inquiry, which would provide an excellent framework for the project—and the students' learning.

Following Jeff Galle's suggestion to involve students in the process of creating and carrying out a community-based course, the professor recruited four undergraduates to be teaching assistants (TAs). All of them had previously taken classes with the professor, and beyond being strong and engaged students, they shared a desire to do something meaningful in and with a community. The idea of the course excited them, but it also generated a lot of questions. Much to their chagrin, the professor did not have many of the answers. The teaching team would have to figure it all out together while also focusing on their primary goal: learning to listen to Clarkston youth and community members.

LISTENING AS SERVICE?

The undergraduate TAs had no experience with IGL or service-based learning classes that sought to engage the community rather than fix it. They assumed their duties would primarily involve logistics such as coordinating teams of volunteers, arranging transportation, taking attendance, and communicating with site leaders about scheduling. The professor's charge, "to work with youth to listen to the stories of the community," initially confused the TAs. Accustomed to community-based courses that had a clear expectation to improve people, they struggled to understand how listening to stories might benefit the community.

The TAs uncertainty echoed a critical concern about if, and how, community-based university courses benefitted the community (Delpit, 2012).

While they did not think sharing stories would harm the community, they could not see what this would solve or help. Of particular concern was the possibility that the class would exploit the community for the sake of research or Emory students' learning.

Over the course of several planning meetings, the TAs slowly came to understand how listening to stories could serve a community. The professor and TAs divided the course into three phases: groundwork, gathering stories, and sharing stories. The TAs came to realize that the first, and perhaps most important aspect of the course, was learning how to listen. Believing the most difficult aspect of the course would be managing the formidable logistics, the TAs ran the risk of focusing on the operation of the class and missing out on connecting with Clarkston youth. They realized that the first step in being of service to the community was examining their ideas about what they were doing in Clarkston.

As they learned, they brought their own stories about service-learning and needed to examine their assumptions too. They came to view listening, *really listening*, as perhaps the best weapon in challenging their assumptions.

PREPARING TO LISTEN: SOCIAL JUSTICE AND THE BLANK SYLLABUS

Most university courses revolve around a detailed syllabus that sets the curriculum by outlining the topics, assignments, assessments, and expectations for the course of study. In the case of the Roving Listener Project, the professor struggled to create a syllabus because of the uncertainty endemic to the project. Following the advice of Jeff Galle, he decided to have the students create the syllabus as they went.

During the first class meeting, the professor and TAs unveiled what would become known as the "blank syllabus." While the document provided an overview of the major goals of the course, it left completely open what the class would do to get there. The raised eyebrows of undergraduates signaled that the document did not meet many undergraduates' expectations for a syllabus. Under the heading "Evaluation," the document explained:

> If you treat this like a standard class, you will do poorly. To succeed in this course you need to show up to every class, do the work and take initiative. We all have better things to do than focus on whether you earned an A− or B+. Basically at the end of the semester I will ask you to grade yourself—and back it up with concrete evidence. ... As I firmly believe students learn as much if not more from each other than they do from the "instructor," I ask students to be both students and teachers. I will strive to do the same. (Downey, 2014)

While the syllabus did not spell out the exact topics and assignments for each class, it did go into detail about the overall structure and purpose of the course.

Lee (2013) stressed the importance of scaffolding in inquiry-guided courses by creating a balance between challenges and supports. Students can find learning through inquiry "unsettling" because "it violates their assumptions about the origins of knowledge and the role of instructors and students in the learning process" (p. 157). While the syllabus did not contain a traditional schedule, it did support the undergraduates' venturing forth into this unfamiliar territory by emphasizing concepts of IBL and shared leadership.

In addition to this, the teaching team created space in the first few classes for students to ask questions and discuss the difference between the Roving Listener Project course and more traditional courses. Students were particularly concerned about how they would be assessed, and the professor and TAs had to gain the trust of the students. Given the uncertainty of the course, the professor promised the students that the grading would be, much like the course, collaborative. The TAs were particularly helpful in assuaging student fears and encouraging the students to take chances and not just look for the right answers.

The "blank syllabus" also made clear that throughout the course the teaching team would aim to make students' assumptions about teaching and learning, as well as community-based service, a part of the curriculum. Kirkland (2014) emphasized that community-based service-learning courses can place students and communities at risk if they do not take an intentional social justice approach to service-learning.

Kirkland found that university service-learning courses often fail to challenge—and in some cases, even exacerbate—students' sense of privilege and their deficit-based assumptions about communities. Kirkland's conclusion resonated with the experiences of one TA, who agreed that "service learning has come to mean something equivalent to an extended and sustained field trip (a kind of localized study away) for privileged learners who often imagine their roles in communities as agents of salvation as opposed to agents of service" (p. 583).

While this deficit-approach is by no means taught in the classrooms, the TA felt that few classes challenged or problematized progressive privileging. In "The Disadvantages of an Elite Education," William Deresiewicz (2008) lamented that far too many graduates leave elite universities with the inability to relate to people "below" them because they have come to think of themselves as "above," as the best and brightest. While a few professors might raise critical questions about students' assumptions about helping underprivileged minority children succeed, these salvos are no match against the institutional championing of undergraduates for volunteering to help poor and minority students. *Noblesse oblige* and resume building aside, these experiences can lead students not only to underestimate others, but also to overestimate themselves and their abilities.

The Roving Listener Project course sought to make the assumptions about what university members were doing in Clarkston visible before the class ever stepped foot into the community. The students read and discussed articles that challenged their assumptions about their role in community service and community change. Initial course readings also sought to have students explore and better understand their own stories.

Watching Chimamanda Adichie's "The Danger of a Single Story" (2009) made class members question how misconceptions and stereotypes prevent people from seeing others as fully human. William Derchsowitz's "The Disadvantages of an Elite Education" (2013) challenged ideas about university privilege. R. McDermott and H. Vareene's "Culture as Disability" (1995) pushed students to consider how culture mediates assumptions about others. A. Portelli's "A Dialogical Relationship: An Approach to Oral History" (2005) disturbed the notion that the class might simply collect stories from people. We also learned about the asset-based community development philosophy of the original Roving Listener model, which revised the conception of community service as fixing deficits.

Throughout the semester, students continued exploring and discussing these issues through Thomas King's *The Truth about Stories* (2008), S. A. Venkatesh's *Gang Leader for a Day* (2008), and Ernesto Sirolli's TED talk, "Want to help someone? Shut up and listen!" (2012). While the course never explicitly addressed social justice per se, the class's commitment to seeing privilege and investigating assumptions helped students to reflect upon who they were and what they were doing in the Clarkston community. As Milner (2015) explained, "Personal stories need to be well connected to broader matters, content, contexts, and constructs to help frame pedagogical relevance. … Stories without theory could leave discussions at the surface level when narrative grounded in and connected to literature can be impactful" (p. 156).

Through reflective group video logs (vlogs) uploaded to a private YouTube page, students discussed the readings in relation to their lives and the course. Students used the comments section of the YouTube channel to dialogue with each other and the teaching team. By explicitly asking the students to connect their experiences in Clarkson to the readings, the vlogs created a safe space for the class to gently challenge and reconsider assumptions.

One Emory student's vlog illustrated how the space offered them the opportunity to raise necessarily uncomfortable questions about their education at Emory: "As in the 'Elite Education' article, many Emory students may have trouble relating with 'real' people—from our cafeteria workers and custodians to Atlanta residents… I'm excited to go to Clarkston. I think hearing these stories over the semester will teach us something about ourselves and the world."

While course readings sought to challenge the implicit deficit-based approach to service that many students had encountered—and to some degree learned—at Emory, using a narrative inquiry framework provided a means for students to listen to stories that would further help them to reconsider their work in Clarkston.

OUR NARRATIVE PROJECTS

Prior to venturing out to listen to the stories of the Clarkston community, the professor tasked the Emory students with not only listening to the stories of the Clarkston students but also sharing their own stories with the Clarkston youth. Drawing upon the methodology and theory of narrative inquiry, the assignments were designed to have the storytelling, and learning, go both ways. Some of the assignments carried over from narrative inquiry methods included having students create timelines of their life, sharing the story of a precious personal belonging, and inquiring into the many stories in and around a family photograph. These methods helped the students grasp that one could not simply "collect" stories, that stories are shared between people in the midst of living their lives.

While the teaching team originally prioritized listening to the stories from the larger Clarkston community, the Emory students and Clarkston youth ended up devoting most of the semester to telling and listening to each other's stories. Following the model of photographer Dawoud Bey's book *Class Pictures* (2007), the teaching team engaged a local photographer to take candid portraits of everyone in the class. Building on the idea that there is always more behind a photograph than what is captured in the frame, the students then had to come up with one hundred words to describe what one could not know about them from the photo. The assignment challenged both Emory students and Clarkston youth to examine their own lives and then share a piece of their story with the class as a whole.

Once students developed a sense of both who they were and how to listen, the class ventured out during the last several weeks of the semester to listen to the stories of the larger Clarkston community. Teams composed of Emory and Clarkston students listened to the stories of community elders, recent refugees, and even the Mayor. The students then invited everyone who had participated in the Roving Listener Project to come and celebrate at the Banquet of Stories.

The course took many unexpected turns over the course of the semester, most of which required students to take risks and improvise. While the

Emory students agreed with Lee (2013) that "taking risks is essential for learning and development" (p. 106), many struggled with stepping into risky or uncertain situations. During the first couple of classes in Clarkston, one TA spent most of her time taking care of details like signing students in and arranging snacks rather than actually getting to know the Clarkston youth. She began to realize that dealing with the logistics provided a convenient means for her to avoid risky or uncertain situations. She recalled a time when the professor asked her to partner with a student on a storytelling activity:

> I imagined I looked a bit dizzy when Naila and I began our conversation. A moment before I'd been playing the part of a walking checklist, roaming the room to ensure every group had supplies and that every student had a partner. Quite suddenly I was standing with Naila introducing myself and getting ready to unpack her photo, an exercise I had thought I was not going to be a part of that day. The sudden shift frightened me. Was I ready? Did I know the assignment well enough? I felt self-conscious and nervous. I found myself retreating into the assignment description, as though that might help. I placed the three dimensions on our poster and hoped they might provide me with some stability. (Personal communication, September 16, 2014)

She was not alone in her trepidation, as the teaching team noted that the word "nervous" appeared many times in Emory students' description of their encounters with the Clarkston youth.

Despite the students' desire to get to know the Clarkston students, the prospect of initiating and sustaining a conversation posed a challenge, especially when the task was to listen and ask questions, rather than talk and provide answers. The TA saw not knowing as a terrifying weakness, a place where she was likely to misstep. In a conversation with a Clarkston student, a misstep might have serious implications for the relationship.

The Emory students discussed the discomfort in their vlogs and came to understand that acknowledging discomfort, and in some cases sharing this with their Clarkston partners, allowed them to be vulnerable and further shed their assumptions about who they were or what they were doing in Clarkston. Recognizing her anxiety allowed the TA to open up to Nailia so that she could then relate to and learn about Naila as a person, a young woman, and a member of the Clarkston community in a more authentic manner.

The TA left Clarkston that day realizing that authentic participation in the Clarkston Roving Listener Project meant she had to do more than plan the classes or handle the logistics. She had to be an active, and sometimes nervous, participant in the process as well. Being present and creating the space for people to make personal connections helped to forge genuine relationships between the Emory and Clarkston participants.

FROM DISCOMFORT TO OWNERSHIP

Reflecting on the course, Emory students spoke of the importance of being present in Clarkston. By present they meant not only being in Clarkston, but also about being attentive listeners and learners. Uncertainty came with the territory, but being present and genuine allowed them to develop a sense of ownership over the experience. By midway through the course, Emory students took the initiative to identify important opportunities for learning, both for themselves and their Clarkston partners, and pursued them. Sometimes being attentive to the lives of the Clarkston youth meant that it took students longer to complete assignments. As one Emory student recalled:

> I remember the week we had to write her 100 words, and my Clarkston partner didn't want to do that and was really stressed cause she was being bullied at school. So that day we got behind, but I helped her get through getting bullied in school and the drama of elementary school. Even though we didn't finish the assignment, I still felt honored because she got to share something personal with me. The fact that she felt comfortable expressing that [story], I felt really touched by that. ([Education and Culture])

The Emory student's sense of control and authority over her work in Clarkston allowed her to make an important judgment call and listen to the student talk about being bullied instead of feeling pressured to complete the assignment. The teaching team emphasized that the Emory students' first priority was to listen to the stories that the Clarkston youth wanted (and sometimes needed) to share.

While Emory students sometimes struggled with how to respond to the stories Clarkston youth told them about their lives, they slowly became more confident in their commitment to listen. As one Emory student commented:

> Because Dr. Downey always emphasized how significant it was to be active and accountable to Clarkston students, it naturally came to me—not just me but us. If we did not do this with confidence, it might lead to pessimistic results. I felt glad and responsible for creating such an enthusiastic, supportive, and encouraging environment. ([Education and Culture])

Students recognized the importance of being present in class, because being distracted by their phones or upcoming tests or life on campus prevented them from connecting with not only the Clarkston youth, but also their learning. In a traditional classroom, mental absenteeism might lead to a lower grade; in community-based courses, it negatively impacts the overall culture of the class.

Personal commitment and connection to the Clarkston students increased the undergraduates' sense of ownership and shared leadership. Several students commented that while they could sit back and allow the professor to assume responsibility for what happened in other classes, in Clarkston they stepped out of their comfort zone to connect with Clarkston youth and community members.

NO SINGLE STORY

Over the course of the semester, the relationships the Emory students forged with the Clarkston youth slowly began to challenge their assumptions about the Clarkston community. The class referred to this process as "challenging the single story" they had bought into the course about the Clarkston community needing outside help (Adichie, 2009). In their final video reflection, two Emory students reflected on how listening to the stories of students interrupted their assumptions:

> *Student 1:* One of the Clarkston students mentioned he would get in a lot of fights with students ... it wasn't so much that he liked fighting people, but he wanted to stick up for friends who were being made fun of.
> *Student 2:* [The story] really told you a lot about his character. Even this little kid has some values he sticks to.
> *Student 1:* I think when you see a kid who gets in a lot of fights you make a lot of judgments. When I got the chance to interview him, I got to understand his reasoning behind getting in fights.
> *Student 2:* I think that's one of the truths we learned about stories. It can give us a chance to hear different sides and perspectives. ([Education and Culture])

The course turned moments like this into learning opportunities by having students inquire into their assumptions. When Emory students mentioned moments when the Clarkston youth "surprised" them, the teaching team asked them to inquire into whether they had bumped up against a tacit assumption, or single story, that they had made about the Clarkston youth and community. When Emory students talked of being surprised by how nice or smart or talented the Clarkston youth are, they were asked to consider if, and why, they had assumed otherwise.

As Thomas King's (2003) text explained, students must not only listen to but also find ways to learn from other's stories: "Take [the story]. It's yours. Do with it what you will. But don't say in the years to come that you would have lived your life differently if only you had heard this story. You've heard it now" (p. 29). When properly acknowledged, a story validates another person's perspective and recognizes their unique viewpoint as a source for new knowledge, and the resulting connections can have a profound effect on both storyteller and listener. As another Emory student explained in her final reflection:

> When groups of people are given the opportunity to tell their story—an opportunity to verbalize their history, the things that are important to them—that really lets them know that their experience is valuable, that its important. I guess what I pulled from the reading is, you accept [the story] as it is, you accept it as truth, and I think that's one of the main takeaways from this class. ([Education and Culture])

While many students reported starting with a single story of Clarkston, intentional and ongoing inquiry into how the class's experience challenged assumptions opened a sometimes uncomfortable but very fertile space for questioning what students thought they knew and for knowing differently.

One Emory student experienced what she described as a profound shift in her thinking over the course of her time in Clarkston. She had arrived at Clarkston thinking she already knew what "problems" plagued the community, such as crime, teenage pregnancy, and gangs. While she had learned about the causes and solutions for teen pregnancy in her sociology classes at Emory, she had never met, or come to know, anyone experiencing it.

This changed when she met Aria. She spent a few classes coming to know her and eventually learned that she was a teenage mom. Coming to know Aria's story caused the Emory student to question what she had learned about teenage pregnancy. Aria's experience created a powerful counterstory to what the Emory student now called her "oversimplified" understanding of teenage pregnancy. The experience made her critically question aspects of her education, like how she had assumed she knew all about people she had never met.

About two months into the course, the teaching team realized that the Emory students had created another space to reflect on and inquire into their experiences in Clarkston. Emory students used the twenty minutes they spent together travelling to and from Clarkston as a generative space to discuss their experiences. When their reflections repeatedly referenced conversations that occurred in transit to or from Clarkston, the teaching staff became aware of the important role that these spaces played in their experience and learning.

In addition to allowing a rare opportunity to form meaningful friendships and connections among Emory students, the carpool became a space for candid reflection. Though official reflections for the class took on the form of vlogs, online comment boards, and short writings, the car ride back to Emory offered an informal space to gather other perspectives on the day's activities. Because scheduling restrictions did not allow a group meeting time outside of class time in Clarkston, the carpool provided a much-needed opportunity for Emory students to bring up thoughts or concerns that they could not voice at the community center. As a student pointed out, the unique conversation space was very different from traditional courses:

> Instead of a regular classroom where you're walking alone [after class], I'm in the backseat of one of the cars, and we are always reflecting on the different assignments for class or the things we are learning from the Clarkston students. It was a good way to reflect in addition to the vlog and watching other students' vlogs and commenting. It really gave me... lots of new perspectives.

It remains important to build in a range of reflective assignments into community-based and service-learning courses (Lee, 2012), but the car rides demonstrate the importance of creating informal spaces for students to process and reflect on their experiences beyond the purview of the professor. Free from the pressure to give the professor "what he wants to hear" these off-the-record reflections allowed students to truly evaluate activities and share their thoughts with each other and the TAs. The car rides encouraged candid and honest responses to the class and each other.

The affective aspect ended up being perhaps the most important difference between the Roving Listener Project course and a traditional course, and it is supported in the research on learning. As Lee (2013) wrote, "in the absence of strong, positive emotions engendered by caring, deep engagement, motivation, and interest, little real learning occurs" (p. 160). Beyond the relationships formed with the Clarkston community, the relationships the Emory students were able to form with each other helped to deepen the learning experience.

As the course went on, the class members sensed a shift not only in how we related to one other, but also in the way the Clarkston youth related to university members. While at first they had expected Emory students to tell them what to do, to tutor or teach them, as Emory students listened to stories and acted on their ideas for the course, the Clarkston students slowly took ownership of their experience, referring to themselves as Roving Listeners. They began to share with the Emory students their many selves, as well as the selves they aspired to be. One Clarkston student showed this vividly, and her performance at the Banquet of Stories became one of the most memorable moments from the semester.

NIKEEMA'S MOMENT

The professor arrived at the community center on the last day of the course to find the Emory and Clarkston students already there and in a flurry of activity. The Banquet of Stories celebrating a semester of work would start in a few minutes. Three weeks earlier, he had challenged the Emory and Clarkston students to plan a banquet that would bring together the Clarkston community and celebrate all of the stories and storytellers they had listened to and learned from over the course of the semester.

The goal was to showcase the stories they had heard as well as what had been learned. Over the course of the semester, the professor had tried to practice "planned obsolescence," or slowly stepping back from his role as professor and empowering students to become leaders and learners. By ceding this ground to the students and trying to support them in their learning, he hoped to make the Clarkston Roving Listener Project a student-led and sustainable community fixture.

As the banquet began, the professor took his place among the hundred guests and watched Emory and Clarkston students take turns sharing stories and honoring community members. While enjoying a gourmet meal catered by the culinary club from the local high school, he felt a tap on his shoulder. One of the TAs informed him that Nikeema had finally arrived.

Two weeks earlier, the banquet planning committee had solicited volunteers to read their stories or poems during the banquet. To everyone's surprise, Nikeema had raised her hand and said in little more than a whisper that she wanted to read one of her poems. Up until this point, Nikeema had been a quiet but steady presence in the class. While her passionate prose hinted at the deep well within her, during class she had not said more than a few words. And yet she had volunteered to read her poetry in front of over 150 people the following week, many of them strangers.

Nikeema's family had fled Sudan during the civil war, like thousands of other refugees, and settled in Clarkston. Nikeema's father had been a child soldier in Sudan, and her brother had already dropped out of high school and joined a gang. Nikeema desperately wanted to graduate from high school and go on to college but sometimes felt that the odds were stacked against her success. Facing setback after setback, she struggled to "stay strong." Her soft smile and calm demeanor gave away little of her inner turmoil.

The professor went to the back of the banquet hall, where Nikeema stood nervously, her eyes wide with fear. She confessed that she had almost not shown up but decided at the last minute that she "needed" to come. She had not yet shared her poem, and the professor worried that she would struggle in front of the audience and retreat to the safety of the crowd as quickly as possible. As Nikeema nervously made her way to the front of the room, the professor returned to his table and continued chatting with the other guests and eating dinner.

A powerful and confident voice boomed from the speakers, gaining power and strength with each word. Everyone looked up to see Nikeema, center stage, her brow knotted as she spit line after powerful line of spoken word poetry into the microphone. The entire hall froze, stunned by her powerful voice and beautiful prose about her struggles, hopes, and dreams. Her poem touched on the power of stories, of listening, believing, and becoming. She spoke for five minutes, pausing for effect, and knew every word by heart. She had written the poem over the course of the semester and practiced it in front of her bedroom mirror for weeks.

Nikeema had found a space to tell and live a different story about herself, her life, and her struggles. As she exhorted us to live with our hearts, to tell and live better stories, the professor realized that a space had been created for everyone to listen and to come to know one another, and ourselves, differently. The class, with its attention to listening and respect for stories, became a space of possibility, a place of learning, and becoming.

By turning what Emory students had expected to be all about them improving Clarkston youth into an inquiry into the stories that we all brought and shared, the teaching team and Emory students ended up surprised by what they learned about the Clarkston youth as well as how this new knowing troubled their previous assumptions about Clarkston youth and service-learning.

CHALLENGING DEFICIT-BASED SERVICE-LEARNING

The Emory students' past experiences with community service and service-learning courses confirmed Kirkland's sobering findings about the failure of service-learning experiences to change students' perspectives of people or communities labeled "underserved" or "underprivileged." As the semester progressed and the relationships deepened, Emory students embarked on the uncomfortable process of questioning their conceptions of community service.

Emory students came to understand that connecting with people and communities means meeting them on their terms and developing common ground. They became more than helpful tourists. One student noted, "I feel like I learned more in this setting because it gave me an opportunity to feel like a *true member* of the Clarkston community" ([Education and Culture]).

Students developed an asset-based approach to interacting with the people of Clarkston. Learning from community members stands in unstated contrast to university learning, where professors carry the power and validation of the institution. Their professor's refusal to "play professor" and provide all of the answers opened the space for all learners to learn from the funds of knowledge in the Clarkston community (Moll, 1992).

INQUIRY-BASED LEARNING AS A MEANS TO MAKING COMMON, YET UNCOMFORTABLE, GROUND

The experience of IGL is akin to incorporating a balancing ball into strength training. Just as there is much to be gained in terms of functional strength from performing exercises with the wobbly discomfort of a balance ball, there is also much to be learned from a course that keeps learners somewhat off-balance in terms of their assumptions about communities and service.

The focus of narrative inquiry on the stories of the Clarkston community and the Emory community kept university members off-balance just enough to prevent them from becoming too comfortable in their work with, or assumptions about, the Clarkston community and service-learning. Traditional classes that contained little uncertainty did not work these learning muscles. Remaining balanced in inquiry learning requires making numerous, quick adjustments that engage the whole self. From time to time, the learner must be prepared to fall.

In the Clarkston Roving Listener Project, Clarkston and Emory students came to embrace, albeit uncomfortably, the unease and uncertainty of inquiry. Every week presented new opportunities for listening, learning, and building relationships. Students learned flexibility, not only in their planning but also in their thinking. To say the class stretched students would be an understatement; it allowed both professor and students to see the gifts, talents, and strengths of students that often go untapped in Emory and Clarkston classrooms.

Settling on the balance ball of inquiry generated many unforeseen questions in the face of uncertainty. Listening to the Clarkston students and the stories of their community tested the class's strengths, knowledge, and beliefs in IGL. Learners sought to support one another while allowing uncertainty and instability to build new strengths in academic knowledge and self-knowledge. The Roving Listeners stood on uncharted, uncomfortable ground that slowly became more common, collaborative, and shared.

Narrative inquiry provided a valuable framework for IGL in the community setting because it encouraged a democratic approach to learning and knowledge making that students had not experienced in the university "bubble." By exploring the discomfort with engaging the Clarkston community on more equitable terms through the experiences of listeners and storytellers, the students ventured out into unchartered territory and collectively created a space for authentic learning. IBL formed the backbone of the community-based undergraduate course, helping to transform what might have been a more traditional service-learning experience into something far less certain or comfortable.

As one Emory student put it, the Clarkston Roving Listener Project would have been "almost impossible without having common ground." By collectively venturing out of the traditional classroom's comfort zones, students created "common ground" where they could reflect upon and question their experiences. They engaged in unique learning that created a space to rethink service, learning, and self.

REFERENCES

Adichie, C. N. (2009, July) Chimamanda Ngozi Adichie: The danger of a single story [Video file]. Retrieved from http://www.ted.com/talks/chimamanda_adichie_the_danger_of_a_single_story?language=en.

Bey, D. (2007). *Class pictures.* New York: Aperture.

Clandinin, D. J., and Connelly, F. M. (2000). *Narrative inquiry: Experience and story in qualitative research* (1st ed.). San Francisco, CA: Jossey-Bass.

Delpit, L. D. (2012). Will it help the sheep? University, community, and purpose. In *"Multiplication is for white people": Raising expectations for other people's children* (pp. 193–206). New York: The New Press.

Deresiewicz, W. (2008). The disadvantages of an elite education: Our best universities have forgotten that the reason they exist is to make minds, not careers. *American Scholar, 77(3)*. Retrieved from https://theamericanscholar.org/issues/summer-2008/.

Downey, C. A. (2014). EDS 308: Education and culture [Course Syllabus].

Education and Culture. (2014). Education and Culture [YouTube Channel]. Retrieved on 2015 from https://www.youtube.com/channel/UCbPTqQbM7o0921Tz-9LfTqw.

Huber, J., Caine, V., Huber, M., and Steeves, P. (2013). Narrative inquiry as pedagogy in education: The extraordinary potential of living, telling, retelling, and reliving stories of experience. *Review of Research in Education, 37(1)*, 212–242.

King, T. (2003). *The truth about stories: A native narrative.* Toronto, ON: House of Anansi.

Kirkland, D. E. (2014) "They look scared": Moving from service learning to learning to serve in teacher education—a social justice perspective. *Equity & Excellence in Education, 47(4)*, 580–603.

Lee, V. S. (2012). What is inquiry-guided learning? *New Directions for Teaching and Learning, (129)*, 5–14.

Lee, V. S. (2013). Supporting students' search for a meaningful life through inquiry-guided learning. In O. Kovbasyuk and P. Blessinger (Eds.), *Meaning-centered education: International perspectives and explorations in higher education* (pp. 154–167). New York: Routledge.

Moll, L. (1992). Funds of knowledge for teaching: Using a qualitative approach to connect homes and classrooms. *Theory into Practice, 31(2)*, 132–41.

Nelson, H. L. (1995). Resistance and insubordination. *Hypatia, 10(2)*, 23–43.

McDermott, R. and Vareene, H. (1995). Culture as disability. *Anthropology & Education Quarterly, 26(3)*, 324–348.

Milner, H. R. (2015). *Rac(e)ing to class: Confronting poverty and race in schools and classrooms.* Cambridge, MA: Harvard Press.

Portelli, A. (2005). A dialogical relationship: An approach to oral history. *Expressions Annual, 14.*

Sirolli, E. (2012, September). Ernesto Sirolli: Want to help someone? Shut up and listen! [Video file]. Retrieved on 2015 from http://www.ted.com/talks/ernesto_sirolli_want_to_help_someone_shut_up_and_listen?language=en.

Venkatesh, S. A. (2008). *Gang leader for a day: A rogue sociologist takes to the streets.* New York: Penguin.

Index

academic performance, xiv, 66, 100, 109–10, 119
academic rigor, 5
accountability, 107–8, 113n12, 151
active learning. *See* inquiry.
active questioning. *See* inquiry.
advanced placement (AP), 98, 101, 104, 109, 114n16
assessment, xix, 12, 14, 24, 28, 34–35, 38, 41, 41nn4–5, 45, 49–51, 57–58, 66, 68, 94, 97–98, 101, 103, 106, 113n12, 119
asset-based community development, 148, 156
assumptions. *See* stereotypes.
attentive listening, 131, 151
attitudes, 73;
 toward learning, 119;
 toward school, 119;
 toward self, 119
awareness and mindfulness. *See* contemplation.

backwards design, 13, 34, 76, 80
Bain, Ken, xvi, xvii, xviii
benchmarks, 27, 99
blank syllabus, 146–47
Bloom's Taxonomy, 76, 79, 87n10, 87n22

bridging, xx, 92, 119
Bowen, Stephen, x, xi, xxi, 5, 161–62
Boyer Report, 11

CAE. *See* Center for Academic Excellence.
cajita, 134–35, 138n1
CAL. *See* cognitive-affective learning.
Center for Academic Excellence (CAE), xi, xii, xviii, xxi, 4, 6, 9, 15, 161
Center for Contemplative Mind in Society, 124, 127, 138n3
Certification. *See* IGL Certification Program.
Chick, Nancy, 74–75
civic engagement. *See* community.
classroom observation, 33–34, 36–37, 71, 103–4, 106
close reading, 14, 109
cognitive-affective learning (CAL), xx, 117, 163
collaboration, xvii, 9–10, 14, 40, 46, 51–4, 65–66, 68, 72, 76, 90, 92, 94, 98, 101, 103, 108, 147, 157
college and career readiness, 110
Common Core, xv, 93, 98, 99, 110–11
community, x, xxi, 5, 89–92, 95–7, 106, 114n15, 118–19, 121–24, 127, 131–35, 137–38, 143–49, 153–57;

community-based learning, xxi, 90,
    143–45, 147, 151, 154, 157;
  development, 118, 148;
  partnership, 92, 97, 143;
  responsibility, 90, 121, 131, 136;
  social problems, 122, 136
community service, 123–24, 132,
    148, 156;
  deficit-based approach, 121, 144,
    147–49, 156
constructivist philosophy, 26, 73, 94
contemplation, 117, 123, 125–27, 153;
  contemplative methods, xx, 118,
    124–27, 129, 132–33, 135,
    138, 163;
  contemplative pedagogy, xx, 118,
    124–27, 130, 132–33, 135;
  contemplative service-learning,
    xx, 117;
  music, 127–29;
  listening, 127, 131–32, 137, 144–46,
    149, 152, 156–57
cooperative classrooms, xvi, 26
counterstory, 144, 153
creativity, ix–x, xiii, xiv, xvi, xvii, xviii,
    xix, xx, xxi, 3–7, 9–10, 12, 15, 45,
    58, 97, 113n4, 125, 164
critical thinking, assessing, 58, 81
critical thinking exercises, 100, 110
critical thinking, nurturing, 48, 67, 83

debate, 9–10, 76, 82–83, 95–96,
    101–2, 113n4
deductive pedagogies, 93–94, 99;
  deduction, 101
dialogic listening, 131
differentiation, 93, 95

educational partnership, xiv, 10, 92, 143
ELA. *See* English and Language Arts.
elementary schooling, 92, 95, 97,
    99–100, 103, 106, 111, 113n7,
    114n20, 134, 151
English and Language Arts (ELA), 93,
    96, 103, 105
empathy, 82, 87n17, 121

environmental science, 45–46, 49–50,
    52–54, 67, 163–64
epistemology, xx, 101, 117, 125–6
existing knowledge. *See* prior
    knowledge.
experiential learning, xxi, 15, 19, 26, 89

faculty development, xvi, xiv, xviii,
    26–27, 32, 72, 84–85
faculty self-assessment, 28, 34–35, 66
flipped classroom, 76, 87n16.
  See also backwards design.
free-writing, 133
full-format inquiry, xiii, 92, 98–101,
    103, 113n1, 113n4, 113n13, 162

Galle, Jeffery, x, xiii, xviii, 1, 3,
    144–46, 161
General Education Program (GEP), 19,
    27, 33, 36
General Education Requirements
    (GER), 16
Gonzales, Joseph, 77–78
graduate students, 68, 71–72, 86n1
group work, xvi, 54, 57, 66, 77.
  See also cooperative classrooms.

history, xx, 2, 9, 10, 27–28, 36, 76–84,
    86n6, 87n13, 87n17;
  historical thinking, 77–78, 81–82,
    84, 86n8b
humanities, xviii, 8, 10, 17, 23, 48
Hutching, William, 96
Hyatt Model, 51

IBL. *See* Inquiry Based Learning.
IGL. *See* Inquiry Guided Learning.
IGL Certification Program, xix, 24,
    28, 32–42
incentives, 27–8, 32, 35–36, 38, 40
independent learning, 19, 20, 29,
    37, 46–47, 58, 73, 91–92, 101,
    110, 113n1
induction, 101, 110–11;
  inductive learning model, 111
innovation. *See* creativity.

Index

INQ. *See* Ways of Inquiry.
Inquiry pedagogical practices;
   active learning, xiv, 11, 26, 40, 46–7, 49, 73–74, 77, 81, 84–85, 86n4, 89, 96, 98, 161;
   active questioning, 92;
   assessments, xix, 12, 14, 50–51, 57–58, 68, 94, 101–3, 106, 112;
   discussions, 6, 18–19, 76–78, 81, 83, 94, 101, 106–9, 113n12;
   framework for, 28–29, 32, 34–38, 40, 76, 96, 145, 157;
   integration, 74, 77–78, 80–81, 83;
   method, 74–75, 100, 107, 109, 149;
   pedagogy, 98, 108, 163;
   practice, xiii, xx, 93, 98, 100, 104;
   hypothesizing, 53, 57, 96.
   See also inquiry based learning (IBL); inquiry guided learning (IGL)
inquiry-based learning (IBL), xiv, xx, xxiin1, 11, 89, 92–111, 113n1, 113n12, 113n13, 114n17, 147, 157;
   institutional support for, 67, 103
inquiry-based approach. *See* inquiry-based learning; inquiry
inquiry circles, 31–32, 35, 37, 43n10
Inquiry Guided Learning (IGL), xix–xx, xxii, 1, 6, 11–12, 24–30, 32–36, 38–49, 51–58, 65–68, 73–75, 77–78, 80, 86n6, 87n13, 90, 112n1, 143–45, 157
Institute for Pedagogy in Liberal Arts (IPLA), ix–xxi, xxiin2-3, 1–4, 6–15, 21n6, 28, 32, 41, 45–48, 57, 67–68, 72–76, 78, 80–89, 91–93, 97–98, 101–2, 105, 111, 117, 134, 144, 161;
institutional initiatives, xi, 12, 15

Justice circles. *See* inquiry circles.

Kirkland, David E., 147, 156

Lane, Jill, 11, 13
learning community, 5, 27, 32, 35, 38,

learning environment, xiii, xvi, 16, 107, 129
learning outcomes, 8, 12–13, 34, 48–51, 72–74, 78–82, 84
learning style, 94
lectio divina, 127, 132–33, 138
lecture, xiv, 25, 45, 49, 72, 76, 78, 80–1, 87n16, 96, 99, 107, 110
Lee, Virginia, 11–12, 13, 19, 26–27, 33, 73–74, 144, 147, 154
level of engagement, 94, 102
Levy model, 30–33, 37, 40, 43n9
lower-level thinking, 101

Mazur, Eric, xvi, 3, 10
memorization, xix, xx, 3, 38, 45, 46, 52, 58, 77, 83–84, 94
metacognition, 73, 127
Mindful Dyadic Dialogue, 131, 137
multicultural awareness, 119, 135

Nadler, Marjorie, 80–81
narrative inquiry, xxi, 144–45, 149, 157.
   See also inquiry
No Child Left Behind, 99

Oxford College of Emory University, ix, xi, xiv, xxi, xxiin3, 1–5, 7, 10–12, 15–18, 20n1, 20n3, 21n8, 46, 72, 75, 97, 117

passivity, xvii, 48, 92–93
patience, 121, 134
pedagogy:
   collegiate, xiv, xix, xx, 90–92, 97–98, 102, 111;
   interdisciplinary, xviii, 18, 20, 23, 48, 122;
   k-12, xiv, xvi, xx, 8, 77, 86n6, 90–91, 97–99, 106, 113n2;
   nontraditional, 98, 120;
   traditional, 25, 120
Performance Standards, 91, 93, 98–100, 107, 110–11, 113n3, 113n13
peer instruction, 10;
   active peer teaching, xvi

peer learning, 27, 32, 38–40
problem-based learning (PBL), ix, xv, 8–11, 26, 47, 53, 99
problem solving, 21n9, 47, 58, 67, 93
prior knowledge, 30, 93–94
public school, xvi, xx, 91–93, 97, 99–100, 107–11, 113n2, 113n9, 113n14

quality enhancement plan (QEP), 15, 24–28, 39, 42n4
questioning, 29, 48, 92–94, 96–7, 100–1, 105, 109, 111, 124, 153, 156;
  active questioning, 92;
  closed-ended questions, 80;
  open-ended questions, 43n16, 51–52, 65, 74–75, 87n15, 97

research-teaching, 96
retention, xx, 83–84
role-play, 82, 84
Roving Listener Project, 143, 145–50, 154–55, 157–58
rubrics, 38, 58–9, 64, 74, 81, 87n14

SACSCOC. *See* Southern Association of Colleges and Schools Commission on Colleges.
scaffolding, xxiin1, 12–13, 21n9, 27, 29, 34, 49, 51, 81, 147
Scholarship of Teaching and Learning (SoTL), xiv, xvi, xviii, 2, 15, 72, 74–75, 84–85, 86n6, 117
scholar-teacher, xv, xvi, xvii, xviii, 14, 96
science, xv, xviii, xix, 1, 8, 10, 17, 45–55, 57, 65, 67–68, 69n1, 84, 96, 100
Scientific Method, 46, 50, 53, 58, 65, 67, 73, 96, 100–101, 113n4
secondary schooling, xiv, xv, xx, 9, 15, 90, 92–93, 97, 98, 104, 107, 111, 113n13, 114n15;
  high school, 5, 46, 92–93, 98, 103–5, 113n7, 114n16, 145, 155;

middle, 105, 113n7, 114n20, 143–4
service-learning, 89–90, 117–24, 126–36, 143–44, 146–47, 154, 156–57;
  community partnership in, 97;
  contemplative, xx, 117, 133;
  deficit-based, 147, 149, 156;
  pedagogy, xx, 120–23, 128, 136. *See also* community; contemplative service learning.
SLO. *See* student-learning outcomes.
sociology, 10, 153
Southern Association of Colleges and Schools Commission on Colleges (SACSCOC), 24
social justice, xx, 21n10, 117–25, 127–36;
  social justice pedagogy, 117–138
social responsibility, 18–9, 119–20, 121, 123
social sciences, xviii, 8, 10, 17, 28, 43n7
social skills, 119
SoTL. *See* Scholarship of Teaching and Learning.
special education, 98, 104–6, 109
standardized testing, 93, 99, 108
STEM, 10, 67
stereotypes, xiii, xxi, 19, 73, 90, 108, 120, 133, 143, 146–48, 150, 152–3, 156, 157
stillness and silence, 127–29
storytelling, 133, 149–50;
  stories, xv, xxi, 9, 133, 143–46, 148–49, 151, 152–58;
  storytellers, 153, 155, 157
strategic planning, 4–5, 15, 16, 18, 20nn1–2
student evaluations. *See* student ratings of instruction.
students:
  at-risk, 94, 147;
  with behavioral issues, 109;
  competitiveness, 10, 76, 120;
  confidence, 109, 151;

empowerment, 74, 99–100, 109, 155;
engagement, xiii–xiv, xix–xx, xxiin1, 5–6, 20n2, 24, 31, 34, 43n14, 54, 57, 67–68, 77, 79, 81–85, 87n17, 91–94, 96, 100–2, 107–10, 113n13, 114n20, 117–20, 129, 132, 145, 154;
high achievers, 57;
nontraditional, 71, 86n2;
ownership, xvi, 39, 48, 54, 68, 79, 91, 108, 111, 151–52, 154;
preparation, 74, 81, 98, 124;
participation, 29, 98, 109, 119, 150;
reluctant readers, 111;
reflection, 27, 34, 38, 77, 85, 89, 119, 122–24, 126–28, 132, 134–35, 138, 143, 152–54;
respect, 94, 109, 121, 128, 132
student-learning habits, 25
student-learning outcomes (SLO), 49–51, 66, 119

student ratings of instruction, 38
student self-assessment, 66

Taylor, Beverly, 80–81
TBL. *See* Team-Based Learning.
Team-Based Learning (TBL), ix, xvi, 8, 26, 73, 75
teaching assistantships, 49, 66, 71, 86n1, 145
transformative learning, 16, 120, 127

undergraduate students, xv, xvii, xxi, 1, 3, 11, 13, 15–16, 18, 25, 27, 33, 45–47, 49, 53, 66, 68, 92, 97, 121, 143–47, 152, 157

Wagner, James, 5
Ways of Inquiry (INQ), xxi, 1, 11, 14, 16–19, 162
Wineburg, Sam, 77

Zones of Proximal Development, 93

About the Contributors

EDITORS

Jeffery Galle is associate professor of English, founding director of the Center for Academic Excellence, and principal organizer of IPLA at Oxford College of Emory University. Co-author of *How to Be a "HIP" Campus: Maximizing Learning in Undergraduate Education* (2015), Galle's scholarship focuses on active learning, particularly inquiry. The Outstanding Professor for the College of Arts and Sciences (ULM 2005), the Scott Professor for Teaching Excellence (ULM 1996–1999), and the Emory Distinguished Teaching Scholar (2009), Galle also serves as a consulting editor for *College Teaching*.

Rebecca L. Harrison, associate professor of English and director of STEAM English at the University of West Georgia, teaches courses in Southern women writers, American literature, pedagogy, and secondary English education. A women's literature specialist, Harrison has published on writers such as Eudora Welty, Beatrice Witte Ravenel, and Mary Dorcey; her most recent book *Inhabiting La Patria*, a critical collection on Julia Alvarez, was published by SUNY Press in 2013. Harrison, the 2015 Robert Reynolds Awardee for Excellence in Teaching, has forthcoming essays on innovative pedagogical practices on teaching Eudora Welty and STEAM pedagogies in English.

CONTRIBUTORS

Stephen Bowen joined Emory University in 2005 as William R. Kenan, Jr. Professor of Biology and dean of Oxford College, in which role he served until his retirement in 2016. He has played a leadership role in higher education as president of the Association for General and Liberal Studies, senior fellow of the American Association of Colleges and Universities, and consultant for the North Central Association's Higher Learning Commission and the Middle States Commission on Higher Education. At Oxford College, Bowen supported faculty pedagogical innovations, including the Institute for Pedagogy in the Liberal Arts and the Ways of Inquiry curriculum.

C. Aiden Downey is visiting professor at Emory University's Division of Educational Studies and a lecturer in the Intercultural Conflict Management Program at Alice Solomon University in Berlin, Germany. A former middle and high school science teacher, he holds a PhD in education, culture, and society from University of Pennsylvania's Graduate School of Education. He cofounded The Workshop School, an innovative public high school in Philadelphia.

Devon Fisher is associate professor of English and director of Lenoir-Rhyne University's Center for Teaching and Learning. He is the author of *Roman Catholic Saints and Early Victorian Literature: Conservatism, Liberalism, and the Emergence of Secular Culture* (2012). He holds a PhD in English literature from the University of North Carolina at Chapel Hill.

Heather Giebeig is a graduate of Florida State University and a veteran teacher with twenty-five years of experience in elementary education. The last fourteen years of her teaching career have been dedicated to facilitating resource gifted education classes for which she discovered and employed full-format inquiry-based learning. She is now a second grade teacher at Mt. Zion Elementary in Mt. Zion, Georgia.

Jennifer Heller is associate professor of English at Lenoir-Rhyne University, where she also serves as the chair of the School of Arts and Letters. She is the author of *The Mother's Legacy in Early Modern England* (2011), and she publishes in the fields of Renaissance literature, drama, material culture, and the scholarship of teaching and learning. She holds a PhD in English literature and women's studies from the University of North Carolina at Chapel Hill.

Angela Suzanne Insenga received her master's degree from Clemson University and her doctorate from Auburn University. She is associate professor of English at the University of West Georgia. Her scholarship comprises Young Adult (YA) literature, adolescent literacies, and pedagogy, both collegiate and secondary. Insenga's work investigates representations of girlhood in YA, and she argues for curricula and teaching practices that engage students' cultural currency and foster critical acumen via the deployment of age-appropriate literature and methodologies.

Daniel W. Kiser holds degrees from Southern Illinois University (BM and MM) and the University of Illinois (DMA). He has released three compact discs with the Lenoir-Rhyne University Concert Band and has performed with or conducted ensembles that have appeared on several WDAV-FM broadcasts. Joining the Lenoir-Rhyne University faculty in 1992 as the Director of Bands, Kiser has held a series of progressive administrative appointments which led to his 2008 appointment as dean of the College of Arts and Sciences.

Virginia S. Lee is principal and senior consultant of Virginia S. Lee & Associates, working with numerous colleges and universities in the United States and abroad. She is a former president of the Professional & Organizational Development (POD) Network in Higher Education, the largest professional organization for faculty and educational developers in higher education in North America. She was selected as a Fulbright Specialist in 2010 for a term of five years. Lee serves on the editorial boards of several journals in the field of inquiry pedagogy and publishes widely in international venues on teaching and learning in higher education.

Kalina Manoylov is associate professor of Biology at Georgia College and an adjunct associate professor at the University of Iowa. For the past ten years, she has been researching teaching and learning through inquiry in her ecology and phycology classes.

Christine Mutiti is assistant professor in the Department of Biological and Environmental Sciences at Georgia College. She uses course-based undergraduate research in her upper-level courses such as wetland and landscape ecology.

Samuel Mutiti is associate professor at Georgia College, where he teaches geology and environmental science courses. He works to increase quality undergraduate research opportunities within the environmental science curriculum through both independent research and course-based research experiences.

Patricia Owen-Smith is professor of Psychology and women's studies at Oxford College of Emory University. She holds a PhD in developmental psychology. In 2000, she was named a Carnegie Scholar by Carnegie's CASTL program for her research project focused on models of insight development in the classroom. Owen-Smith founded and continues to direct Oxford College's Women's Studies and Service-Learning programs. She also directed the *Center for Cognitive-Affective Learning*, an initiative sponsored by the CASTL program. Owen-Smith is the recipient of the Emory Williams Teaching Award. Her current scholarship centers on contemplative practices in higher education.

David Ratke is professor of Religious Studies and chair of the School of Humanities and Social Sciences at Lenoir-Rhyne University. He teaches and researches in the areas of Christian thought and history, world religions, and interfaith relations.

Lia Schraeder is assistant professor of History at Georgia Gwinnett College. She completed a PhD in history at the University of California, Davis, in 2009. Her interest in educational innovation also led her to complete an MEd in learning, design, and technology at the University of Georgia in 2015.

Catherine Chiappetta Swanson is an educational consultant at McMaster Institute for Innovation and Excellence in Teaching and Learning. She is also an instructor of Social Sciences at McMaster University, where she has worked with some of the early innovators of the inquiry approach. As an educational consultant, she supports instructors and graduate students in developing curricula, refining courses, and facilitating workshops on inquiry-guided learning. Chiappetta Swanson is a member of a multidisciplinary team working to transform the first-year experience institutionally through the development of a foundational blended-learning course.

Allison Rick VandeVoort is assistant professor of Environmental Science at Georgia College. Her research includes course-based, community-centered research in soil science.

Emily R. Yowonske graduated from Emory University with a BA in English and educational studies. During her time in Atlanta, Yowonske was a teaching assistant for the Clarkston Roving Listener Project and an English teacher's assistant at the Ben Franklin Academy. Yowonske earned her master's degree in special education and English education from the University of Pittsburgh. She teaches eleventh grade cultural literacy in Pittsburgh, PA.

Caralyn B. Zehnder was professor in the Department of Biological & Environmental Sciences at Georgia College and the Environmental Science Program Coordinator for eight years. She is currently the Professional Development Coordinator at Springfield Technical Community College.

www.ingramcontent.com/pod-product-compliance
Lightning Source LLC
Chambersburg PA
CBHW021850300426
44115CB00005B/93